Class Acts

Series Board

James Bernauer

Drucilla Cornell

Thomas R. Flynn

Kevin Hart

Richard Kearney

Jean-Luc Marion

Adriaan Peperzak

Thomas Sheehan

Hent de Vries

Merold Westphal

Michael Zimmerman

John D. Caputo, *series editor*

Perspectives in
Continental
Philosophy

MICHAEL NAAS

Class Acts
Derrida on the Public Stage

FORDHAM UNIVERSITY PRESS
New York ■ 2021

Fordham University Press gratefully acknowledges financial assistance and support provided for the publication of this book by DePaul University.

Copyright © 2021 Fordham University Press

An earlier version of Part I of this book appeared in French as Michael Naas, *Derrida à Montréal: Une pièce en trois actes* Copyright © 2019 Les presses de l'Université de Montréal.

All rights reserved. No part of this publication may be reproduced, stored in a retrieval system, or transmitted in any form or by any means—electronic, mechanical, photocopy, recording, or any other—except for brief quotations in printed reviews, without the prior permission of the publisher.

Fordham University Press has no responsibility for the persistence or accuracy of URLs for external or third-party Internet websites referred to in this publication and does not guarantee that any content on such websites is, or will remain, accurate or appropriate.

Fordham University Press also publishes its books in a variety of electronic formats. Some content that appears in print may not be available in electronic books.

Visit us online at www.fordhampress.com.

Library of Congress Cataloging-in-Publication Data available online at https://catalog.loc.gov.

Printed in the United States of America

23 22 21   5 4 3 2 1

First edition

*For Marine,
First in Paris, now in Septeuil,
always in a class of her own.*

Contents

Abbreviations of Works Cited   *xi*

Introduction: The Program   *1*

PART I: DERRIDA IN MONTREAL
(A PLAY IN THREE SPEECH ACTS)

Argument and Dramatis Personae   *13*

Act 1. The Context (1971)   *15*

    Intermission 1: Glyph 1   *41*

Act 2. The Signature (1979)   *45*

    Intermission 2: Glyph 2   *55*

Act 3. The Event (1997)   *59*

    Encore: Cocoon   *69*

PART II: THE OPEN SEMINAR

The Counter-Program (Syllabus)   *75*

Class 1. *Agrégations*: The Chance of *Life Death* (1975–76)   *93*

Class 2. Education in *Theory and Practice* (1976–77)   *111*

Class 3. Grace and the Machine: *Perjury and Pardon* (1997–98) 127

Conclusion: *Actes de naissance* 149

Acknowledgments 157
Notes 159
Index 183

Abbreviations of Works Cited

Works by Jacques Derrida

All works subsequently cited with the English pagination followed by the French.

"AC"   "Aphorism Countertime." Trans. Nicholas Royle, in *PSY 2*, 127–142. ("L'aphorisme à contretemps," in *PSY* 2, 131–144.) First published in 1986 on the occasion of a production of *Romeo and Juliet* by Daniel Mesguich at the Théâtre Gérard-Philipe in Saint Denis.

AF   *Archaeology of the Frivolous*. Trans. John P. Leavey Jr. Lincoln: University of Nebraska Press, 1980. (*L'archéologie du frivole: Lire Condillac*. Paris: Éditions Galilée, 1973.)

AFF   *Archive Fever: A Freudian Impression*. Trans. Eric Prenowitz. Chicago: University of Chicago Press, 1996. (*Mal d'Archive: Une impression freudienne*. Paris: Éditions Galilée, 1995.)

"ANC"   "L'autre nom du Collège," in *RB*, 201–221. An essay written for the tenth anniversary of the CIP, first published in *Rue Descartes* 7 (1993): 9–25.

"ATE"   "Afterword: Toward An Ethic of Discussion." Trans. Samuel Weber, in *LI*, 111–154. ("Postface: Vers une éthique de la discussion," in *LI*, Galilée, 199–285.)

"BR"	"Bâtons rompus." Public discussion with Hélène Cixous of March 15, 2003, in *Derrida d'ici, Derrida de là*. Ed. Thomas Dutoit and Philippe Romanski. Paris: Éditions Galilée, 2009, 177–221. Excerpt published in English under the title "Deconstruction and Childhood." Trans. Peggy Kamuf. In *The Oxford Literary Review* 41, no. 2 (2019): 149–159.
BS 1	*The Beast and the Sovereign*. Volume 1, Seminar of 2001–2002. Trans. Geoffrey Bennington. Chicago: University of Chicago Press, 2009. (*La bête et le souverain, Volume 1, 2001–2002*, ed. Michel Lisse, Marie-Louise Mallet, and Ginette Michaud. Paris: Éditions Galilée, 2008.)
BS 2	*The Beast and the Sovereign*. Volume 2, Seminar of 2002–2003. Trans. Geoffrey Bennington. Chicago: University of Chicago Press, 2010. (*La bête et le souverain, Volume 2, 2002–2003*, ed. Michel Lisse, Marie-Louise Mallet and Ginette Michaud. Paris: Éditions Galilée, 2009.)
CFU	*Chaque fois unique, la fin du monde*. Ed. Pascale-Anne Brault and Michael Naas. Paris: Éditions Galilée, 2003.
"CHM"	"Cogito and the History of Madness." In *WD* 31–63. ("Cogito et histoire de la folie." In *ED* 51–97.) First given as a lecture at the Collège Philosophique on March 4, 1963.
"CIP"	"A Certain Impossible Possibility of Saying the Event." Trans. Gila Walker. In *The Late Derrida*. Ed. W.J.T. Mitchell and Arnold I. Davidson. Chicago: University of Chicago Press, 2007, 223–243. First published in *Critical Inquiry* 33.2 (Winter 2007): 441–461. ("Une certaine possibilité impossible de dire l'événement." In *Dire l'événement, est-ce possible? Séminaire de Montréal, pour Jacques Derrida*. With Gad Soussana and Alexis Nouss. Paris: L'Harmattan, 2001, 79–112.)
CL	*The Calculus of Languages*. Trans. Katie Chenoweth and Rodrigo Therezo. Chicago: University of Chicago Press, 2021. (*Le calcul des langues: Distyle*, ed. Geoffrey Bennington and Katie Chenoweth. Paris: Editions du Seuil, 2020.)
DDP	*Du droit à la philosophie*. Paris: Éditions Galilée, 1990. (For the English translation, see *WAP* and *EU*.)
"DI"	"Declarations of Independence." Trans. Tom Keenan and Tom Pepper. In *N* 46–54; first published in *New Political Science* 15 (Summer 1986): 7–15. ("Déclarations d'indépendance," in *O* 11–32.)

DIS	*Dissemination.* Trans. Barbara Johnson. Chicago: University of Chicago Press, 1981. (*La dissémination.* Paris: Éditions du Seuil, 1972.)
DP 1	*The Death Penalty.* Volume 1, Seminar of 1999–2000. Trans. Peggy Kamuf. Chicago: University of Chicago Press, 2014. (*La peine de mort, Volume 1, 1999–2000.* Ed. Geoffrey Bennington, Marc Crépon, and Thomas Dutoit. Paris: Éditions Galilée, 2012.)
DP 2	*The Death Penalty.* Volume 2, Seminar of 2000–2001. Trans. Elizabeth Rottenberg. Chicago: University of Chicago Press, 2017. (*La peine de mort, Volume 2, 2000–2001.* Ed. Geoffrey Bennington, Marc Crépon, and Thomas Dutoit. Paris: Éditions Galilée, 2015.)
"EE"	"L'école a été un enfer pour moi: Conversation avec Jacques Derrida." With Bernard Defrance. In *Cahiers Pédagogiques* 270 (January 1989): 41–42. See "LC" for the second part of this interview.
EO	*The Ear of the Other: Otobiography, Transference, Translation.* Trans. Peggy Kamuf and Avital Ronell. Ed. Christie V. McDonald. New York: Schocken Books, 1985. (*Otobiographies: L'enseignement de Nietzsche et la politique du nom propre.* Paris: Éditions Galilée, 1984.) See also *OA*.
EU	*Eyes of the University: Right to Philosophy 2.* Trans. Jan Plug et al. Stanford, CA: Stanford University Press, 2004. (*Du droit à la philosophie*, 281–659.)
"FK"	"Faith and Knowledge: The Two Sources of 'Religion' at the Limits of Reason Alone." Trans. Samuel Weber. In *Religion.* Ed. Jacques Derrida and Gianni Vattimo, 1–78. Stanford, Calif.: Stanford University Press, 1998. Also published in *AR*, 40–101. ("Foi et savoir." In *La religion*, ed. Jacques Derrida and Gianni Vattimo. Paris: Éditions du Seuil, 1996, 9–86; reprinted in *Foi et Savoir* suivi de *Le Siècle et le Pardon*, Paris: Éditions du Seuil, 2001, 7–100.) All references are to section (§) numbers.
FWT	*For What Tomorrow. . . .* With Elisabeth Roudinesco. Trans. Jeff Fort. Stanford, CA: Stanford University Press, 2004. (*De quoi demain . . . Dialogue.* With Elisabeth Roudinesco. Paris: Libraire Arthème Fayard et Éditions Galilée, 2001.)
G 3	*Geschlecht 3.* Trans. Katie Chenoweth and Rodrigo Therezo. Chicago: University of Chicago Press, 2020. (*Geschlecht III, Sexe, race, nation, humanité*, ed. Geoffrey Bennington,

Katie Chenoweth, and Rodrigo Therezo. Paris: Éditions du Seuil, 2018.)

GL *Glas.* Trans. John P. Leavey Jr. and Richard Rand. Lincoln: University of Nebraska Press, 1986. (*Glas.* Paris: Éditions Galilée, 1974.)

"LC" "Libérer la curiosité, susciter du désir." In *Cahiers pédagogiques* 272 (March 1989): 44–47. This is the second of a two-part interview; see "EE" for part I.

LD *Life Death*, Seminar of 1975–1976. Trans. Pascale-Anne Brault and Michael Naas. Chicago: University of Chicago Press, 2020. (*La vie la mort*, Séminaire (1975–1976), ed. Pascale-Anne Brault and Peggy Kamuf. Paris. Éditions du Seuil, 2019.)

LI *Limited Inc.* Trans. Samuel Weber. Evanston, IL: Northwestern University Press, 1988. (*Limited Inc.* Paris: Éditions Galilée, 1990.)

"LI" "Limited Inc a b c . . ." Trans. Samuel Weber, in *LI* 29–110. (*LI*, Éditions Galilée, 61–197.) First published in *Glyph 2* (1977): 162–254.

LLF *Learning to Live Finally: The Last Interview.* Trans. Pascale-Anne Brault and Michael Naas. Hoboken, NJ: Melville House Publishing, 2007. (*Apprendre à vivre enfin: Entretien avec Jean Birnbaum.* Paris: Éditions Galilée/Le Monde, 2005.)

"MC" "My Chances / *Mes chances*: A Rendezvous with Some Epicurean Stereophonies." Trans. Irene Harvey and Avital Ronell. In *PSY* 1 344–376/353–384.

MP *Margins of Philosophy.* Trans. Alan Bass. Chicago: University of Chicago Press, 1982. (*Marges de la philosophie.* Paris: Éditions de Minuit, 1972.)

MPD *Memoires for Paul de Man.* Revised edition. Trans. Cecile Lindsay, Jonathan Culler, Eduardo Cadava, and Peggy Kamuf. New York: Columbia University Press, 1989. (*Mémoires pour Paul de Man.* Paris: Éditions Galilée, 1988, 41.)

"MS" "Marx & Sons." Trans. G. M. Goshgarian. In *Ghostly Demarcations: A Symposium on Jacques Derrida's Specters of Marx.* Ed. Michael Sprinker. London: Verso Press, 1999, 213–262. (*Marx & Sons.* Paris: Presses Universitaires de France/Galilée, 2002.)

N *Negotiations: Interventions and Interviews, 1971–2001.* Trans. and ed. Elizabeth Rottenberg. Stanford, CA: Stanford University Press, 2002.

O	*Otobiographies: L'enseignement de Nietzsche et la politique du nom propre*. Paris: Éditions Galilée, 1984. (See *EO* and *OA*.)
OA	*L'oreille de l'autre: Otobiographies, transferts, traductions*. Textes et débats avec Jacques Derrida. Eds. Claude Lévesque and Christie V. McDonald. Montréal: VLB Éditeur, 1982.
OG	*Of Grammatology*. Trans. Gayatri Chakravorty Spivak. Baltimore, MD: Johns Hopkins University Press, 1976. (*De la grammatologie*. Paris: Éditions de Minuit, 1967.)
OS	*Of Spirit: Heidegger and the Question*. Trans. Geoffrey Bennington and Rachel Bowlby. Chicago: University of Chicago Press, 1991. (*De l'esprit: Heidegger et la question*. Paris: Éditions Galilée, 1987. Also published in *Heidegger et la question: De l'esprit et autres essais*. Paris: Flammarion, 1990, 9–143.)
P	*Positions*. Trans. Alan Bass. Chicago: University of Chicago Press, 1981. (*Positions*. Paris: Éditions de Minuit, 1972.)
"PaF"	"Politics and Friendship: An Interview with Jacques Derrida." Trans. Robert Harvey. In *N* 147–198. An interview conducted by Michael Sprinker in April 1989 at the University of California, Irvine. (*Politique et amitié: Entretiens avec Michael Sprinker sur Marx et Althusser*. Paris: Éditions Galilée, 2011.)
PC	*The Post Card: From Socrates to Freud and Beyond*. Trans. Alan Bass. Chicago: University of Chicago Press, 1987. (*La carte postale: de Socrate à Freud et au delà*. Paris: Flammarion, 1980.)
PG	*Pourquoi la guerre aujourd'hui?* With Jean Baudrillard (Fécamp: Lignes, 2015).
"PP"	"Plato's Pharmacy." In *DIS* 61–171. ("La pharmacie de Platon." In *Dissémination*, 69–197.)
PP 1	*Perjury and Pardon*, Seminar of 1997–1998. Trans. David Wills. Chicago: University of Chicago Press, forthcoming 2022. (*Le parjure et le pardon*, Volume 1, *Séminaire (1997–1998)*, ed. Ginette Michaud and Nicholas Cotton. Paris: Éditions du Seuil, 2019.)
PP 2	*Perjury and Pardon*, Seminar of 1998–1999. Trans. David Wills. Chicago: University of Chicago Press, forthcoming 2023. (*Le parjure et le pardon*, Volume 2, *Séminaire (1998–1999)*, ed. Ginette Michaud, Nicholas Cotton, and Rodrigo Therezo. Paris: Éditions du Seuil, 2020.)
"PSS"	"Psychoanalysis Searches the States of Its Soul: The Impossible Beyond of a Sovereign Cruelty." In *WA* 238–280. (*États d'âme*

	de la psychanalyse: L'impossible au-delà d'une souveraine cruauté. Paris: Éditions Galilée, 2000.)
PSY 1	*Psyche 1: Inventions of the Other.* Ed. Peggy Kamuf and Elizabeth Rottenberg. Stanford, CA: Stanford University Press, 2007. (*Psyché*, volume 1, Paris: Éditions Galilée, 1987–1998.)
PSY 2	*Psyche 2: Inventions of the Other.* Ed. Peggy Kamuf and Elizabeth Rottenberg. Stanford, CA: Stanford University Press, 2008. (*Psyché*, volume 2, Paris: Éditions Galilée, 1987–2003.)
"R"	"Rams: Uninterrupted Dialogue—Between Two Infinities, the Poem." Trans. Thomas Dutoit and Philippe Romanski. In *SQ* 35–163. (*Béliers: Le dialogue ininterrompu—Entre deux infinis, le poème.* Paris: Éditions Galilée, 2003.)
R	*Rogues: Two Essays on Reason.* Trans. Pascale-Anne Brault and Michael Naas. Stanford, CA: Stanford University Press, 2005. (*Voyous*. Paris: Éditions Galilée, 2003.)
RB	*Le rapport bleu : Les sources historiques et théoriques du Collège international de philosophie.* By François Châtelet, Jacques Derrida, Jean-Pierre Faye, Dominique Lecourt. Paris: Presses Universitaires de France, 1998.
"SEC"	"Signature Event Context." In *MP* 307–330. ("Signature événement contexte," in *Marges*, 365–393.)
"SH"	"Shibboleth: For Paul Celan." Trans. Joshua Wilner; revised Thomas Dutoit. In *SQ* 1–64. (*Schibboleth: Pour Paul Celan.* Paris: Éditions Galilée, 1986.)
SM	*Specters of Marx: The State of the Debt, the Work of Mourning, and the New International.* Trans. Peggy Kamuf. New York: Routledge, 1994. (*Spectres de Marx*. Éditions Galilée, 1993.)
"SOO"	"A Silkworm of One's Own: (Points of View Stitched on the Other Veil)." Trans. Geoffrey Bennington. In *Veils*. With Hélène Cixous. Stanford, CA: Stanford University Press, 2001, 17–92; reprinted in *AR*, 309–355. ("Un ver à soie: Points de vue piqués sur l'autre voile." In *Voiles*. With Hélène Cixous. Paris: Éditions Galilée, 1998, 23–85.)
SQ	*Sovereignties in Question: The Poetics of Paul Celan.* Ed. Thomas Dutoit and Outi Pasanen. New York: Fordham University Press, 2005.
TP	*Theory & Practice*, Seminar of 1976–1977. Trans. David Wills. Chicago: University of Chicago Press, 2019. (*Théorie et pratique: Cours de l'ENS-ULM 1975–1976* [sic]. Ed. Alexander García Düttmann. Paris: Éditions Galilée, 2017.)

TS	*A Taste for the Secret.* With Maurizio Ferraris. Trans. Giacomo Donis. Ed. Giacomo Donis and David Webb. Cambridge: Polity Press, 2001.
"UG"	"Ulysses Gramophone: Hear Say Yes in Joyce." Trans. Tina Kendall and revised by Shari Benstock. In *Acts of Literature.* Ed. Derek Attridge. London: Routledge, 1992, 253–309. ("Ulysse gramophone: Ouï-dire de Joyce," in *Ulysse gramophone: Deux mots pour Joyce.* Paris: Éditions Galilée, 1987, 55–143.)
"UWC"	"The University Without Condition." In *WA* 202–237. (*L'Université sans condition.* Paris: Éditions Galilée, 2001.)
WA	*Without Alibi.* Ed. and trans. Peggy Kamuf. Stanford, CA: Stanford University Press, 2002.
WAP	*Who's Afraid of Philosophy? Right to Philosophy 1.* Trans. Jan Plug. Stanford, CA: Stanford University Press, 2002. (*Du droit à la philosophie,* 9–279.)
WD	*Writing and Difference.* Trans. Alan Bass. Chicago: University of Chicago Press, 1978; London: Routledge & Kegan Paul, 1978. (*L'écriture et la différence.* Paris: Éditions du Seuil, 1967.)

Other Works

HTD	John Austin, *How to Do Things with Words.* Cambridge, MA: Harvard University Press, 1975.
LL	François Jacob, *The Logic of Life: A History of Heredity.* Trans. Betty E. Spillman. New York: Random House, 1973. (*La logique du vivant. Une histoire de l'hérédité.* Paris: Gallimard, 1970.)
"RD"	John R. Searle, "Reiterating the Differences: A Reply to Derrida." In *Glyph* 1 (1977): 198–202.

Class Acts

Introduction: The Program

The life of a professional philosopher is, it is commonly thought, one of solitude, reflection, and introspection, a life of reading, writing, and thinking far from the public eye. Such a view is surely not incorrect. It is hard to imagine a philosopher who does not spend a good part of his or her day poring over a text trying to understand an argument, hunched over a keyboard trying to turn a phrase, or just looking out the window trying to put some order into his or her thoughts. But there are also philosophers who, in addition to this more private life, spend much of their time in public, before the public eye, teaching, lecturing, and speaking with students, or else giving papers and presentations at various universities, professional conferences, and public meetings. Jacques Derrida was one of those philosophers. Indeed, it is hard to imagine a more visible or more public philosopher, especially during the last three to four decades of his life.

This work aims to bear witness to these two aspects of Derrida's work—his public presentations and his teaching—by focusing on some of the questions that link these two things, beginning with the question of the "speech act," the question of just what one is *doing* when one *speaks* in public in this way. This is especially appropriate insofar as Derrida himself never ceased, in both of these settings, to interrogate this relationship between speech and act, words and deeds, language and action, the thought or ideas of a philosopher and the milieu or context in which those thoughts and ideas are communicated. Whether it was in the classroom or a conference hall, Derrida was always interested in the way in which spoken or written words might do more than simply communicate some meaning or intent but promise to give rise to something like an *event*. This is a book about the possibility of such events in Derrida's work.

While traces of Derrida's many public interventions or presentations, whether in France, the United States, or elsewhere throughout the world, have long been visible through Derrida's published works, many of which were first presented in some kind of public forum, the full scope of his pedagogy is only now beginning to come into view. The publication of approximately ten of Derrida's seminars over the course of the last fifteen years (there are more than thirty to come) has already given us a much better sense of Derrida's practice of teaching, that is, his deep commitment to that other form of public presentation that is a course or a seminar. Already we are beginning to understand much better the way Derrida combined reflections on the philosophical topics under discussion with an interrogation of the approach being taken to consider them and the milieu or the context in which they were being pursued. In classical philosophical terms, we are beginning to understand the interest Derrida took in questions of pedagogy and of the public speech act in both theory and practice—and, of course, in the ways these two things overlap in both theory and practice.

Given this interest in the context for *doing* philosophy, it is hardly surprising that Derrida would eventually take up many of the questions that are central to speech act theory, questions about the way we use language not only to talk about the world and communicate with others within our world but also *to do things* or *to bring things about* within the world. Those are the very questions that John L. Austin had taken up in his seminal text of 1962 *How to Do Things with Words*.[1] Back in 1971, therefore, at a conference in Montreal, Derrida delivered "Signature Event Context," an essay that would initiate his long engagement with speech act theory and, especially, with Austin. In that work, Derrida at once praises Austin for opening up an entirely new approach to language and yet criticizes some of the metaphysical assumptions behind that approach. Six years later, in the wake of a scathing critique of Derrida's essay by the American philosopher John Searle, Derrida would take up speech act theory yet again in a long essay entitled "Limited Inc a b c . . ." In that essay, Derrida attempts both to respond to Searle's criticism and to clarify and deepen his own reading of Austin.

This engagement with Austin in 1971 and with Searle in 1976 has long been known to readers and scholars of Derrida. But what has been much less known are all the ways in which Derrida would continue to use the language and raise the questions of speech act theory throughout his work, beginning with his frequent use of terms such as "constative," "performative," and "use and mention," terms or distinctions borrowed from Austin and those who would follow him.[2] But well beyond a simple borrowing of terms, everything from Derrida's analysis of the inauguration and legitimation of political institutions, his taking up of questions of law and sovereignty, of juridical performatives (in, for example, his texts on perjury and pardon and on human rights), his emphasis on an originary affirmation or performativity at the heart of all language (the "yes, yes")—all these gestures and questions will have been informed by Derrida's reading of Austin and motivated by the question of how we do things with words. It was this same rethinking of speech act theory that also informed and motivated some of Derrida's most original reinterpretations of such classical philosophical problems as the relationship between possibility and impossibility, activity and passivity, essence and accident, and so on.

True to the work or to the event of deconstruction, that is, true to the way a deconstructive reading is essentially open, as it were, to the accidental encounter, Derrida's work came to be indelibly marked by the works of speech act theory, and especially by the work of Austin, by the language and thought of this encounter, just as it came to be marked by the works of all those thinkers or texts that Derrida read closely. Whether we are considering the influence on Derrida's philosophical vocabulary or his unique philosophical project, the work of Austin will have been an important, even a privileged site of deconstructive investigation, just as formative or decisive in some respects as the works of Plato, Rousseau, Hegel, Husserl, or Heidegger. And that would have been the case from 1971 right up until the end.

In "The University Without Condition," a text first presented at Stanford University in April 1999, right at the same time Derrida was completing the second year of his seminar *Perjury and Pardon* in Paris, all the themes that will be at the center of this work—pedagogy, performativity, speech acts, context, the accident, the event, and so on—are brought together in a particularly precise and powerful way. Derrida there says in the context of a rethinking of the university:

> One will therefore have to ask oneself what "professing" means. What is one doing when, performatively, one professes, but also when one exercises a profession, and singularly the profession of professor? I will thus rely often and at length on Austin's now classic distinction between performative speech acts and constative speech acts. This distinction will have been a great event in this century—and it will first have been an academic event. It will have taken place *in* the university. ("UWC" 209/23–24)

Even if Derrida will go on here, as he did elsewhere, to criticize the terms in which the speech act has been traditionally understood and framed, beginning with Austin, he will never abandon the terms of speech act theory and will never cease to avow or, better, to profess his debt to them. In this work from 1999, Derrida makes quite explicit the connection between the work of the professor, the professing of the professor, in public, in the university, and speech act theory, the way in which, in both the classroom and in lecture halls or at conferences, which themselves often take place at universities, one does things with words in order to make things happen, that is, in order to produce something like an event. This is a book, as I suggested, about those events or about the possibility of such events, about those that will have "taken place" during Derrida's lifetime but also, and perhaps especially, those that promise to take place beyond it.

Since this book revolves around Derrida's appropriation and critique of traditional speech act theory from the early 1970s onward in both his public presentations and his seminars, that is, in his acts as both a public intellectual and a pedagogue or professor, it is divided into two distinct parts, each one a sort of prolonged speech act in its own right. The first part, under the pretext of a play in three "acts," looks at three key moments in Derrida's confrontation with and development of Austinian speech act theory, all three acts taking place, curiously, as if by accident, in Montreal, that is, all three based on public presentations in Montreal that were subsequently published. The first act in this "play," titled "Derrida in Montreal (A Play in Three Speech Acts)," follows Derrida as he delivers in August 1971 in Montreal the above-mentioned "Signature Event Context," the first and most decisive work on speech act theory in Derrida's corpus. Particular attention is here paid to themes such as presence, intention, repetition, power, and the opposition between speech and writing, themes that are continuous with Derrida's works prior to 1971 but that, in the context of a rethinking of speech act theory, begin to take on new forms and move in new directions.

The second act of this single play takes place some eight years later, in 1979, at a colloquium at the University of Montreal. It is there that Derrida delivers a lecture on Nietzsche and the question of the signature, and particularly the political implications of the signature, a lecture subsequently published as "Otobiographies."[3] After a brief intermission that considers Derrida's return in 1977 in "Limited Inc a b c . . ." to the reading and critique of Austin that began in "Signature Event Context," and that was the object of John Searle's fiery criticism, the second act demonstrates how Derrida began using speech act theory in order to rethink the foundation of political and professional institutions (in "Otobiographies" but also in "Declarations of Independence" from three years earlier). As in the first act, questions of the speech act but also of the written act, of the signature, of context and translation, and, in this unique case, of the relationship between French, Quebecois French, and English will be front and center.

Finally, in the third act, we see Derrida, some eighteen years later, in April 1997, yet again in Montreal, speaking at the Canadian Center for Architecture, giving a series of improvised remarks that would later be published as "A Certain Impossible Possibility of Saying the Event." We here see Derrida returning yet again to the question of the speech act, some twenty-six years after "Signature Event Context," this time with a renewed emphasis on the event. We thus see how Derrida's earlier appropriation of speech act theory eventually turned into a rethinking of the event as what comes before every speech "act" and all performativity in general, the event as what involves a certain passivity rather than activity and a lack of performative power rather than a special form of it. Through this reading, we are able to take the measure of both the continuity in Derrida's work from the early 1970s through the late 1990s and the important shifts or transformations—the chance mutations, perhaps—within it.

What we have, then, are three acts, corresponding to three events in Montreal, all three of these acts and events revolving, by accident or design, around questions of the speech act, questions of the signature, the event, and context. In retrospect, these three conferences or events signed by Derrida in more or less the same context give the appearance of being part of a single play spread out over twenty-six years, a single performance on the performativity of the speech act. That is why I thus read these three acts, beginning in the early 1970s and running through the late 1990s, as if they were of a piece, three acts or three speech acts in a neatly circumscribed corpus within the massive corpus of Derrida, three acts in which Derrida rethinks, through speech act theory, questions of possibility and actuality, activity and passivity, essence and accident.

Part II of this work, "The Open Seminar," has a different, though not wholly unrelated, genesis and design. It looks at three recently published seminars of Derrida's, two from the mid-1970s when Derrida was teaching at the École Normale Supérieure (ENS) and one from the late 1990s when he was at the École des Hautes Études en Sciences Sociales (EHESS). The dates of these three seminars correspond roughly to the dates of the three acts of Part I, "Derrida in Montreal." But even more, all three turn explicitly around questions of pedagogy and the event, along with questions of act, production, the speech act, and performativity more generally. Just as the three acts or speech acts of Part I were thus read as part of a single play, presented over some quarter of a century, these three recently published seminars—of 1975–76, 1976–77, and 1997–98—are here read together as three pedagogical acts in an on-going "open seminar."

This notion of an "open seminar" comes from Derrida himself. During the years he taught at ENS and the EHESS, Derrida typically taught two seminars, both on Wednesday afternoons and evenings, a "closed" or "restricted" seminar (*Le séminaire restreint*), reserved for students doing their masters or doctorates with him, and, before that, from 5:00–7:00 p.m., an "open" seminar (*Le séminaire ouvert*), that is, a public seminar open to anyone who wished to attend, the only requirement being, as I recount later in this work, signing a notebook to testify to one's attendance. Now while each year of this ongoing "open seminar" was unique in terms of theme or, in cases where the theme carried over from one year to the next, the figures and texts studied, there were inevitable correspondences and connections between the years. There were often moments during a particular seminar when Derrida would look forward to what he would be doing the following year or backward at what he had done in previous years, thereby linking one seminar to others.

But each seminar was "open" to the others in an even more essential way, each inviting comparison to and contrast with the others in terms of themes, argumentative strategies, terms, and so on. It is a point that Derrida sometimes made with regard to his published texts, with certain works calling out to be read in conjunction with or even inside others. The point is made in a particularly poignant way in an interview back in 1967, later published in 1972 in *Positions*:

> One can take *Of Grammatology* as a long essay articulated in two parts (whose juncture is not empirical, but theoretical, systematic) *into the middle* of which one could staple *Writing and Difference*. . . . Inversely, one could insert *Of Grammatology into the middle* of *Writing and Difference*. . . . In any case, that two "volumes" are to be inscribed one *in the middle of* the other is due . . . to a strange geometry, of which these texts are doubtless the contemporaries. (*P* 3–4/12)

What Derrida says here about his written works holds just as much, if not more, for his seminars, each of which was unique and yet fundamentally related to all the others. It is thus not only possible but, often, desirable, even necessary, as I propose doing here, to read together various seminars from the 1970s when Derrida was at ENS, or even those seminars from the 1970s with seminars from the late 1990s and beyond. It is in this way that we might consider the entire series of seminars to be one endless "open seminar," a seminar open at once to whoever comes or wants to come and to other seminars in certain ways that are already now quite visible and in others that will become clear only over time. Derrida himself seems to suggest something similar near the beginning of the first year of his seminar on hospitality, in 1995–96, when he actually relates the "openness" of the open seminar to the theme of that year, that is, to hospitality. He begins, "*Nous ne savons pas ce que c'est que l'hospitalité*" ("We do not know what hospitality is"), and he goes on to relate this phrase about hospitality to the hospitality of language itself, in this case the French language, and then to the seminar itself:

> *Nous ne savons pas ce que c'est que l'hospitalité.* This is a phrase that I am addressing to you in French, in my language, *chez moi*, in order to begin and in order to welcome you to this seminar, where I am the first to speak, in my language, which seems to presuppose that I am home [*chez moi*] here, master in my own home, and that I am welcoming you in, into what is called this "open" seminar, that I am inviting you, accepting or greeting you, letting you come in and cross over the threshold, by saying to you "welcome" [in English], *bienvenue*.

The seminar is thus "open," Derrida suggests, to whoever wants to attend, to all those whom Derrida then greets on the threshold of this seminar on "hospitality." But because every seminar was essentially "open" in that way, even those that did not have "hospitality" as their explicit theme, every seminar was in effect related to every other through this "openness," this "hospitality." And so just as Derrida's published texts might be thought to refer to or, better, to contain one another in unexpected ways, so his seminars might be seen to intersect and coincide, to invite comparison and contrast, in ways that are more or less predictable and ways that, in the future, will be completely surprising to all of us. As Derrida himself testifies in the midst of the recently published seminar *Life Death*, "I never fail to be surprised when I give a course. Surprise is that structure that draws metalanguage back, that always surprises it in its naiveté, surprises it at the moment of its withdrawal, shows it that it is no longer virginal, that it is already violated. . . . One never knows where a course will go" (*LD* 58/86). That is the case, as Derrida says, of every course or seminar, every seminar, as he liked to say, "worthy of the name," that is, *digne de son nom*. It is also the case for the seminars taken as a whole.

"The Open Seminar" begins with an introduction that attempts to combine a general account of Derrida's teaching career, one that can be gleaned from the public record, with some more personal reflections about it. It also tries to make the case that the first two seminars under consideration here, both from the mid-1970s, are particularly important in Derrida's teaching career. For they coincide exactly, as Derrida himself will confess, with his first *explicit* consideration of philosophical and educational institutions in France and elsewhere and of his own role within them. They also coincide with various initiatives, such as GREPH, that aimed either to combat proposed reforms in teaching, and particularly the teaching of philosophy in France, or to institute new reforms. In this introduction to "The Open Seminar," I attempt to give a brief account of these initiatives through the lens of Derrida's *Du droit à la philosophie*, a massive volume of 1990 that combines many of Derrida theoretical works on education with texts documenting Derrida's role in these more practical interventions, from the formation of GREPH to the founding of the Collège International de Philosophie.

After this brief history of Derrida's long engagement with questions of pedagogy and pedagogical practice, I turn to the three most recently published seminars in order to find traces both of this engagement with questions of pedagogy and, not coincidentally, with questions regarding the speech act. It also turns out that each of these three seminars coincides chronologically with one of the three acts of "Derrida in Montreal," each of them taking up at the very same time the questions of signature, event, and context that we will have seen in the first part of this work.

The first chapter or "class" in "The Open Seminar" focuses on Derrida's 1975–76 seminar *Life Death* and the dual notion of "program" that informs it. In that seminar, Derrida juxtaposes a reading of the notion of "program" used by French biologist François Jacob in his depiction of the workings of DNA with reflections on the "program" of the *agrégation* exam that had set as its topic for that year "Life and Death." The chapter thus begins by looking at the critical role played by the *agrégation* exam in the production or reproduction of philosophy as a discipline in France. It then analyzes Derrida's reading of Jacob's *The Logic of the Living* in terms of two supposedly distinct programs, the putatively inflexible program of DNA, a program shared by all living beings, and the supposedly freer, more flexible program of human culture and institutions, including pedagogical institutions such as the *agrégation*. Central to this seminar is the question of the accident in relation to the foreseeable or the programmable, in this case, the relationship between genuine change, innovation, or mutation and the program, be it the educational program of the *agrégation* or Jacob's understanding of the program of DNA. The result, I argue, is a complete rethinking of the forms of production or reproduction at stake in both genetics and education.

The second chapter of "The Open Seminar" analyzes Derrida's questioning of the relationship between "theory and practice" in his recently published seminar of 1976–77 of this same title. It traces Derrida's reading of this relationship in Marx and Marxism, beginning with various interpretations (beginning with Louis Althusser's) of the famous line from Marx's "Theses on Feuerbach": "Philosophers have only *interpreted* the world, in various ways; what is important is to transform it." I go on to argue here that Derrida's reading of theory and practice in Marx should be used in the end to reread Derrida himself and so rethink the relationship between theory and practice in deconstruction and, especially, in Derrida's pedagogy. The chapter then tracks the places where Derrida's seminar, first presented in Paris to help prepare students for the 1977 *agrégation* exam in philosophy on the theme of, precisely, "Theory and Practice," repeated, overlapped with, or anticipated many prior and subsequent treatments of similar themes in Derrida's published works, beginning with Derrida's 1993 *Specters of Marx*. The chapter thus concludes that no seminar can be truly "restricted" to the time in which it was first given or "reserved" for a select audience. In the end, every seminar, like Derrida's "specters of Marx," or like all the seminars in Derrida's "open seminar," remains forever noncontemporaneous with itself, in a word, "out of joint," always holding in reserve more than it was ever able to communicate or teach during the class for which it was intended, more than it was ever able to "profess" before its "original audience."

After two chapters that concentrate on two seminars presented in the 1970s at the ENS while Derrida was exercising his functions as *agrégé répétiteur* preparing students for the *agrégation* exam, the final chapter jumps ahead in time some two decades, to 1997–98, the first year of the seminar on *Perjury and Pardon*. By this time Derrida had been teaching for more than a dozen years at the EHESS, giving a seminar, unrelated to the *agrégation* this time, on questions related, once again, to speech acts, to the very particular acts of perjuring oneself and pardoning or forgiving others. Chronologically, this chapter brings us right back to the time of the final act of "Derrida in Montreal," the seminar on *Perjury and Pardon* beginning just a few months after that third act at the Canadian Center for Architecture in April 1997. Thematically as well, then, the themes of the seminar bring us right back to what is at stake in "Derrida in Montreal," questions involving speech act theory and the philosophical underpinnings of it. As I try to show in this final chapter of "The Open Seminar," Derrida here in 1998 seems to remark or rewrite Austin's notion of "infelicity" as "perjury" or, rather, as *parjure*, and his notion of the "speech act" as the "written work" or, rather, as the *oeuvre*. The consequences of this rewriting or this reinscription could not be more profound, for tied to Austin's notion of the speech act are the philosophical values of presence, life, proximity, and the oppositions between success and failure, essence and accident, the origin and the supplement, possibility and actuality, and so on, values and oppositions that an emphasis on the oeuvre and on an originary *parjure* will completely overturn or disrupt.

In the end, all three of these chapters address in some way the question of pedagogy, of what it means to give a seminar, the possibility of turning a seminar into something like an event. And they all address in some way the question of when, exactly, a seminar "takes place," and so the question of the relationship between the live event and its reproduction. Like the three acts of Part I, these three chapters related to three recently published seminars—two of them from the 1970s, just like the first two acts of "Derrida in Montreal," and one from 1997–98, the same time frame as the third act—raise questions regarding the continuities and discontinuities in Derrida's work. In both parts of this work, therefore, all three acts or speech acts raise questions about the relationship between time and the event.

That, in short, is what is on the program for this work, that is, on the agenda, the playbill or the syllabus. In each case, as we will see, the *context*—which is always contingent, always an accident of sorts (Montreal or Paris, a public presentation or a seminar)—determines the kind of act or speech act, the kind of unique *event*, that takes place, at the same time as it raises the question of the common *signature*, in this case, the signature of "Jacques Derrida," that invites us to read these acts together. As we will see in the conclusion, it is perhaps this signature—the possibility of a work, of an oeuvre—that always takes us beyond the context in which a given talk or seminar was given, this signature that always promises to give rise or, indeed, give birth to other works and other events.

PART I

Derrida in Montreal
(A Play in Three Speech Acts)

Argument and Dramatis Personae

> Although *Sec* ["Signature Event Context"] never suggested beginning with theatrical or literary fiction, I do believe that *one neither can nor should begin by excluding* the possibility of these eventualities. ("LI" 89/166)

I am no playwright, and I have absolutely no pretensions to ever becoming one, but as I began to write about Derrida and speech act theory, and so, inevitably, about Derrida and Montreal, I began to get the impression that I was in the process of writing not so much an essay, lecture, or talk but a play. Or rather, I began to get the impression that I was not writing at all but rather witnessing or transcribing a play that had already been written by Derrida himself, that had even been staged by him, a play that might have gone under the title *Derrida in Montreal*, a play that had been performed or played out in three distinct *acts* on the topic, as chance would have it, of the *speech act*, that is, on so-called speech act theory, three acts not only written and staged by Derrida but actually performed by him *live* over the course of some twenty-six years in Montreal. While there may be other acts, that is, other colloquia or conferences in Montreal that Derrida participated in over the course of his long career, these are the three of which I am aware, and all three have the particularity of addressing this question of the speech act and of the kind of event that takes place in or through it.

What follows, then, is, as it were, a single play, divided into three acts, with three different set designs, two quick costume changes, and two intermissions that, let me tell the reader in advance, will take place not in Montreal, or even in Canada, but down below the border, in the United States. For while everything that happened in Montreal with Derrida was absolutely unique, singular, and without comparison with anything Derrida did or experienced in the United States or elsewhere, there was nonetheless always a back-and-forth, a kind of shuttle diplomacy or free trade agreement between the two countries that was constantly being negotiated or renegotiated, and that will be true, as we will see, from the first act of this play right through to the end—and even beyond. Three acts, then, two intermissions, and perhaps, if anyone is still here by the end, an encore or two, and the whole thing, with just a few exceptions, written in and for a single language, namely, the French language, *la langue française*, which will turn out to be in this production not just the medium or the element for the play but, in Quebec, one of its dramatis personae.

Act 1: The Context (1971)

This first act is the one most everyone knows best. It is August 1971, and Derrida is in Montreal, at the University of Montreal, to be precise, delivering a lecture or, as one would say in French, a "*communication*" to the Congrès International des Sociétés de Philosophie de Langue Française, which had set for itself that year the theme of, precisely, "Communication."[1] It was there that Derrida would first deliver "Signature Event Context," his most significant work—his signature work—on speech act theory, and in particular on John L. Austin's *How to Do Things with Words*. It is a lecture that would stir up a lively debate at the time with Paul Ricoeur, who had opened the Congrès the day before, and that would in the years following lead to an even livelier debate, or, truth be told, to a polemical and even acrimonious exchange, between Derrida and the American philosopher John Searle over the reading and the legacy of the speech act theory of John Austin.[2] We will get just a taste of this latter during our first intermission.

Derrida begins "Signature Event Context" by recalling, precisely, the *context* of his talk—a talk, that is, a *communication* on the theme of "communication." He begins with this question: "Is it certain that there corresponds to the word *communication* a unique, univocal concept, a concept that can be rigorously grasped and transmitted: a communicable concept?" ("SEC" 309/367) In other words, does there correspond to the word *communication* a single, univocal concept that might then be conveyed, transmitted, and communicated without loss or remainder? And if there is such a concept,

15

how would it be communicated exactly? In what language? What context? And what might this language or this context already assume about the nature of communication itself? For it may be, Derrida already seems to be suggesting, that the very context for such a question, namely, a colloquium in which participants give talks aimed at communicating a certain *meaning* with regard to communication, will have already predetermined its object by excluding or setting aside other meanings of the word *communication* in ordinary language (already a first gesture in Austin's direction), for example, says Derrida, the "communication" of a movement, of a shock or a tremor, a disease or a force—this word "force," just like "context," being a key notion for John Austin, whose name has not yet appeared or been uttered by Derrida beyond the epigraph to the essay, which we will come to in a moment ("SEC" 309/367). Derrida is asking, in effect, whether these nonsemantic notions of *communication* can be so readily excluded from a conference that is seeking to define or understand the *meaning* of the word or the concept "*communication*," that is, the French word *communication* and the (univocal) concept to which it would supposedly refer.

It is at this point—we are just a few paragraphs into the essay—that Derrida brings on stage for a first time that French language I mentioned earlier. Here he is, putting the question of language into the context of his questions about communication and context:

> It seems to go without saying that the field of equivocality covered by the word *communication* permits itself to be reduced massively by the limits of what is called a *context* (and I announce . . . between parentheses, that the issue will be, in this communication, the problem of context, and of finding out about writing as concerns context in general). For example, in a *colloquium of philosophy* in the *French language*, a conventional context, produced by a kind of implicit but structurally vague consensus, seems to prescribe that one propose "communications" on communication, communications in discursive form, colloquial, oral communications destined to be understood and to open or pursue dialogues within the horizon of an intelligibility and truth of meaning, such that in principle a general agreement may finally be established. ("SEC" 310/368)

Drawing attention once again to the *context* of his talk in Montreal, a Congrès des Sociétés de Philosophie de Langue Française, Derrida recalls that the word "*communication*" is, obviously, a French word, a word of the French language, and that it cannot be so easily communicated—or translated—into other languages without loss or ambiguity. And that is true even for languages such as English that seem to have the same word available to it. For if it is common to speak in French of a paper, talk, or lecture as an oral "*communication*," in this case a *communication* about the nature or meaning of "communication," it would be very unusual, indeed hardly ordinary, to speak in English of a talk as a "communication." One might speak, say, of a White House press or news release as a "communication" or, probably better, a "communiqué," but it is not common to speak of an academic talk at a conference or congress as a "communication." At the same time as he raises questions of meaning and of context, therefore, Derrida evokes the fundamental and obviously related question of translation.³

Having thus raised in his own unique way, that is, having at once used and mentioned notions of *language* and *communication*, Derrida announces that his talk, his communication, will focus on the question of *context*. In short, he will attempt "to demonstrate why a context is never absolutely determinable, or rather in what way its determination is never certain or saturated" ("SEC" 310/369). And he will want to show that this is the case not simply in fact but in principle, that this "structural nonsaturation" belongs to the very nature of a context ("SEC" 310/369). While the organizers of the conference might thus have thought that the theme of "communication" had been sufficiently delimited or circumscribed by the context and through an "implicit consensus" on the part of participants that they would deliver communications on "communication" as *discourse* "within the horizon of an intelligibility and truth of meaning" ("SEC" 310/368), Derrida is already suggesting that some of the most important work in communication theory is being done by those who, like Austin—though, again, his name has not yet come up beyond the epigraph—have questioned this horizon and introduced other questions regarding the communication not so much of truth or of meaning but of *force*.

Hence Derrida says that in what follows he must first show "the theoretical insufficiency of the *usual concept of context*" ("SEC" 310/369), and then, in line with what he argues in *Of Grammatology* and elsewhere, the necessity of "a certain generalization and a certain displacement of the concept of writing" ("SEC" 310/369). This displacement, that is, this reinscription and redeployment of the concept or, as we will see, the quasi-concept of writing within a new context will then require a complete rethinking of the category of *communication* as the transmission of meaning. Instead, therefore, of considering writing to be a secondary, limited form of communication understood as the transmission of meaning, Derrida will want to show that it is actually "within the general field of writing thus defined that the effects of semantic communication will be able to be determined as particular, secondary, inscribed, supplementary effects" ("SEC" 310–311/369). Derrida will thus at once describe or explain the necessity of criticizing the notion of context and, through a sort of performative of his own, displace and reinscribe that notion of context within a rethinking of the problematic of writing, writing in general and the signature in particular. And all of this occurs, recall, before any explicit mention of Austin apart from the epigraph, which—and we here begin to catch a glimpse of Derrida's strategy—makes reference to writing, or more precisely, to the *exclusion* of writing. Here is the epigraph, which in addition to addressing writing and not speech is drawn not from the main body of Austin's text but from a footnote about three quarters of the way through the text: "Still confining ourselves, for simplicity, to *spoken* utterance" ("SEC" 309/367).

After this preamble of sorts, which at once comments on the frame or the context of the communication and introduces the major themes of his own *communication*, Derrida begins the first and longest of his essay's three sections, "Writing and Telecommunication," with a brief overview of the ways in which *writing* has typically been understood in the Western philosophical tradition. As Derrida's subtitle already suggests, it has been understood as a kind of "tele-communication," a powerful means for the communication of meaning that "*extends* very far, if not infinitely, . . . the field and powers [*pouvoirs*] of a locutionary or gestural communication" ("SEC" 311/369–370). It is a claim that Derrida had been making in various other contexts since at least *Of Grammatology* (1967), published four years before. According to the tradition that Derrida had been analyzing in those texts, a philosophical tradition that begins in Plato, if not before, and extends up to Hegel and Saussure, if not beyond, writing is considered to be a *supplement* to speech, a powerful supplement capable of extending the *powers* of spoken and gestural communication in a space and time that are essentially *homogeneous* with those of spoken and gestural communication ("SEC" 311/370). It is a supplement that thus introduces no fundamental break, no discontinuity, in tele-communication, only a greater and greater extension of the space and time of spoken discourse.

To illustrate these claims, Derrida takes up the example of Étienne Bonnet de Condillac (1714–80), who, in his *Essay on the Origin of Human Knowledge* (*Essai sur l'origine des connaissances humaines*) of 1746, developed a theory of writing that exemplifies many of the fundamental traits of the traditional view. It is a work that was "inspired," Derrida notes, by Condillac's contemporary, the English philosopher William Warburton—a Frenchman and an Englishman, notice, already a foreshadowing or an echo, perhaps, of Derrida and Austin, the former taking his inspiration from the latter.[4] We thus find in Condillac a philosophical discourse that, "like all philosophy," says Derrida, "presupposes the simplicity of the origin and the continuity of every derivation, every production, every analysis, the homogeneity of all orders" ("SEC" 311/370). We will want to keep our eye on this word *origin*, which will attract Derrida's attention when he turns to Austin a bit later in the essay, the simplicity of an origin—or source—that will account for the continuity within space and time of every production of meaning, in short, the continuity in space and time of all *communication*, written or spoken.

Like other philosophers before him, then, Condillac wishes to maintain the homogeneity of written and spoken discourse but then define the specificity of writing in terms of *absence*: writing is used to transmit meanings to those who are *absent* from us in space and time with an efficacy that is unavailable to speech. Insofar as language is, for Condillac, essentially representative, that is, a sort of picture, reproduction, or imitation of some content, writing extends in time and space the powers of representation to those who are absent to us in space, who may in fact be very far away, or absent in time, those in the future, perhaps in a very distant future, who may one day gain access to our original meaning through a series of written signs ("SEC" 312/371).

According to Condillac, then, who is, for Derrida, representative of an entire philosophical tradition, writing must first be understood in relation to the "absence of the addressee": "one writes in order to communicate something to those who are absent" ("SEC" 313/372). Writing is understood in terms of the absence of the addressee, though this absence—and this will be a second trait that Condillac shares with others in the tradition—is understood as merely *temporary*, that is, as the modification and progressive extension of some presence (see "SEC" 313/373). Absence is thus always understood in terms of a deferred but *eventual presence*, and the supplement of writing is what repairs or remedies that absence, thereby restoring an original presence. In other words, absence is understood as the deferred presence of some meaning, idea, or ideal content, and writing is that which conveys or communicates that content in a way that is homogeneous with speech but more powerful than speech in terms of its extension in space and time.

But then what is the *specificity* of writing when understood as simply a modification or deferral of presence, that is, as a kind of deferred speech? Condillac can say that "a written sign is proffered in the absence of the addressee" ("SEC" 315/374), but if there is to be a specific difference to writing, if "absence in the field of writing" is to be "of an original kind" ("SEC" 314/374), then that absence must be not only deferred but also, Derrida contends, brought to an "absolute degree" ("SEC" 315/374). Only in this way would writing be something more or something other than a mere modification or deferral of presence or a mere extension of speech.

The real specificity of writing or of written communication is thus to be found in the fact, Derrida argues, that writing "must remain legible [or readable, *lisible*] despite the absolute disappearance of every determined addressee in general" ("SEC" 315/375). That is, in order to be something different than speech, writing must be "repeatable—iterable—in the absolute absence of the addressee"; it "must be able to function in the radical absence of every empirically determined addressee in general" ("SEC" 315–316/375).

After recalling that the word *iterability* comes from the Sanskrit *itara*, meaning *other*, Derrida suggests that writing must always remain repeatable or iterable for some *other*, some third party, in the absence of any empirically determined addressee. "The possibility of repeating, and therefore of identifying, marks is implied in every code," even the most seemingly idiosyncratic and secret ("SEC" 315/375). While some particular writing or code may thus *in fact* remain secret or unreadable for a very long time, perhaps even forever, it must remain *in principle*, in its structure as writing, iterable and thus readable for some third party, that is, beyond or in the absence of any empirically determined addressee.

Writing would thus not be writing if it were not essentially—and not just simply accidentally—related to *death*. As Derrida can now argue, "a writing that was not structurally legible—iterable—beyond the death of the addressee would not be writing" ("SEC" 315/375). Only such a radical absence of the addressee, only the death of every empirically determined addressee, can make writing something more than or different from a modification or deferral of presence. The absence or death of the addressee is, therefore, not some empirical possibility that might befall my writing (my pen pal dying before receiving my letter) but a possibility that structures all writing. In short, the possibility of the death of the addressee is inscribed *structurally* in every written mark.

That is the specificity of writing understood in terms of the absence of the addressee. But Derrida then goes on to argue, unlike Condillac, who speaks only of the addressee, that "what holds for the addressee holds also, for the same reasons, for the sender or the producer" ("SEC" 316/376).[5] Having suggested that writing would not be writing if it could not function, if it were not readable, in the absence of every empirically determined addressee or reader, Derrida goes on to argue that writing would not be writing if it did not imply the radical absence of the *addressor*. Hence Derrida writes, or will have written, in 1971, and we read today:

> To write is to produce a mark that will constitute a kind of *machine* that is in turn *productive*, that my future disappearance in principle

will not prevent from functioning and from yielding, and yielding itself to, reading and rewriting. ("SEC" 316/376; my emphasis)

Insofar as any writing must be able to function, that is, be productive, beyond its origin, beyond the future disappearance of its sender or its producer, that is, beyond his or her life, then the absence or the death of the addressor seems to be just as central to writing as the absence of the addressee. As soon as I begin to write or even, as we will see, speak, my nonpresence, that is, my nonpresent intentionality, some absence within my "intention-to-signify," in short, my nonpresent life, my death, is implied in the very readability of what I write. Hence Derrida's reference to a machine: writing is writing by virtue of the fact that "it must continue to 'act'"—already a redefinition of action, it would seem—"and to be legible even if what is called the author of the writing no longer answers for what he has written, for what he seems to have signed, whether he is provisionally absent, or if he is dead" ("SEC" 316/376).[6]

There is, therefore, says Derrida, an "essential drifting" ("SEC" 316/376) to writing as a repeatable or iterable structure—cut off from all absolute responsibility, from consciousness, an orphan separated from its father's assistance, as Plato's *Phaedrus* once put it. We do not need to read Derrida's important 1968 essay "Plato's Pharmacy" on the question of writing in Plato to begin to suspect that the question of this seemingly extrinsic, marginal thing called "writing" is, in the end, inseparable not only from questions of communication and meaning in general but also from questions of space and time, presence and absence, not to mention life and death, legitimacy and illegitimacy, fathers and sons, and so on. As Derrida says, "If Plato's gesture is, as I believe, the philosophical movement par excellence, one realizes what is stake here" ("SEC" 316/376).

Understood in this more radical way, writing suggests a "break with the horizon of communication as the communication of consciousnesses or presences, and as the linguistic or semantic transport of meaning"; as such, it suggests a break with "the semantic horizon or the hermeneutic horizon," a shot across the bow, it seems, of hermeneutics, the kind for which Paul Ricoeur, who, we recall, had opened the Congrès the day before, was the best known advocate at the time ("SEC" 316/376). The concept of writing will thus ultimately call for distinguishing the notion of *polysemia*, that is, a notion of multiple meanings controlled or regulated by context, from what Derrida had elsewhere called *dissemination*, a notion that, as we will see, compromises or renders illegitimate every supposedly rigorous determination or delimitation of a context ("SEC" 316/376). But before that,

Derrida wants to argue that these traits of writing are in fact generalizable and so can apply to "all languages in general" and even to "the entire field of what philosophy would call experience, that is, the experience of Being: so called 'presence'" ("SEC" 317/377).[7] This is, of course, the famous "critique of the metaphysics of presence," a critique that begins, at least here, with the notion of writing. Without trying to justify this larger claim regarding experience, Derrida will go on to argue that the absence of writing can be found in "every species of sign and communication," so that writing is no longer simply a species of communication, that is, a deferred presence beholden to speech, but the general or generalizable structure of all communication, including speech, as we will see in a moment.

What, then, are these characteristics of writing and how are they generalizable? First, the written sign implies absence and a beyond of every present or determined *context*. As Derrida argues, "a written sign . . . is a mark which remains, which is not exhausted in the present of its inscription, and which can give rise to an iteration both in the absence of and beyond the presence of the empirically determined subject who, in a given context, has emitted or produced it" ("SEC" 317/377). For writing to be writing, it must be able to *function*, as we saw, in the absence of the addressee, the addressor, and, thus, beyond every determinate or determinable context. The very notion of iterability in the absence of any empirically determined addressee entails "the radical destruction . . . of every context as a protocol of a code" ("SEC" 316/375–376). This suggests that "a written sign carries with it a force of breaking with its context, that is, the set of presences which organize the moment of its inscription" ("SEC" 317/377). This set of presences includes not only the putatively present moment of inscription but also the presence of meaning to a subject or a speaker in a *vouloir-dire* or a meaning-to-say. The written sign thus breaks with the presence and power that are typically assigned to or rooted in consciousness or intention, in a speaker who is assumed to be the living source and origin of his or her written communication and who thus is assumed to be the organizing center of a context. For it is of the very essence of the written sign to remain legible "even if the moment of its production is irremediably lost, and even if I do not know what its alleged author-scriptor meant consciously and intentionally at the moment he wrote it, that is, abandoned it to its essential drifting" ("SEC" 317/377).

This force of breaking with context also means that central to the very notion of the written sign is its essential iterability in *another context*. For one can always lift a sign and inscribe it into other chains, other contexts. As Derrida writes of the written sign, "no context can enclose it" ("SEC" 317/377). This possibility of breaking with any particular context is thus not some accident that may someday befall some particular sign but, again, a *structuring* possibility. Derrida writes:

> this force of rupture is due to the spacing [*espacement*] which constitutes the written sign: the spacing which separates it from other elements of the internal contextual chain (the always open possibility of its extraction and grafting), but also from all the forms of a present referent (past or to come in the modified form of the present past or to come) that is objective or subjective. ("SEC" 317/377–378)

Force and *spacing*: here are two more notions that Derrida seems himself to be reinscribing and remarking, placing them in a new context and giving them a new force.

Having shown all of this with regard to writing, Derrida now goes on to claim that the thesis regarding the arbitrariness of the sign implies that what holds for writing holds in fact for all signs, spoken as well as written. In order for a sign, any sign, to be "readable," that is, comprehensible, it must be repeatable, iterable—and thus, in a certain sense, *productive*—in the absence of every determined addressee or every determined context and, thus, beyond the presence of its emitter or producer. It is this structural possibility of iterability that makes every sign, spoken as well as written, susceptible to being cited, lifted out of one context and grafted onto another. In fact, it is this repeatability or iterability that accounts for the very identity or self-identity of any sign, written or spoken, this identity being determined only through a series of self-differences, a series of inscriptions in other contexts.[8] It is the very notion of iterability, Derrida can now argue, that makes not only writing but speech meaningful, meaningful because repeatable, iterable, in the absence not just of the addressor and of every empirically determined addressee in general but in the absence of the referent or the signified.[9] As Derrida writes, the "unity of the signifying form is constituted only by its iterability, by the possibility of being repeated in the absence not only of its referent, which goes without saying, but of a determined signified or current intention of signification, as of every present intention of communication" ("SEC" 318/378). Hence a sign, any sign, becomes recognizable as the sign that it is only through a series of iterations; as such, it must always be able to function in the absence of its referent or its signified. It is this "structural possibility of being severed from its referent or signified (and therefore from communication and its context)" that seems "to make of every mark, even if oral, a grapheme in general, that is, . . . the nonpresent *remaining* of a differential mark cut off from its alleged 'production' or origin" ("SEC" 318/378).[10]

We will focus on this notion of *origin* in a moment when we turn to Austin, but let me simply note yet again the emphasis placed here on *production* in Derrida's argument. In speaking of "the nonpresent *remaining* of a differential mark cut off from its alleged 'production'" ("SEC" 318/378), Derrida seems to be rethinking the notion of production as the capacity or power of a living subject to produce something, an utterance, for example, and reinscribing the notions of power and production on the side of the utterance or the mark itself, the "capacity" or the "power," the *pouvoir*, of a statement, sign, or trace to function on its own, to have effects, cut off from its supposed origin or source.[11] This notion of power, of *pouvoir*, will be essential to Derrida's understanding of the speech act, not to mention the *event*, from the first act of this little play right through to the end in 1997, and—precisely because of this power—beyond.[12]

Hence, the ability to break with context characterizes not just the written sign but all signs in general, including spoken ones. The written sign simply makes more readily apparent or explicit what is always already the case for any sign, namely, that it *is* and *must be* repeatable, iterable, transferable from one context to another, iterable in the absence of both the addressor and any addressee in general. Moreover, it must always be able to function in the absence of its referent or its signified, a point Derrida dwells on at some length through a reading of a few passages from Husserl's *Logical Investigations* where it is argued that certain statements can still function and have meaning (and so not be non-sense) without having either a reference or signification ("SEC" 318–321/379–381). Even in the case of a completely agrammatical utterance, the possibility still remains for that utterance to be repeated, iterated, taken up and cited in other contexts—for example, as an example of agrammaticality. It is, then, this possibility of iterability in general, but then also the possibility of the graft, of citation, of citationality, that has the power to break with context and so compromises from the word go any intention or *vouloir-dire* ("SEC" 320/381). For every sign can be not only repeated but *cited*, that is, lifted, extracted, put between quotation marks, in order to break with its given context and so "engender infinitely new contexts in an absolutely nonsaturable fashion" ("SEC" 320/381). This possibility of grafting or citing structures even the "original" utterance, since in order for it to be taken up, for it to be recognized as what it is, that is, as resembling itself, it must be "cut off . . . from its 'original' meaning and from its belonging to a saturable and constraining context" ("SEC" 320/381). Inasmuch as every mark is essentially citable, the origin or the source is lost or at least doubled, repeated, from the beginning, and any "normal" functioning of the sign will be conditioned upon this citational, non-normal, "parasitical" possibility—all these terms being borrowed, cited, if you will, from Austin.

It is at this point, then, that Derrida finally turns to Austin. It happens in the second of the three parts of "Signature Event Context," this one titled, somewhat strangely and, as Derrida explains elsewhere, parasitically, "The Parasites. Iter, of Writing: That Perhaps It Does Not Exist."[13] But before looking at Derrida's reading of Austin, it will perhaps be worth asking how it is that Derrida, speaking in Montreal in 1971, comes to speak of John L. Austin in the first place. For it is a curious choice insofar as Austin is hardly a thinker in the "Continental" tradition with which Derrida was most familiar, the tradition that runs from Plato and Aristotle to Hegel, Husserl, and Heidegger. It is also a curious choice insofar as Austin is not just any ordinary English philosopher but an ordinary language philosopher whose context is the English language and, lest we forget, Derrida is speaking before the Congrès International des Sociétés de Philosophie de Langue Française.

So, how does Derrida come to speak of Austin and of speech act theory? Well, we know that Austin first delivered the series of lectures that would become *How to Do Things with Words* in 1955 at Harvard University as the William James Lectures. We also know that Derrida spent the academic year 1956–57 doing research at Harvard, just a year after Austin's lectures. While Derrida would thus not have heard those lectures, it is not impossible that he would have heard Austin's name because of his visit the year before and that word of those lectures was "still in the air" in Cambridge, Massachusetts, during the time of Derrida's stay. But it is also likely that Derrida had no real access to those lectures before their English publication in 1962, two years after Austin's death. In fact, it is most likely that Derrida did not read those lectures before their translation into French by the Quebecois philosopher Gilles Lane as *Quand dire, c'est faire* in 1970, that is, the year just before "Signature Event Context."[14] It is this translation that Derrida cites throughout "Signature Event Context" (even though he refers to the work throughout by its English title), and Derrida begins his reading of Austin by citing a passage from the French translator's introduction (see "SEC" 321/382). So it is not impossible that Derrida had heard of Austin as early as 1956 and had read him as early as 1962 but that he decided to write on him only after the appearance of the French translation in 1970. Finally, it has to be said that Derrida was not the first to have spoken of Austin in Montreal: Paul Ricoeur had already evoked him in his inaugural address the day before. Whether the overlap was intentional on Derrida's part or an interesting coincidence is unclear.

Whatever the reason for or the cause of his interest, Derrida seems to have understood right from the start the significance of Austin to philosophy, the importance of this turn to what Austin calls "ordinary language." This interest might be understood in terms of the infamous "linguistic turn" in philosophy, which is evident in philosophers as diverse as, say, Wittgenstein and Heidegger, or else in terms of the emphasis, from Nietzsche onward, on the *conditions* of truth or of truth statements and on forms or functions of language that exceed questions of truth and falsity, possibilities for thinking communication in terms not simply of *meaning* but of *force*. Austin himself, of course, mentions none of these so-called Continental philosophers, at least not in *How to Do Things with Words*, but when he begins his first lecture by speaking of a certain constative or "descriptive" fallacy that consists in reducing all utterances of philosophical interest to statements of truth or falsity, Derrida could have hardly been indifferent, and he would have quickly seen the implications of Austin for the philosophy that interests him.

Austin thus affirms the significance of other kinds of utterances, juridical utterances, for example, that are not simply true or false, and he affirms their significance for philosophy. Austin, who is usually not given to hyperbole, will go so far as to call this turn to such utterances a "revolution in philosophy," perhaps "the greatest and most salutary in history" (*HDT* 3).[15] It is a sentiment with which Derrida would probably agree, though, as we will see, he will want to show that that "revolution," if revolution it really was, is far from complete in Austin, who, despite his originality, carries a good deal of prerevolutionary metaphysical baggage along with him. What is certain is that everything Derrida ended up saying about juridical performatives, about the essentially performative nature of all law, about human rights, declarations of statehood, perjury and pardon, promises and testimony, all these things seem to bear the influence of Austin. Derrida actually says as much during a discussion in 1994 of his recently published *Specters of Marx*. In order to explain his use of the word "quasi-performativity" in that work and elsewhere, Derrida says:

> In *Specters of Marx*, as in all of my texts of at least the past twenty-five years, all my argumentation has been everywhere determined and *overdetermined* by a concern to take into account the performative dimension (not only of language in the narrow sense, but also of what I call the trace and writing).
>
> *Overdetermined*, because, at the same time, the aim has been other than to apply an Austinian notion as it stood (here too, I hope that I have been faithful-unfaithful, unfaithful out of faithfulness, to a heritage,

to "Austin," to what is one of the major bodies of thought or main theoretical events—undoubtedly one of the most fertile [*féconds*]—of our time). I have for a long time been attempting to transform the theory of the performative from within, to deconstruct it, which is to say, to overdetermine the theory itself, to put it to work in a different way, within a different "logic"—by challenging, here again, a certainly "ontology," a value of full presence that conditions (*phenomenologico modo*) the intentionalist motifs of seriousness, "felicity," the simple opposition between felicity and infelicity, and so on. ("MS" 224/27)

Derrida thus begins this second section of "Signature Event Context" by listing several reasons why Austin's notion of the *performative* is or should be so compelling. First, unlike most philosophers, Austin is interested less in the truth and falsity that is supposedly conveyed by a certain class of utterances called statements or constatives than in the ways in which all utterances, performatives first but also constatives in the end, *communicate* something. (Once again, notice, Derrida is bringing us back to the *context* of the Congrès in Montreal, whose theme for that year was *communication*.) Next, what is rather unique about the performative as opposed to most other utterances, such as the constative, is the fact that "the performative's referent is not outside it." That is, the performative "does not describe something which exists outside and before language. It produces or transforms a situation, it operates" ("SEC" 321/382). In a word, the performative *does* something with words rather than simply using words, as in a constative, to designate or connote or to speak of a state of affairs outside or beyond it. While Derrida will ultimately challenge this distinction between the performative and the constative, and he will find in Austin himself certain resources for doing so, he will never simply abandon the distinction, not here and, as we will see, not anywhere, opting instead to resituate or recontextualize the distinction within a more general field of "performativity" or, indeed, within a rethinking of the "event." As Derrida recalls some twenty-eight years later, in "The University Without Condition": "Even while recognizing the power, the legitimacy, and the necessity of the distinction between constative and performative, I have often had occasion, after a certain point, not to put it back in question but to analyze its presuppositions and to complicate them" ("UWC" 209/24).

Finally, says Derrida, "this category of communication is relatively original," for in the category of utterances designated by Austin as performatives what is communicated is not "a content of meaning" but "an original movement" or "a force by the impetus of a mark" ("SEC" 321/382). Austin thus frees the analysis of the performative from the distinction between true and false, that is, from the value of truth, from that "constative fallacy" he refers to in the opening pages of *How to Do Things with Words* (3). In a somewhat Nietzschean fashion, says Derrida, Austin substitutes *force* for truth, the force of an utterance for its truth-value. For all these reasons, says Derrida, "it could appear that Austin has exploded the concept of communication as a purely semiotic, linguistic, or symbolic concept" ("SEC" 322/383). The performative communicates something more than a semantic content that is to be judged in accordance with its truth-value, the correspondence between what is being said and "the thing itself."[16]

But then it comes, the critique we have all been prepared to expect. "And yet [*Et pourtant*]," writes Derrida by way of transition. Having praised Austin for all the ways in which speech act theory seems to depart from—and be an advance over—traditional philosophical conceptions of communication, having complimented him for "an analysis that is patient, open, aporetic, in constant transformation, often more fruitful in the recognition of its impasses than in its positions," Derrida claims that, in the end, Austin's whole analysis seems to be guided by a "common root" ("SEC" 322/383), namely, a certain concept of *context* linked to presence, self-presence, full consciousness, intentionality, and so on. It is this concept of context that will explain Austin's attempt to exclude all those traits or characteristics we just saw Derrida attribute to writing, that is, all those traits Derrida refers to as the "*graphematic in general*" ("SEC" 322/383). It is this exclusion, this ultimately failed exclusion, Derrida will argue, that accounts for many of the confusions of Austin's analysis and that contaminates the purity of many of the oppositions he tries to maintain in relation to the speech act.

It is, in the end, the value of *context*, Derrida contends, that commands Austin's entire analysis, the value of a "total" or "an exhaustively determinable context, whether de jure [*en droit*] or teleologically." For one of the central elements of this total context is "consciousness, the conscious presence of the intention of the speaking subject for the totality of his locutionary act" ("SEC" 322/383). What that then means, Derrida concludes, is that the "performative communication once more becomes the communication of an intentional meaning" ("SEC" 322/383–384). After having thus credited Austin with identifying the performative as a particular kind of locutionary act that communicates a *force* rather than a *meaning*, as the constative seems to do, Derrida now suggests that there is within the communication of this force another kind of meaning linked once again to presence and intention. And so, having credited Austin with opening the door to an understanding of communication that radically breaks with the tradition, Derrida criticizes him for using problematic metaphysical notions of presence and intentionality, of intentional meaning as presence, to define that communication—the very notions that Derrida demonstrated to be at the center of the philosophical tradition's understanding of speech and writing. Hence, Derrida will now show the way in which Austin, despite the radicality of speech act theory, nonetheless tries to bring performative communication back to an "intentional meaning," to a conscious and intentional presence that "implies teleologically that no *remainder* escapes the present totalization" ("SEC" 322/384); that is, that there is no excess over, above, or beyond the present context, or beyond the conventions and linguistic, grammatical, and semantic determinations in operation in that context. In a word, Derrida claims, "*intention* remains the organizing center" of the total field of the speech act, that is, "a free conscious present for the totality of the operation," "an absolutely full meaning that is master of itself" ("SEC" 323/384). As a result, in the discourse of Austin there is "no irreducible polysemia, that is, no 'dissemination' escaping the horizon of the unity of meaning" ("SEC" 322/384).

In the final analysis, Austin's understanding of the speech act is secured by means of a double operation that, writes Derrida, is "typical of the philosophical tradition that [Austin] prefers to have little to do with" ("SEC" 323/384). Since the operation is so "typical" in Derrida's eyes, it is essential to pay close attention to Derrida's treatment of it here since it will be repeated elsewhere—indeed pretty much *everywhere*—in his work. On the one hand, Austin recognizes "that the possibility of the negative (here *infelicities*) is certainly a structural possibility, that failure is an essential risk in the operation under consideration" ("SEC" 323/384–385). Austin's long list of infelicities, that is, of ways in which a speech act can fail, seems to be ample evidence of this. But, says Derrida, "with an almost *immediately simultaneous* gesture made in the name of a kind of ideal regulation, [there is] an exclusion of this risk as an accidental, exterior one that teaches us nothing about the language phenomenon under consideration" ("SEC" 323). This is a crucial moment in Derrida's reading of Austin and, as a result, a crucial moment for understanding Derrida. The negative of a phenomenon is always, for Derrida, a "structural possibility" or an "essential risk" that can never simply be excluded from the positive version of that phenomenon. On the contrary, the possibility of the negative or of the unsuccessful continues to condition even the positive or the successful phenomenon and so is essential, in Derrida's view, to understanding that positive or successful phenomenon. One could say that just as the spoken utterance becomes a species, on Derrida's analysis, of a generalized writing, so the successful performative becomes a species of a generalized unsuccess or failure. The negative is thus not the opposite of the positive, an opposite that can be excluded from it, or else a simple possibility that *might* befall it, but an ever-present possibility that structures or conditions the positive.

In the present context, such an understanding of the negative is the result of "everything that might quickly be summarized under the problematic heading of the 'arbitrariness of the sign'" ("SEC" 323/385), an arbitrariness that, to summarize in turn, introduces iterability, difference, otherness, and thus absence into every mark, every convention, and so every speech act—including the successful or the felicitous one. It is through this notion of a structuring negative that Derrida will attempt to displace several of Austin's key distinctions. Whereas Austin recognizes that all conventional acts (and not just speech acts) are "*exposed* to failure," that they are exposed to circumstances or to contextual surroundings that *might* lead to failure, he does not consider that there is "a certain intrinsic conventionality which constitutes locution itself," a conventionality that introduces into all language everything implied by the "arbitrariness of the sign" ("SEC" 323/385). While Austin thus recognizes the possibility of failure, of the speech act being *open* to failure, he does not see failure as "an essential predicate or *law*" ("SEC" 324/385). As a result, he "does not ask himself what consequences derive from the fact that something possible—a possible risk—is *always* possible, is somehow a necessary possibility." In short, he does not ask the critical question, "What is a success when the possibility of failure continues to constitute its structure?" ("SEC" 324/385).[17]

This is in many ways the nub or the core of Derrida's critique of Austin. It is this understanding of the nature of locution itself as *intrinsically* iterable, open to variation, to reinscription and citation, to parasitism, open, therefore, to other contexts, that radically distinguishes Derrida's approach to the speech act from Austin's. Take, for example, the category of seriousness, one of the essential traits of the successful speech act in Austin. For Derrida, it is the possibility of nonseriousness in a speech act, the kind of nonseriousness that characterizes, say, a poem or a play—a play like this one, for example—that conditions or haunts every so-called serious performative. As Derrida asks, "is not what Austin excludes as anomalous, exceptional, 'non-serious,' that is, *citation* (on the stage, in a poem, or in a soliloquy), the determined modification of a general citationality—or rather, a general iterability—without which there would not even be a 'successful' performative" ("SEC" 325/387). The "paradoxical, but inevitable consequence" of all this, Derrida can conclude, is that "a successful performative is necessarily an 'impure' performative, to use the word that Austin will employ later on when he recognizes that there is no 'pure' performative" ("SEC" 325/388).[18]

For Derrida, then, Austin's "opposition" success/failure (*succès/échec*) is "insufficient or derivative" ("SEC" 324/385) for the simple reason that the possibility of failure will continue to condition even the successful performative. Equally insufficient will be the opposition between *normal* and *parasitic* utterances. Derrida will argue that just as the possibility of failure continues to condition or to haunt every success, or nonseriousness the serious, so the possibility of citation continues to condition or to haunt every speech act, every utterance, indeed every sign—even the most supposedly unique or original ("SEC" 324/386). Like failure, then, parasitism or citation is not something that *might* happen to some original, successful performative, something that might *eventually* befall it, but that which conditions the performative from the beginning. In other words, the possibility of citationality, of parasitism, of iterability that Austin tries to exclude from the successful performative is the condition of every successful speech act.

For Austin and this entire philosophical tradition, success is *opposed* to failure, and the possibility of failure is considered to be an *accident* that simply supervenes upon the successful. Austin's entire understanding of "ordinary language," Derrida argues, is marked by this opposition and this exclusion.[19] For Derrida, on the contrary, failure must be thought as a structuring possibility of success, a speech act *without* full consciousness, for example, as the conditioning possibility of every successful performative.

But then how to explain the positive or "successful" performative, Derrida asks, in the form of a possible objection to his own argument? Since he has focused so much on failure, how can he account for what seems not to fail, that is, for what seems to be the success of a great number of speech acts? Derrida imagines someone posing him the question:

> You cannot deny that there are performatives that succeed, and they must be accounted for: sessions are opened, as Paul Ricoeur did yesterday, one says "I ask a question," one bets, one challenges, boats are launched, and one even marries occasionally [a bit of dry Austinian humor, it seems, chez Derrida]. Such events, it appears, have occurred. And were a single one of them to have taken place a single time, it would still have to be accounted for. ("SEC" 326/388)

Derrida's answer to this self-posed objection is telling in the context of "Signature Event Context" but also in the context of all of Derrida's subsequent work on the nature of the *event*. It is an answer that, as we will see, anticipates certain things that will be said about a quarter of a century later, again in Montreal, about the event and the speech act as event:

> I will say "perhaps." Here, we must first agree upon what the "occurring" or the eventhood of an event consists in, when the event supposes in its allegedly present and singular intervention a statement which in itself can be only a repetitive or citational structure, or rather ... an iterable structure. Therefore, I come back to the point which seems fundamental to me, and which now concerns the status of the event in general, of the event of speech or by speech, of the strange logic it supposes, and which often remains unperceived. ("SEC" 326/388)

After thus aligning here the "event" and, already in 1971, the "perhaps," Derrida returns to his "fundamental" point, the one that "often remains unperceived," namely, that "a performative statement" would not be possible "if a citational doubling did not eventually split, dissociate from itself the pure singularity of the event" ("SEC" 326/388), a doubling that can be found not only in the speech act of a poem or a play but also in so-called ordinary language. In other words, no "performative statement" could succeed if "its formulation did not repeat a 'coded' or iterable statement," that is, if it were not "identifiable as *conforming* to an iterable model, and therefore were not identifiable in a way as 'citation'" ("SEC" 326/388–389). In order for a formulation to be recognized, identified, in order for there to be, as Austin will call it, *uptake*, the speech act must be recognized as conforming to a particular code or convention. And so, in being recognized as what it is, that is, as the successful performative that Austin wants it to be, the success of the performative is already eroded by the possibility of failure, citation, parasitism, and so on.

Derrida's intention here is not, of course, to equate or conflate what happens on a stage with what happens off it. He is well aware that promises or oaths made on a stage do not engage one as they do when made in front of a priest, pastor, or judge in "real life." The point is, rather, that the stage cannot be distinguished from what is off the stage by means of categories such as seriousness, intention, and so on, since the iterability—or the spacing—of a sign, any sign, begins to erode the singularity of the supposedly serious, intentional speech act or event. While the category of intention would thus not disappear from a rigorous analysis of speech acts, it would have to be resituated, according to Derrida, within a more general topology of iterability. It would thus still have its place, but "it will no longer be able to govern the entire scene and the entire system of utterances" ("SEC" 326/389). For "given this structure of iteration, the intention which animates utterance will never be completely present in itself and its content" ("SEC" 326/389).[20] The written sign thus cannot be *opposed* to the oral sign on the basis of intention or consciousness or presence, even though the written sign, and in an exemplary fashion the *signature*, the topic of the last section of the essay, no doubt demonstrates more clearly than the spoken sign how iterability, absence, and a certain lack of presence structure every sign. Hence, intention would not be eliminated as a category, but, since it is no longer the controlling category, the door is open to thinking the speech act in relation not just to the parasitical practices of theater or jokes but, for example, to a certain unconscious, a "structural unconscious if you will," that "prohibits every saturation of a context" ("SEC" 327/389).[21]

Every successful performative will thus be unsuccessful, abnormal, impure to some degree insofar as a certain citationality or iterability conditions it. The real live promise always has something rehearsed, repeated, mechanical, and non-self-present about it. What this means is that "one will no longer be able to exclude, as Austin wishes, the 'non-serious,' the *oratio obliqua*, from 'ordinary' language" ("SEC" 327). In defining the conditions for success, Austin projects or imagines the possibility of a speech act that actually takes place, fully and completely, without the least bit of parasitism, non-seriousness, or citationality affecting it. By excluding "citationality or general iterability," by not taking fully into account the intrinsic or structural conventionality of all language, Austin's ordinary language, says Derrida, "harbors a lure, the teleological lure [*leurre*] of consciousness whose motivations, indestructible necessity, and systematic effects remain to be analyzed" ("SEC" 327/389).[22] In the end, it is consciousness or intention, the category of conscious intention, that establishes or anchors this notion of context in Austin. Derrida writes:

> For a context to be exhaustively determinable, in the sense demanded by Austin, it at least would be necessary for the conscious intention to be totally present and actually transparent for itself and others, since it is a determining focal point of the context. ("SEC" 327/389)

Derrida is suggesting here that the very notion of context, like that of ordinary language, is linked to "an ethical and teleological discourse of consciousness" ("SEC" 327/389), of a consciousness that is itself linked to presence, self-presence, spontaneity, life, and so on. It is at this point that Derrida introduces the word that serves as a title for one of his most important and widely read essays, also published in *Margins of Philosophy* (see *MP* 1–27/1–29), "Différance," an essay from 1968:

> *Différance*, the irreducible absence of intention or assistance from the performative statement, from the most "event-like" statement possible, is what authorizes me, taking into account the predicates mentioned

just now, to posit the general graphematic structure of every "communication." ("SEC" 327/390)

This reference to "the general graphematic structure of every 'communication'" leads directly to the third, final, and by far the shortest section of the essay, entitled simply "Signatures." Derrida begins: "This general space is first of all spacing [*espacement*] as the disruption of presence in the mark, what here I am calling writing" ("SEC" 327/390). *Writing* is thus the name for spacing as the disruption of presence in any mark, spoken or written, the spacing that is found both between and within elements, at once synchronically and diachronically. It is no coincidence, then, that all of the difficulties in Austin's analysis of the speech act come to converge in his exclusion of writing from consideration. This exclusion is more than merely strategic (as John Searle, as we will see, will claim) but symptomatic of that teleology just mentioned and of the philosophical tradition's understanding, as we saw earlier, of writing as a mere modification of presence and the tradition's emphasis on presence, self-presence, and so on, in speech and, in a modified form, in writing.

Derrida begins the final section of "Signature Event Context" by recalling Austin's preference in speech act theory for "the forms of the first-person present indicative in the active voice," that is, for acts such as "I do," I promise," "I declare," and so on ("SEC" 328/390). Such a preference for this first-person present active stems, Derrida argues, from what Austin considers to be the "*source* (origin) of the utterance" ("SEC" 328/390), namely, a present or self-present conscious speaker. This notion of *source* is what governs or grounds Austin's analysis and, on Derrida's account, it remains unquestioned by him: "Austin does not doubt that the source of an oral statement in the first-person present indicative (active voice) is *present* in the utterance and in the statement" ("SEC" 328/390–391). Derrida, of course, already has reason to doubt that which Austin takes for granted. He will thus go on to question this source in terms of its alleged presence or self-presence and, at least implicitly, its supposed power or ability to *produce* a speech act.

But, even more significant for Derrida, Austin also does not doubt that "this link to the source in written utterances is simply evident and ascertained in the *signature*" ("SEC" 390–391). As Austin says, and Derrida cites, the "I" of the signatory is "referred to . . . in written utterances (or 'inscription'), *by his appending his signature* (this has to be done because, of course, written utterances are not tethered to their origin in the way spoken ones are)" (*HDT* 60–61; cited at "SEC" 328/391). The written signature is thus, for Austin, what links the utterance to the "I"; it is what substitutes for that tethering to the origin that is found in spoken discourse.[23] As such, the signature in Austin functions as a sort of surrogate for the spoken "I," that is, for the first-person present indicative active. It confirms the presence or past presence of the author or the signer, just as the "I" does in spoken discourse. The category of writing, then, and of the signature in particular, will have thus oriented Derrida's entire analysis of speech acts from the very beginning, indeed already from the exergue, because it will have surreptitiously oriented Austin's entire teleological understanding of the speech act.

Derrida begins questioning Austin's assumptions about the signature, including what is here called the "oral 'signature'" ("SEC" 328/391), a notion that Derrida introduces in order to suggest that there will be a kind of graphematics, a sort of "signature effect," even in spoken utterances. As for the written signature, "by definition" it "implies the actual or empirical nonpresence of the signer" ("SEC" 328/391). A certain absence is implied in the written signature in a way that it is not in the spoken utterance or the "oral" signature, which, by seeming to be "tethered" to the speaking subject, gives access (or seems to give access) to the source of the utterance ("SEC" 328/391). Like the spoken performative, the signature *does* things with words. Unlike the spoken performative, it already implies, both for Derrida *and* for Austin, though, as we will see, in different ways and with varying degrees of radicality, the *absence* of the signer or the signatory.[24] As a result, it raises in an exemplary fashion all the questions of absence, iterability, and so on, that Derrida claims characterize not only writing in the restricted sense but also language in general.

The signature is thus, for Derrida, exemplary, though not unique, in its ability to, as Derrida said earlier in the essay, "continue to 'act' and to be legible even if what is called the author of the writing no longer answers for what he has written, for what he seems to have signed, whether he is provisionally absent, or if he is dead" ("SEC" 316/376). Though Austin excludes, marginalizes, or defers writing from consideration in *How to Do Things with Words* for what may *seem* to be strategic reasons, the exclusion is much more revelatory. Austin can, in a first moment, exclude writing from his analysis, in accordance with the entire philosophical tradition, insofar as it is but the temporary modification of a present and, thus, merely an extension of speech. Any problems associated with the written signature can thus be set aside and later resolved once the spoken utterance—the "oral signature," if Austin were to accept such a term—has been understand and explained. It is therefore not at all problematic for Austin to mention early on in *How to Do Things with Words*, as part of his very first list of performatives, not only "I do" (as in a wedding ceremony), or "I name this ship," or "I bet you *x*," but "'I give and bequeath my watch to my brother'—as occurring in a will" (*HDT* 5). The example, which, curiously, Derrida does not mention, poses no problem to the general theory of the speech act so long as writing is understood as a simple modification of a presence. But if writing is instead understood in terms of a general iterability that conditions not just writing but also speaking, then it becomes not just a problematic, supplementary example that can be cleared up once the rules of the speech act have been definitively established, but the very structure and rule of every speech act, a rule that would call for a complete rethinking or reinscription of all of Austin's categories.

The signature is not, in the end, some derivative case of a speech act that can be explained once the general principles of the speech act, that is, of the spoken speech act, have been understood and determined. It is, on the contrary, exemplary of all those things we saw attached to the written and spoken sign—lack of intention, iterability in the absence of the producer, the absence of both the addressor and the addressee, and so on. It is not the example that confirms the rule but the example that determines the rule. Derrida writes:

> in order to function, that is, in order to be legible, a signature must have a repeatable, iterable, imitable form; it must be able [*pouvoir*] to detach itself from the present and singular intention of its production. It is its sameness which, in altering its identity and singularity, divides the seal [*sceau*]. ("SEC" 328–329/392)

Notice here once again the way in which power or capacity, *pouvoir*, has been displaced from the putative origin or source of the signature, that is, from the signer, to the signature "itself," which is itself only insofar as it is iterable and divided. Whereas, for Austin, the *signature* is but the mark or the trace of a past *event* whose illocutionary force is ultimately determined by *context*, for Derrida the signature is itself an event, a nonsaturable signature-event, if you will, that is conditioned not by some determined context but by a general iterability that has the force of breaking with any determined context. As paradoxical as it may seem, the agent or the signatory of any speech act (whether in speech or in writing), the producer of any speech act, is but the *effect* of a nonsaturable signature-event, the effect of a general structure of iterability. It is by this same logic that, as we saw earlier, speech came to be seen as the effect of writing, but of a "writing" that has itself been displaced, remarked, and reinscribed within a new context.

As he nears his conclusion, Derrida discreetly returns not just to the *concept* of context in Austin but, once again, to the particular context of his talk, of his "communication" on communication in Canada. He says that he would like to conclude his, he says, rather *dry* discourse on the speech act—that is, in French, his *sec* discourse, as in *S*ignature *E*vent *C*ontext—by noting that what we are today witnessing is not at all an Austinian teleology moving toward greater and greater univocity in the statement and greater and greater explicitness and non-equivocation in the performative but the multiple effects of a more generalized writing. Derrida then adds, referring once again, albeit obliquely, to the Canadian context, not Montreal or Quebec this time but Toronto:

> we are not witnessing an end of writing which, to follow [Marshall] McLuhan's ideological representation, would restore a transparency or immediacy of social relations; but indeed a more and more powerful historical unfolding of a general writing of which the system of speech, consciousness, meaning, presence, truth, etc., would only be an effect, to be analyzed as such. It is this questioned effect that I have elsewhere called *logocentrism*. ("SEC" 329/392)

Instead of transparency, then, instead of a global village, we have a greater and greater force of dissemination: speech, writing, email, internet, texting or text messaging, bots and robocalls *avant la lettre* . . .

After this brief allusion to Marshall McLuhan, who was not Francophone or Quebecois but who at least had the distinction of being Canadian, Derrida goes on to make a few more programmatic statements that serve to link "Signature Event Context" even more explicitly to his earlier work. He gives us, as it were, some of the ABCs of deconstruction. He writes, for example, that

> the semantic horizon which habitually governs the notion of communication is exceeded or punctured by the intervention of writing, that is of a *dissemination* which cannot be reduced to a *polysemia*. Writing is read, and "in the last analysis" does not give rise to a hermeneutic deciphering, to the decoding of meaning or truth. ("SEC" 329/392)

As Derrida has hinted all along, *writing* in the more general sense that he has developed must cause us to rethink the very notion of *communication* as the transmission of an identifiable, univocal meaning. Even the notion of *polysemia* will not suffice, therefore, since it is simply a more complex version of univocity, where signs with more than one meaning are parsed out and clarified by means of intention and context. *Dissemination*, on the contrary, in combination with everything that comes along with it under the name of "the arbitrariness of the sign," will pose a challenge, for all the reasons we have seen, to this understanding of meaning and will give us a new way of understanding everything that is called "communication."

Finally, Derrida argues that in order to bring about a "displacement of the classical, 'philosophical,' Western, etc., concept of writing," it is necessary to retain this name *writing*, as least "provisionally and strategically"—in line with what Derrida calls "an entire logic of *paleonymy*" ("SEC" 329/392)—to refer to this notion of a general writing or iterability that is, now, the condition of both speech and writing. Derrida thus goes on to argue that a classical philosophical opposition, such as that between speech and writing, is also always a hierarchical ordering, with, in this instance, speech being privileged over writing. In order to intervene effectively in the system, therefore, in order to effect a displacement within it, it is not enough to try to neutralize the opposition. One must instead "practice an *overturning* of the classical opposition and a general *displacement* of the system" ("SEC" 329/392). Speech must thus be displaced and relocated within a notion of generalized *writing*. It is only in this way that deconstruction is able to "*intervene* in the field of oppositions that it criticizes, which is also," adds Derrida, and the addition is crucial, "a field of nondiscursive forces" ("SEC" 329/392). Such an intervention would thus have effects on the entire system insofar as "each concept belongs to a conceptual chain, and itself constitutes a series of predicates" ("SEC" 329/392). Since there is, in the end, "no metaphysical concept in and of itself" ("SEC" 329/392) but only a conceptual order that can itself be displaced by reinscribing a term such as *writing* within it, deconstruction "does not consist in passing from one concept to another, but in overturning and displacing a conceptual order, as well as the nonconceptual order with which the conceptual order is articulated" ("SEC" 329/393). The notion of writing is thus not some isolated concept, but a classical concept that "carries with it predicates which have been subordinated, excluded, or held in reserve by forces and according to necessities to be analyzed" ("SEC" 329/393), predicates, as we have seen, such as absence, nonpresence in space and time, lack of intention, the accident, the machine, and death. Derrida concludes:

> It is these predicates . . . whose force of generality, generalization, and generativity find themselves liberated, grafted onto a "new" concept of writing which also corresponds to whatever always has *resisted* the former organization of forces, which always has constituted the *remainder* irreducible to the dominant force which organized the—to say it quickly—logocentric hierarchy. ("SEC" 329–330/393)

Hence, deconstruction seems to *do* or to *perform* the very grafting that Derrida describes as a structural possibility for any utterance, the possibility of grafting old philosophical terms onto "new" concepts. This is, as it were, the deconstructive version of the speech act, but rather than "dubbing" or "naming" or "christening" this new concept of iterability by some new or other name, Derrida remarks or reinscribes an old name, namely, *writing*. It is in this sense that Derrida will attempt at once to describe *and* perform a notion of *dissemination* that will displace Austin's notion of *polysemia* and the concepts of intention, consciousness, presence, and context that determine it. That is how Derrida here does things with words in a way that at once recognizes Austin and breaks with him. Derrida argues:

> To leave to this new concept the old name of writing is to maintain the structure of the graft, the transition and indispensable adherence to an effective *intervention* in the constituted historic field. And it is also to give their chance and their force, their power [*pouvoir*] of *communication*, to everything played out in the operations of deconstruction. ("SEC" 330/393)

Retaining the old name thus gives to this "new concept" of writing its "chance" and its "force," its "power of *communication*." Having thus displaced without abandoning the notion of writing, Derrida again, notice, retains and remarks the notion of *power*: it is not the one who performs a speech act who has a power but the structure of the graft, a power that is now aligned with force and chance, that is, with the possibility of reinscription, above and beyond any consciousness or intentional structure, and with the possibility—beyond or at least separated from any fully conscious intention, from any fully self-present consciousness—of a signature. It is, therefore, not a capability or power on the part of the producer but an "ability" in the thing or in the trace, the possibility of a trace functioning in the absence of its producer.

It is here, close to his conclusion, that Derrida pens one of those provocative, somewhat oracular and yet, if we are patient enough, perfectly comprehensible lines about what he has been arguing all along in his essay:

> But what goes without saying will quickly have been understood, especially in a philosophical colloquium: as a disseminating operation *separated* from presence (of Being) according to all its modifications, writing, if there is any, perhaps communicates, but does not exist, surely. Or barely, hereby [*par les présentes*], in the form of the most improbable signature. ("SEC" 330/393)[25]

Writing communicates but it does not exist, *perhaps*, because it is not *present* in the sense that philosophy has understood presence. If it thus does exist, it does so only barely, and "hereby"—this word "hereby," typically translated into French by *par les présentes*, being flagged by Austin himself in *How to Do Things with Words* as one of the words frequently used in writing to suggest a performative (see *HDT* 57/82).

That, then, is the end of the essay—"in the form of the most improbable signature"—the end, at least, of the *argument* that Derrida seems to have been making about writing and the signature. But there is something else just after this line, a "remark," set in parentheses, a rather unconventional gesture for this kind of writing, where Derrida recalls that the philosophical colloquium for which "Signature Event Context" was prepared required that the written text of the communication be sent in advance to the organizers and *signed* by the author. At which point Derrida adds, echoing the substance if not the title of Austin's work, *Quand dire, c'est faire*, in French: "Which I did [*Ce que j'ai fait*], and counterfeit [*contrefais*: counter-do] here. Where? There. J.D." ("SEC" 330/393)

After thus attaching his initials, "J.D.," to this remark, Derrida signs his text, his essay, which is now also our text, our essay, this time outside the remark and outside the parentheses. He appends his signature, his "John Hancock" as one says in the United States, and then he types his name below it "J. Derrida."

It is with this triple signature, this triple countersignature—in script, in type, with initials—that "Signature Event Context" ends, and, with it, the first of our three acts of "Derrida in Montreal," by far the longest, I assure you, of the three, since it introduces all the major themes and characters and since everything that follows will follow in a predictably unpredictable manner from it.

Intermission 1: Glyph 1

> What is the nature of the debate that seems to begin here? Where, here? Here? Is it a debate? Does it take place? Has it begun already? When? Ever since Plato, whispers the prompter promptly from the wings, and the actor repeats, ever since Plato. ("LI" 29/64)

Before beginning our second act, I propose a brief intermission to recall just a little bit of the publishing history surrounding "Signature Event Context." The essay was first published not long after the conference itself in Montreal in the conference's proceedings, that is, in what are called appropriately enough in French the *actes du colloque*. It was then republished in 1972 as the final essay of the collection *Marges de la philosophie*, so that the signature or signatures that conclude and sign the essay can be read as concluding and signing the entire volume of essays. The collection *Marges de la philosophie* was then translated into English by Alan Bass and published in 1982 with the University of Chicago Press as *Margins of Philosophy*. Between 1972 and 1982, however, some of the volume's essays were translated, often by different translators, and published in other venues, that is, in various academic journals. Such is the case of "Signature Event Context," which was translated by Samuel Weber and Jeffrey Mehlman and published in 1977 in the very first issue of the journal *Glyph*, along with a little supplement that would generate a great deal of controversy and cause the spilling of a prodigious amount of ink, a ten-page essay by the American philosopher John R. Searle titled "Reiterating the Differences: A Reply to Derrida." So began the so-called debate between Derrida and Searle.

Searle establishes the acrimonious tone of the debate right at the outset of his "Reply." He suggests in his opening lines that Derrida has "misunderstood and misstated Austin's position at several crucial points" ("RD" 198). It is the type of retort one finds in many an academic essay. But that is just the beginning, just the opening salvo, in a long series of criticisms, complaints, and insults that would be sprinkled liberally over the ten pages of the "Reply." According to Searle, Derrida "confuses iterability with the permanence of the text" ("RD" 200); he gives a "mistaken account of the nature of quotation" ("RD" 203) and fails to "understand the distinction between use and mention" ("RD" 203); he has "completely mistaken the status of Austin's exclusion of parasitic forms of discourse" ("RD" 204), and he demonstrates "a misunderstanding of the attitude Austin had to such discourse" ("RD" 205); he "confuses no less than three separate and distinct phenomena: iterability, citationality, and parasitism" ("RD" 206). In the end, "Derrida has a distressing penchant for saying things that are obviously false" ("RD" 203), and the result is that "Derrida's Austin is unrecognizable. He bears almost no relation to the original" ("RD" 204).

Searle does not assign Derrida a letter grade for his essay "Signature Event Context," but had he done so we can assume it would not have been A, B, or C. Of course, to be fair, Searle does begin it all with this concession: "I should say at the outset that I did not find his arguments very clear and it is possible that I may have misinterpreted him as profoundly as I believe he has misinterpreted Austin" ("RD" 198). So there is that, a caveat that seems to come from the same school of speech acts as the well-known pseudo-apology, "I'm sorry if you were offended by my comments."

As for Derrida, he would have gotten the gist of the critique after the first few sentences of the "Reply." As he later wrote:

> The overture in *mis* will have set the tone. This is then incessantly replayed throughout the *Reply*, with an insistence and a compulsive force that can hardly be simply external to the contents of the argumentation. It is as though it were imperative to recall all the *mis*takes, *mis*understandings, *mis*statements, etc. ("LI" 40/82–83)

But Derrida hears something else in Searle's criticism. The insistence and compulsiveness of the critique suggest to Derrida that what is at stake here for Searle is not simply how best to understand Austin but who should inherit Austin's thought, that is, who should become the rightful heir to Austin's theory of speech acts. It is a question or concern that can be heard reverberating behind all of Searle's "Reply."[1]

Now I will be incapable here of responding adequately to each of Searle's criticisms of Derrida, incapable of rigorously determining all the places where Searle misrepresents or misunderstands Derrida in his claims that Derrida has misrepresented or misunderstood Austin.[2] Fortunately, as we will see in our second intermission, Derrida himself would respond to these criticisms, one by one, slowly and patiently, criticisms concerning, for example, the place of intention or intentionality in his reading of Austin, the role of iterability, citationality, and parasitism in writing, in speech, in the speech act, and in language more generally.

But before beginning Act 2, let me simply recall two things regarding Searle's "Reply." First, while there is no absolute difference between speech and writing for either Derrida or Searle, this is for wholly different reasons. For Derrida, as we saw, there is no absolute difference because absence, lack of intention, the possibility of iterability, of citation, and so on, are to be found in both speech and writing, albeit in different ways and to different degrees. For Searle, who also seems to recognize the importance of iterability, "intentionality plays exactly the same role in written as in spoken communication" ("RD" 201) inasmuch as it is truly absent in neither, intentionality being at the center of all communication.

For Searle, then, it is not intentionality or iterability or absence that really distinguishes the written from the spoken sign but, simply, a certain *permanence* of the former, that is, "the (relative) permanence of the written text over the spoken word" ("RD" 200). Permanence, therefore, not the absence of the addressee or the addressor or intention, is the distinguishing feature of writing. It is a point on which Searle insists because, according to him, Derrida "confuses iterability with the permanence of the text" ("RD" 200). But without ever himself explaining what this permanence means, Searle claims that it is "this phenomenon of the permanence of the text that makes it possible to separate the utterance from its origin, and distinguishes the written from the spoken word" ("RD" 200). It is thus this vague notion of permanence that then allows Searle to make the following, truly extraordinary claim about writing: "Writing makes it possible to communicate with an absent receiver," but "it is not necessary for the receiver to be absent. Written communication can exist in the presence of the receiver, as for example, when I compose a shopping list for myself or pass notes to my companion during a concert or lecture" ("RD" 200).

This example of the shopping list has, to be sure, its own enormous problems (for it is not at all certain, for example, that the recipient of that list, the person there in the supermarket, is exactly the "same" person as the one who wrote the list[3]), but since we are at the theater, let me say just a word about passing notes "to my companion during a concert or lecture" or, why not, a play. The reason for passing such notes is, I take it, that I do not want to speak openly and disrupt the performance. I thus write out my comments not in the presence of my companion but in his or her (relative) absence.[4] Were he or she not absent, I would not take the trouble to write out those comments and pass them along in the first place. And, of course, the fact that these notes can be passed along to others beside my companion, the fact that they can always be misunderstood, misinterpreted, or lost, suggests that they always imply my own (relative) absence, even when they reach their intended destination in my companion sitting right there beside me. As Derrida writes in "Limited Inc": "Even if it is sometimes the case that the mark, in fact, functions *in-the-presence-of*, this does not change the structural law in the slightest" ("LI" 48/96).

Were one to continue to maintain that the category of absence is irrelevant when I am sitting right there next to my companion, "present" to him or her, it would be legitimate to ask Searle when exactly it does become relevant. Would the recipient of my note be absent from me if I were two rows behind him or her? Would I myself be absent to him or her if I had my message delivered from outside the theater? Or from halfway around the world? Or if it were delivered by someone unbeknownst to me, perhaps even after my death? It is clear that absence begins, as we saw in "Signature Event Context," already with the first mark, the first written mark but also, of course, to a different degree and in a different way, the first spoken mark.[5] It is thus not at all clear what the "presence" of my companion at a concert or play could possibly mean and even less clear when that presence begins to shade into absence.

We will see how Derrida responds to this "Reply" by Searle, because he will reply, and reply at length and with force, but since the lights are already blinking I invite everyone to return to their seats and to stop talking to their neighbors (one can still pass notes) so that we can begin our second act.

Act 2: The Signature (1979)

> A promise that could not be reiterated (was not reiterable) a moment afterwards would not be a promise, and therein resides the possibility of parasitism, even in what Sarl calls "real life," . . . as though the meaning of these words ("real life") could immediately be a subject of unanimity, without the slightest risk of parasitism, as though literature, theater, deceit, infidelity, hypocrisy, infelicity, parasitism, and the simulation of real life were not part of real life! ("LI" 90/167)

As we have just seen, Derrida speaks a great deal in "Signature Event Context" about both the signature and the event, though it is the notion of context that is really at the center of his analysis and thus at the center of our first act of "Derrida in Montreal." This second act will be devoted essentially to the signature, and to an exceptional event made possible by the signature, as the context will soon make clear. It is October 22–24, 1979, some eight years after our first act, and Derrida is once again in Montreal, at the University of Montreal, having been invited by Christie V. McDonald and Claude Lévesque for a public lecture—a public "communication"—and a couple of roundtable discussions. Derrida kicks off that encounter or that series of events by presenting a long text on the theme of autobiography, the proper name, and—as if he were picking up right where he left off in "Signature Event Context"—the signature, in this case Nietzsche's name and signature in his early unpublished work *On the Future of Our Educational Institutions* and, especially, his late text *Ecce Homo*. At issue in these texts is thus the name of Nietzsche and the legacy of his thought, the uses and abuses—in Nazi ideology, for example—of his writings, which can always be *cited*, precisely, in order to make them say something other than what a more patient reading would show. It is a question, then, of the writings of Nietzsche, but then also of the name of Nietzsche, his proper name or proper names and, of course, his signature.

Derrida's text is titled "Otobiographies," *oto*, from the Greek *ous*, meaning "ear," a homonym of *auto*, meaning "self" or "same," a homonym that Derrida will trade on throughout the essay, a trade, a play, that can be seen with the eye—in writing, in *graphy*—but not really heard or picked up by ear. This difference between *oto* and *auto* already says more or less everything about Derrida's argument: autobiography—and Nietzsche's *Ecce Homo* will be exemplary in this regard—is never a more or less immediate or transparent presentation of the self by itself but a representation that requires a detour through language, through writing, through the other, or, as Derrida says, through the ear of other, even when the first other is the self who is writing about him or herself.

Now, I am not going to be able to read this essay "Otobiographies" with anything near the attention and detail it deserves. Let me simply pick out a couple of brief passages that concern the context and that lead more or less directly to the question of the signature. Derrida announces early on that, "since life is on the line, the trait that relates the logical to the graphical must also be working between the biological and biographical, the thanatological and thanatographical" (*EO* 5/39/*OA* 16). It so happens, says Derrida in 1979, that "all these matters are currently undergoing a reevaluation—all these matters, that is to say, the biographical and the *autos* of the autobiographical" (*EO* 5/39/*OA* 16). Nietzsche's texts will demonstrate this in an exemplary way. As Derrida will go on to show, there is an original duplicity that complicates everything here, everything from the name or names used by the author of *Ecce Homo* to refer to himself in this autobiographical text, the name or names that are staged (mise-en-scène) in this text, to the time or times of its writing. Derrida writes of the opening lines of *Ecce Homo*:

> This narrative that buries the dead and saves the saved or exceptional as immortal is not *auto*-biographical for the reason one commonly understands, that is, because the signatory tells the story of his life or the return of his past life as life and not death. Rather, it is because he tells *himself* this life and he is the narration's first, if not its only, addressee and destination—within the text. (*EO* 13/56–57/*OA* 25)

It is not long thereafter that Derrida brings this question of autobiography and of the signature into the context of the event. Still speaking of the preface to *Ecce Homo* in which Nietzsche, late in life, is evoking his entire work and life, Derrida notes, "This is why it is so difficult to determine the *date* of such an event," and "this difficulty crops up," he continues, "whenever one seeks to make a *determination*: in order to date an event, of course, but also in order to identify the beginning of a text, the origin of life, or the first movement of a signature" (*EO* 13/57–58/*OA* 26).[1]

"Otobiographies" is a fitting first scene for this second act of "Derrida in Montreal," and it is followed in the next couple of days by two wide-ranging roundtable discussions about autobiography and the signature, sexual difference, hermeneutics, translation, and literature—with figures such as Joyce, Borges, Ponge, Benjamin, and Blanchot up for discussion. At issue too is the unexpected fate—even for Derrida himself—of the word "deconstruction,"[2] and, in addition to all that, the French language or, rather, this time, the Quebecois language. Having himself already put the question of context on the table, and the difference between French French and Quebecois French, Derrida gets a question from Claude Lévesque about literature and the "so-called Quebecois language [*la langue dite québécoise*]" (*EO* 144/*AO* 190). Derrida's answer, perhaps not surprisingly, evokes questions of translation and of literature but then also, discreetly, of politics:

> It is time for us to take our bearings from the linguistic place in which we find ourselves, this strange linguistic place that is Quebec where, after all, the problem of translation is posed in forms and with a force, a character, and an urgency—in particular a political urgency—that are altogether singular. I think that if anything in this colloquium constitutes an *event*, it is in relation to the linguistic position of Quebec, where, at every moment, at every step, texts arrive not only in translation—that is obviously the case everywhere—but in a translation that is remarked and underscored. (*EO* 145/*AO* 192; my emphasis)[3]

After questions of the signature in Nietzsche and in general, we thus return yet again to the context and to the question of the event. It's "Signature Event Context," or *Sec*, all over again, in duplicate, a second iteration of *Sec*. Derrida brings all three terms to bear here on a thinking of the linguistic and political situation of Quebec, and though the word "independence" is never uttered, one can nonetheless hear it, at least in retrospect, in the background, just below the surface, or just below the border.

For it just so happens that Derrida's reading of "Otobiographies" for this second act of "Derrida in Montreal" was actually a third reading of this same text. First presented during the second session of his 1975–76 seminar in Paris that went under the title *Life Death*, much of this reading of Nietzsche was also presented, well before Montreal, in the summer of 1976 at the University of Virginia in Charlottesville during a conference celebrating the bicentennial of the United States' Declaration of Independence. For that occasion, Derrida would have presented not only the entirety of the text "Otobiographies," the reading of Nietzsche taken from the seminar *Life Death*, but also an additional, introductory section titled "Declarations of Independence," later published in 1984 by Éditions Galilée in the book

Otobiographies, though it is included in neither *L'oreille de l'autre* (the Canadian publication of the proceedings of that 1979 conference in Montreal) nor *Ear of the Other* (the English translation of that Canadian publication).[4] It is not included in these latter for the very good reason that it was not presented by Derrida at the conference in Montreal in 1979, and it was no doubt not presented either because Derrida thought it would have made the talk too long or because he deemed it somehow ill suited to the context. But once one knows it *could* have been there, it is difficult not to hear echoes of it in the version of "Otobiographies" that Derrida presented in Montreal, whose third chapter is entitled, precisely, "The Otograph Sign of State" (*De l'État—Le signe autographe*). Just like the sections of *Otobiographies* on Nietzsche, "Declarations of Independence" is also a text about context, about the event—in this case the event to found a nation—and, in an exemplary way, about the signature.

In "Declarations of Independence," Derrida follows and analyzes in detail the complex relay of names and authorities, of signatures and countersignatures, in the founding document of the United States. There is thus, first of all, at least according to a certain commonsense order that Derrida will ultimately question, Thomas Jefferson, the principal author of the document and thus the one who must take responsibility in signing it. But Jefferson is not, as Derrida recalls, simply writing a document in his own name. He does not simply author and then sign the Declaration of Independence on his own behalf. "Secretary and draftsman, Jefferson represents" ("DI" 52/28), writes Derrida, since he is not only the author of the document but also one of the fifty-six representatives who ultimately signed it. He wrote, then, not only in his own name but in the name of the other representatives; he was thus a representative of these representatives, who themselves, therefore, signed with their own name but as representatives of the people they represented.

Now, it is also worth noting at this point, though Derrida himself makes no reference to this historical curiosity, that this founding document is well known in the United States not only for what its "declaration" brought about or made possible but also for its signatures and its signatories, one of whose names would become a synonym for the signature in general. For among those fifty-six representatives who signed the Declaration of Independence was John Hancock, president of the Continental Congress at the time and the one who, as legend has it, signed the document first and with such flourish so that "old King George will be able to read it without his spectacles." As a result, the name "John Hancock," forever attached to this singular, extraordinary signature, has come to mean the signature in general. Still today, it is not uncommon in the United States for someone to be asked to "give their John Hancock" at the moment of signing a check, receipt, or some official document.

It is thus already not entirely obvious who is doing the *declaring* in the Declaration of Independence. There are Thomas Jefferson and the other representatives of the Continental Congress, including Hancock, but then there are also those who are being represented, the "good people" in whose name the representatives are acting and for whom they are speaking or declaring. But this "good people" too seems to need some justification or legitimation, some principle or foundation to which to appeal in order to authorize the declaration they are making through their representatives. The "good people" too needs some authorization in order even to affirm themselves, or to first recognize themselves, as the "good people" they are. That authorization comes, says Derrida, in the form of the "laws of nature," which in effect allow the good people or their representatives to recognize themselves as a distinct people worthy of the independence they are in the process of declaring, that is, to recognize "the separate and equal station to which the Laws of Nature and of Nature's God entitle them." It is these laws of nature, therefore, that allow the good people or their representative to denote or to declare: "We hold these truths to be self-evident, that all men are created equal, that they are endowed by their Creator with certain unalienable rights, that among these are life, liberty and the pursuit of happiness."

But, of course, this reference to a "Creator," the Creator who has endowed men with the rights that are now being claimed, suggests that there is yet another level of endorsement, another countersignature in addition to Jefferson, the representatives, the good people, and the laws of nature, one *final* relay that would also be the *first*. That first and final signatory is God, God who will have created not only man but also the laws of nature that grant man his freedom. Derrida writes, summarizing the series of relays, beginning with Jefferson:

> Secretary and draftsman, he [Jefferson] represents. He represents the "representatives" who are the representatives of the people in whose name they speak: the people themselves authorizing themselves and authorizing their representatives (in addition to the rectitude of their intentions) in the name of the laws of nature that are inscribed in the name of God, judge and creator. ("DI" 52/28)

According to Derrida, the ultimate guarantor of the Declaration of Independence, its final signatory, as it were, is God, who countersigns what will have *already* been the case, namely, that all men are created equal by their Creator and have been endowed with certain inalienable rights, rights that will have been authorized or granted from the very beginning, as it were, well before any explicit declaration on the part of those who are now claiming those rights. Hence the ultimate ground of the Declaration's performative utterance, the ground of the instituting moment of the United States, the ground of this human law, would be, in the end, natural laws and the God who created them. These natural laws did not have to be invented but, it seems, only discovered; they did not have to be declared or performed but simply discovered and recognized, made into the object of a constative, "all men are created equal," before then being declared. Hence the object of the constative, natural laws and God, would be the ground or the foundation of the performative, the ground or foundation that the Declaration itself is trying to affirm or, perhaps—a hypothesis—to invent:

> "We, therefore, the Representatives of the United States of America, in General Congress assembled, appealing to the Supreme Judge of the world for the rectitude of our intentions, do in the Name and by the authority of the good People of these Colonies solemnly *publish* and *declare*, that these united Colonies are and of right ought to be *free and independent states*." (Cited at "DI" 51/26)

It is thus God who is able, as this guarantor, to bridge the gap—or at least that is the phantasm, as we will see—between what *is* and what *ought to be*, between the constative and the prescriptive, between what is or has been and what must be declared, allowing the representatives to say that "these united Colonies *are* and of right *ought to be* free and independent states" (cited at "DI" 51/26). It is Derrida who emphasizes the "are" and the "ought," constative and prescriptive, that which was, is, and forever will be, on the one hand, and that which, precisely because of this prior state of affairs, ought to be and so calls for a declaration of independence, on the other. Derrida writes: "'Are and ought to be': the *and* articulates ["articulates" meaning here, it seems, at once to "say" and to "link," to show the lines or the "articulations," precisely, between "are" and "ought to be"] and conjoins here the two discursive modalities, the *to be* and the *ought to be*, the constation and the prescription, the fact and the right" ("DI" 51–52/27).

It is just after this that Derrida gives us one of those short little equations like "America *is* deconstruction" (*MPD* 18/41) or, as we saw in Act 1, "writing, if there is any, perhaps communicates, but does not exist, surely," one of those little phrases that is meant to surprise and to provoke. He writes: "*And* is God [*Et* c'est Dieu]: at once creator of nature and judge, supreme judge of what is (the state of the world) and of what relates to what ought to be (the rectitude of our intentions)" ("DI" 52/27). In other words, God is the articulation between *is* and *ought*, what *is* and what *ought to be*, *fact* and *right*, *natural law* and *human law*, the law we *discover* and the law we *declare*, the law that is *found* and the *founding* of the law, the *constative* and the *prescriptive*, that which is the object of a *constative* and that which must be invented or produced by a *performative*. Conclusion: "One can understand this Declaration as a vibrant act of faith, as a hypocrisy indispensable to a political-military-economic, etc. 'coup de force'"—that is, indispensable to the phantasm, to the fable—"or more simply, more economically, as the analytic and consequential deployment of a tautology: for this Declaration to have a meaning *and* an effect, there must be a last instance. God is the name—the best one—for this last instance [*instance*] and this ultimate signature" ("DI" 52/27).

God would be the ultimate signatory who guarantees all the others. Who gives Jefferson authority to draft the Declaration? The representatives. Who gives the representatives authority? The good people. Who gives the good people authority? The laws of nature? But who authorizes or creates the laws of nature? God. And that is where the series of relays ends. The buck always stops at the top, with God—or at least is the phantasm. Derrida thus concludes: "One cannot decide—and this is the interesting thing, the force and 'coup de force' of such a declarative act—whether independence is *stated* or *produced* by this utterance" ("DI" 49/20; my emphasis). In other words, one cannot decide whether the declaration simply *states* the case that these are or indeed already were by right free and independent states, or whether the declaration produces or *performs* the independence of these states. One would be tempted to lean toward the former were it not for that series of signatures and countersignatures, of signatories, leading up to God as the guarantor of the entire process, that is, were it not for the *time* it takes this series of relays to *simulate* that single instant that would guarantee it all. In the Declaration of Independence, that single instant—or the simulacrum of that instant—is also named "God." Derrida writes:

> There is a differential process here because there is a countersignature, but everything should concentrate itself in the *simulacrum of the instant*. It is still "in the name of" that the "good people" of America call *themselves* and declare *themselves* independent at the moment at which they invent (for) themselves a signing identity. They sign in the name of the laws of nature and in the name of God. They *pose* or *posit* their institutional laws on the foundation of natural laws and by the same "coup" (the interpretative "coup de force") in the name of God, creator of nature. He comes, in effect, to guarantee the rectitude of

popular intentions, the unity and goodness of the people. He founds natural laws, and thus the whole game that tends to present performative utterances *as* constative utterances. ("DI" 51/24–25)

Derrida seems to suggest through his analysis of this founding document that it is, in the end, the signatory or signatories who *perform* the event, the signatory or signatories who actually *invent* that which they feign only to be endorsing. In other words, the performative tries to pass itself off as a constative in order to suggest that what is happening thanks to the signature, thanks to the performative, is simply the recognition of a state of affairs that is already in nature or that is already brought about from time immemorial by God. This is the mystical foundation, the performative fiction, if you will, of all sovereignty, from the sovereignty of God to that of the nation state and the individual. One could say that the long list of signatures and signatories linking Thomas Jefferson to God has no other purpose than to invent the ultimate guarantor of those signatories, the instant named "God," just as the signature, the unique signature that then has to be repeated in order to be what it is, invents the signatory. It is the signature, which seems to come in a second time to affirm the prior existence of a self or a subject who signs, that thus actually *invents* the signatory, who then feigns to authorize in a founding instant his or her signature.

The *event*, if there is one, would thus appear to be produced by the context or through the context, even though it must also always exceed that context, in the form of either a fiction, the fiction of a founding instant, or else, perhaps, a moment that is always to come, a moment that eludes the text or the context, a moment that thus cannot but repeat itself. Almost everything we have just spoken about can therefore already be gleaned from Derrida's title, "Declarations"—in the plural—"of Independence." The plural is explained in part by the fact that Derrida had originally planned to do a "comparative reading" of the American Declaration of Independence and the French Déclaration des Droits de l'Homme. That never happened, for reasons Derrida explains at the outset of the essay. But Derrida no doubt decided to keep the plural because, as we have seen, a declaration is never single or singular, never just once and for all, but always marked by multiplicity, by a multiplicity of times and, as we see in an exemplary way in the American Declaration of Independence, a multiplicity of authorities, authors, and signatories. While a text such as the Declaration of Independence would thus like to present itself as being produced at one particular moment in time, at a particular, originary, founding instant, the unique instant of a unique speech act, it takes time for this speech to take place, to be produced, time for this act to be justified, legitimated, or authorized, time for the speech act to be, precisely, spoken and heard, uttered and taken up.

The speech act takes time and this time, while necessary to establishing the authority of the act, already begins to compromise that authority. Time and authority are in a necessary and necessarily antinomic relation: the time of the speech act compromises the authority of the speech act, and the authority or the taking effect of the speech act fights against and tries to annul the time that makes it possible. One could perhaps say, looking ahead to Derrida's work beginning in the 1990s right up through *Rogues* in 2003, that the speech act is always *autoimmune*: in trying to perform itself, in trying to legitimate and justify its performance, every speech act—and, in an exemplary way, a founding speech act like the Declaration of Independence—must always take time and take place in time, that is, in a time that begins right from the start to undo the authority of that act. The only speech act that would be immune, so to speak, from the ravages of time would be an act that takes place in an instant, in a punctual present that needs neither time nor language, an act that appeals to no other, not even to the other in oneself, a putatively pure speech act that would be closed to all reading, all interpretation, and all contestation. Because the moment that some other can say to the one who performs a speech act: "But who are you to be naming or marrying?" "Who are you to be declaring independence?"—and this is possible in principle as soon as the one who speaks presents himself as an authority, or indeed presents himself at all—the immunity or inviolability of that authority is threatened or compromised. Hence the speech act, and especially a speech act such as the Declaration of Independence, tries always to take time and to use the time of the speech act in order to simulate or to give the illusion of an annulment of time, to set up in the place of this time the *phantasm* of a punctual, unassailable, absolutely immune instant, the phantasm of an authority outside of time or productive of time itself.

The only way, therefore, to see that this phantasm *as* a phantasm is to *read* it, to see that it takes place and has its possibility in time, that it is the result of a performative that takes time. Such reading will never in and of itself do away with the force of the phantasm—and that would not always be, in fact, desirable—but it will, perhaps, attenuate the authority, the often unquestioned authority, that comes from believing in the reality of the phantasm, believing that it is a real, embodied, concrete presence, a founding punctual body, in the case of the Declaration of Independence, a perfect, punctual, instantaneous coincidence between the signers of the declaration, the good people who authorize and are authorized by the signing, the laws of nature, and God.

Here is how Derrida concludes "Declarations of Independence," a text first presented, I recall, at the University of Virginia, an institution founded by Thomas Jefferson in 1819: "How is a state made or founded, how does a state make or found itself? And independence? And the autonomy of one that both gives itself and signs its own law? Who signs all of these authorizations to sign?" ("DI" 53/31) All these questions will have to wait, says Derrida, who will instead turn to something closer to home, something he knows a bit more about, the proper names of Nietzsche, the question, again, of the signature, questions of teaching and of academic freedom, birthdays and autobiography—hence the transition to the rest of *Otobiographies*.

"Declarations of Independence" is thus yet another text about the signature, the event, and context, or rather, if one hears the title of Derrida's essay from 1971 not as a series of three nouns but, as he suggests in "Limited Inc," as a dependent clause, it is a text about "the signature event that one texts," "the signature event that one puts into text [*signature événement qu'on texte*]," the signature event that, in the case of the Declaration of Independence, has provided a nation with its founding document, its founding text.[5] It is thus yet another text about the speech act, and though Derrida did not present it in Quebec for all the reasons I have suggested, it can be heard in the background, being spoken or whispered just offstage, in the wings, by the Quebecois *souffleur* of "Derrida in Montreal."

Intermission 2: Glyph 2

> If the police is always waiting in the wings, it is because conventions are by essence violable and precarious, *in themselves* and by the fictionality that constitutes them, even before there has been any overt transgression . . . ("LI" 105/195; see 77/145)

> . . . had we both been together in Montreal while I was reading *Sec*, I would surely have sent off a note to help Sarl's wandering attention. ("LI" 51/102)

During our first intermission, we noted the 1977 publication, in the first issue of the journal *Glyph*, of a first English translation of Derrida's "Signature Event Context" and John Searle's "Reply" to that essay. Well, as we know, Derrida would not—could not—let that reply go unanswered. The second issue of *Glyph*, published later in the same year, would thus feature Derrida's eighty-five-page response to Searle's ten-page "Reply." That response was called "Limited Inc a b c. . . ."[1] By turns brilliant, biting, hilarious, and, for those inclined to read it this way, devastating on pretty much every count for Searle, it addressed point for point the arguments, criticisms, and insults of Searle's "Reply."

"Limited Inc a b c . . ." is the continuation of what Derrida calls an "improbable debate" ("LI" 30/65), an echo of the phrase "improbable signature" with which "Signature Event Context" ended, a debate or an encounter that, from Derrida's point of view, never really takes place because of all the misunderstandings and misstatements, whether witting or unwitting, that prevented any real communication between himself and Searle. Derrida argues: "The speech acts of the *Reply* do their utmost, apparently, to insure that this confrontation will not have taken place and, moreover, that it shall not (ever) take place, or at least not quite" ("LI" 35/74).[2] And yet an encounter does take place, sort of, or to some degree, between Jacques Derrida and John Searle, the representative of a certain Anglo-American philosophical tradition, the *representative*, Derrida insists, because Searle seems to suggest that he is speaking not only for himself but others (such as "H. Dreyfus and D. Searle," whom Searle thanks in his first footnote) and because, as Derrida notices, when Searle sent his "Reply" to the editors of *Glyph* he wrote at the bottom of his text the following inscription, the following speech act in written words, "Copyright © 1977 by John R. Searle" ("LI" 30/64). It is as if Searle were representing not just himself and a couple of colleagues but an entire tradition or body of thought, a corporation, as it were, that had incorporated under the name "John R. Searle." All this explains why Derrida in "Limited Inc" begins referring to Searle and Company by the acronym Sarl:

> In order to avoid the ponderousness of the scientific expression "three + n authors," I decide here and from this moment on to give the presumed and collective author of the *Reply* the French name "Société à responsabilité limitée"—literally, "Society with Limited Responsibility" (or Limited Liability)—which is normally abbreviated to *Sarl*. ("LI" 36/75)

It is, to be sure, rather playful and more than a bit "polemical" (see "LI" 36/76), but there is a serious philosophical point behind it. As Derrida suggests, "The whole debate might boil down to the question: does John R. Searle 'sign' his reply?" ("LI" 30/65).[3] That is, does Searle solely sign his reply? Is Searle solely responsible? And then, does anyone ever sign a reply, or produce a speech act, all by themselves, as Searle, following Austin, seems to believe? That is, does anyone ever sign in a fully present or absolutely conscious way, all by oneself and without the intrinsic possibility of repetition by oneself or another, without the possibility of iterability or citation, of parasitism or nonseriousness, coming to compromise or contaminate the act? Derrida's debate is thus indeed with Sarl, that is, with a *Société anonyme*, a society of limited responsibility, not only because, as Searle says, he is "indebted" to others ("H. Dreyfus and D. Searle") but also because, as Derrida already suggests in "Signature Event Context" and will develop more fully here, no speech act is ever undivided and signed once and for all, as it were, by a single individual ("LI" 31/66). It is another way of saying that the "origin" is never single and undivided:

> This is only another reason why, at the "origin" of every speech act, there can only be Societies which are (more or less) anonymous, with limited responsibility or liability—Sarl—a multitude of instances, if not of "subjects," of meanings highly vulnerable to parasitism—all phenomena that the "conscious ego" of the speaker and the hearer

(the ultimate instances of speech act theory) is incapable of incorporating as such and which, to tell the truth, it does everything to exclude. ("LI" 75–76/143)

This critique of the capability or ability, the responsibility or liability, of the "'conscious ego' of the speaker and the hearer" also brings us back to the themes of power and possibility that we have been following throughout this work. As Derrida writes in "Limited Inc," recalling some of the initial premises of "Signature Event Context": "if one admits that writing (and the mark in general) *must be able* to function in the absence of the sender, the receiver, the context of production, etc. that implies that this power, this *being able*, this *possibility* is *always* inscribed, hence *necessarily* inscribed *as possibility* in the functioning or the functional structure of the mark" ("LI" 48/96).[4]

Once again, I am unable to relitigate or readjudicate the entire debate here, unable to disentangle and clarify all the assumptions and all the conclusions, all the accusations and all the defenses, regarding Derrida's reading of Austin, Searle's reading of Derrida's reading, and then Derrida's response in "Limited Inc" to Searle's reading. I would especially be unable to clarify to anyone's satisfaction all the *levels* of argument and analysis in Austin, Derrida, and Searle, which sometimes intersect or overlap but often operate at such a distance from one another that no real "communication" between them is really possible.[5] Unable, incapable, though also, uninterested, in the final analysis, because I am inclined to believe with Derrida that in those places where he has, according to Searle, "misread" or "over-read" or "misinterpreted" Austin, all those places he has been "unfaithful" to him, it has been out of a kind of fidelity to Austin or to something within Austin's text. I am inclined to think that if Derrida says things that Austin (or Searle) would simply suggest are wrong and are not *in* Austin, if Derrida takes Austin's work in places Austin could not have imagined, then it is because Derrida remains the most Austinian of all contemporary philosophers, doing things with words that the author of *How to Do Things with Words* could not have imagined and might well have rejected. And while Derrida marshals a whole series of well-articulated and very convincing arguments in his defense against the criticisms of Searle, it is all too obvious that Derrida is here doing thing with words that exceed the mere production of valid arguments or true and false claims. Derrida himself alerts us to this in "Limited Inc" when he writes, apparently with a certain Austin and against this particular Searle:

> a theoretician of speech acts who was even moderately consistent with his theory ought to have spent some time patiently considering

questions of this type: Does the principal purpose of *Sec* consist in being *true*? In appearing true? In stating the truth?

And what if *Sec* were *doing something else*? ("LI" 43/87–88)

Hence Derrida can say, "I consider myself to be in many respects quite close to Austin, both interested in and indebted to his problematic" ("LI" 38/78). He is interested and indebted to this original work and yet, as we have seen, he is also willing to "raise questions or objections" where necessary, for example, in those places where he recognizes "in Austin's theory presuppositions which are the most tenacious and the most central presuppositions of the *continental* metaphysical tradition" ("LI" 38/78).[6] It is a curious claim. What Derrida finds most objectionable in Austin are not the ways in which he breaks with the continental tradition but the ways in which he conforms most closely, albeit unwittingly, to it. Derrida will thus go so far as to suggest that Austin is, in the end, more continental, more French or Parisian even, than he himself. And the case of Searle, an American philosopher who once studied with Austin in Cambridge, is even worse. As Derrida writes in "Limited Inc": "isn't Sarl ultimately more continental and Parisian than I am? . . . Sarl's premises and method are derived from continental philosophy" ("LI" 38/79–80). In his understanding of concepts or conceptuality, for example, Searle "reacts much as, in appearance at least, the great philosophers of the tradition have always done (Austin being in this respect a partial exception)" ("LI" 67/130; see 69/132). Derrida can thus conclude: "Metaphysics in its most traditional form reigns over the Austinian heritage: over his legacy and over those who have taken charge of it as his heirs apparent" ("LI" 93/173).

Incapable, then, as I said, of summarizing this debate or this polemic to anyone's satisfaction, I suggest simply listening to Derrida for a moment when he writes in "Limited Inc": "Since Sarl does not devote a single word to signature, event, context, I ask the reader interested in this debate to consult 'Signature Event Context,' which I do not want to cite or to mention in its entirety, so that he can judge for himself the effects of such serious negligence" ("LI" 46/92–93; see 59/116). Let us thus follow Derrida's advice, his plea, and return, not exactly to "Signature Event Context" but to another Derrida text—another Derrida event—for the third and final act of "Derrida in Montreal."

Act 3: The Event (1997)

> What the *Reply* never takes into account is that the most insistent question in *Sec* (I suggest this as an abbreviation for *Signature Event Context*) seeks to discover what an event—which, in the case of a speech act, is supposed to take place—might be, and whether or not the structure of such an event leaves room for certitude or for evidence. ("LI" 37/76)
>
> A pure event, worthy of the name, defeats the performative as much as the constative. One day we will have to come to terms with what this means. ("CIP" 242/109)

While Acts 1 and 2 were also, as we have seen, about the event, in addition to context and the signature, this third act will be devoted almost exclusively to the notion of the event, a notion that had been at the center of many of Derrida's works in the 1980s and 1990s. It is April 1, 1997—April Fool's Day, if you can believe it, *Poisson d'avril*, as it is commonly called in French—and Derrida is at the Centre Canadien d'Architecture in Montreal for a discussion that will later be published under the title "A Certain Impossible Possibility of Saying the Event." Given the setting or the context, one might have imagined that the discussion would revolve around architecture, a topic that Derrida had also addressed a great deal in the 1990s. But, no, the discussion revolves instead around the event, around the performative, and even the political performative, as if Derrida were picking up the conversation right where he had last left it in 1979. Unlike "Signature Event Context" and "Otobiographies," however, Derrida's remarks are here more or less improvised, more like the two roundtables of the second act, consisting essentially of two extended responses to presentations by two Quebecois scholars.[1] As Derrida says later in the conversation, bringing the notion of event into the context of their conversation:

I'm not the author of the topic of our debate.... I must say that, ultimately, what is happening here, to the extent that it was unforeseeable, that it was unanticipated for me—since we improvised to a large extent—is that an event will have taken place. It is happening and it wasn't arranged in advance; a lot was arranged but not everything. ("CIP" 238/104)

After evoking friendship, "an event of friendship [*l'événement d'amitié*]," that would seem to be the element, the milieu, the context, for all his comments ("CIP" 223/81), Derrida begins to address the notion of the event itself, defining it in a way that seems to signal something of a departure from "Signature Event Context." Speaking of the event in general but then also, it seems, of the very event that such an improvised talk might occasion, Derrida says that "if there is an event, it must never be something that is predicted or planned, or even really decided upon." An event, he continues, "implies surprise, exposure, the unanticipatable" ("CIP" 223/81). As "unforeseeable" and "absolutely singular," it always "disrupts the ordinary course of history" ("CIP" 228/89). As such, an event is "always exceptional," always "an exception to the rule" ("CIP" 239/106). It can be neither seen nor predicted in advance, for "a predicted event is not an event" ("CIP" 233/97). But if an event cannot be foreseen or predicted, can it nonetheless be "dicted," Derrida wonders aloud, that is, can it nonetheless be *said*? That is in effect the question that has lent itself to the title given to the event at the Canadian Center for Architecture: "Is saying the event possible [*Dire l'événement, est-ce possible*]?" ("CIP" 224/82) In a certain sense, that is also precisely the question of "Signature Event Context."

To address this question of the event, the event in relation to language and possibility, the possibility of saying the event, Derrida begins by asking about the question of the question, that is, the question of philosophy's traditional privileging of the form of the question (and particularly the "What is?" question) from Plato to, as Derrida puts it, "a certain Heidegger" ("CIP" 224/83). For there are, of course, as Derrida recalls, other ways of addressing a topic than by posing questions to it, especially when the question always seems to involve a certain "violence" with regard to its object ("CIP" 226/86). Hence Derrida suggests, in the spirit of a line of thinking developed more fully in *Of Spirit*, whose subtitle is "Heidegger and the Question," that there is something that precedes the question, something that, even in Heidegger, corresponds to a sort of "acquiescence (*Zusage*)" or "consentment, an affirmation of sorts" ("CIP" 225/83). There is, in short, a "'yes' before the question" ("CIP" 225/83), an originary affirmation that inhabits or haunts the question—the question in general and the question of the event in particular. Derrida affirms:

> There is, then, a certain "yes" at the heart of the question, a "yes" to, a "yes" to the other, which may not be unrelated to a "yes" to the event, that is to say, a "yes"' to what comes, to letting-it-come. . . . A "yes" to the event or to the other, or to the event as other or as the coming of the other, is something that is said, whether this "yes" is said or not. ("CIP" 225/84)

One can do things with words, yes, but is it possible to say, with words, this doing? That is what has been at issue from as early as "Signature Event Context" right through "Declarations of Independence."

It is not long after this point in these improvised, that is, unprogrammed remarks on the performative "yes," that Derrida launches into a lesson that could have come right out of "Signature Event Context." He continues: "There is a saying that is close to knowledge and information, to the enunciation that says something about something. And then there is a saying that *does in saying*, a saying that does, that enacts" ("CIP" 227/87–88). It is a lesson about the constative and the performative that Derrida no doubt repeated, iterated, many times before and in many different contexts since that first iteration in Montreal in 1971 in "Signature Event Context." It is also, perhaps, a lesson about the date, about the *singularity* of a date and its inevitable repetition. For example, 1971, 1979, 1997, three dates that are singular, distinct from one another, and yet already in relation, already a repetition. As we read in "Limited Inc," "the time and place of the *other time* [is] already at work, altering from the start the start itself, the *first time*, the *at once*" ("LI" 62/120).[2]

But something else happens immediately after this repeated lesson on the speech act, something more unforeseeable, something one might be tempted to call an *event*, this time in the form of an illustration or an example, as is so often the case, an anecdote regarding something more recent, closer to the context at hand, in this case, closer to Quebec:

> This morning, I was watching television—I'm going to speak about television, about the news [*les informations*], because it is also a matter of information, of knowledge as information—I was watching the Quebecer news and I happened upon on a short sequence about René Lévesque, an archive document, a synopsis that showed his rise, his action and his relative failure, and what happened before and after the failure. The journalist, or whoever was presenting the program, made

the following comment: "after making the news [*faire l'événement*], René Lévesque had to comment on the news." Whereas he spoke about events after his resignation, beforehand he produced them notably through speech. ("CIP" 227–228/88)[3]

Without venturing any further in this direction, further in the direction of the political speech act or the declaration of independence, further toward the person or the politics, the adventure or the fate, of René Lévesque, Derrida returns from this improvised and unprogrammed example taken from a Quebecois news program to the lesson on speech act theory that was, as it were, already in progress, a part of the regularly scheduled programming. But notice how, once again, the context, that is, Quebec, the French language, has entered onto the scene and gotten inscribed in the program, just as it had in the two preceding acts. It is almost as if there were some *souffleur* in the wings introducing and encouraging the unexpected entrance of the French language, of *la langue française*, or of Quebec herself, onto the stage. It might be said, of course, that it was just a coincidence, just an example, an anecdote from a TV program seen earlier in the day. And yet, as we all know, and thanks in large part to Derrida, the example or the anecdote is never innocent or neutral, always saying more—always doing more—than what it says. Derrida continues after this reference to Lévesque:

> And, as you know (I don't intend to give you a class on the constative and the performative), there's an utterance that is called constative, a theoretical speech that consists in saying what is, describing or noting what is, and there's an utterance that is called *performative* and that does in speaking. For instance, when I make a promise, I'm not saying an event; I'm producing it by my commitment. I promise or I say. ("CIP" 228/88)

And then he adds, linking the promise to the "yes" that he had spoken of earlier:

> I say "yes," I started out by saying "yes" earlier. The "yes" is performative. The example that is always cited in speaking about performative utterances is that of marriage, the "I do" [*oui* in French] in answer to "Do you take this man or this woman . . . ?" does not say the event, it makes it, it constitutes the event. It's a speech-event, a saying-event [*une parole-événement, c'est un dire-événement*]. ("CIP" 228/88)

There it is, a saying-event, like the signature-event that one *texts*, that one puts in text, a saying that somehow says "the singularity of the event" ("CIP" 228/89). But then what is the nature of this saying? Is it a more like a constative or a performative? Neither one nor the other, Derrida seems to suggest, for "every time that *saying the event* exceeds this dimension of information, knowledge, and cognition, it enters the night . . . the 'night of non-knowing,' something that's not merely ignorance, but that no longer pertains to the realm of knowledge" ("CIP" 230/92). As such, "the event defeats [*met en déroute*] both the constative and the performative" ("CIP" 238/105). If speech act theory was in a certain sense about the *ability* or the *power* to say the event, to *produce* the event through saying, the emphasis here is on the impossibility of saying, or, indeed, of producing the event. An event that I could say or produce would not be an event at all. Singular, unforeseeable, unprogrammable, the event always exceeds our capacity for saying and producing, as well as all our grids of interpretation and understanding.

But then what about everything Derrida said in "Signature Event Context" about the necessary repeatability of the event, about the structural iterability of the speech act as event? As Derrida argued in "Limited Inc," is it not necessary for the speech act to "repeat and deport an allegedly original 'event' that is itself divided and multiple"? ("LI" 33/71) It could easily seem as if Derrida's emphasis on the unforeseeable and the unprogrammable has displaced or caused him to forget those early lessons of deconstruction, what I called earlier the ABCs of deconstruction. But Derrida goes on to suggest that, despite the change in vocabulary and accent, there is no contradiction between what was said in those texts and what is now being argued in "A Certain Impossible Possibility of Saying the Event." Here, for example, is Derrida articulating the general rule of iterability in relation to hospitality:

> When I welcome a visitor, when I receive the visitation of an unexpected visitor, it must be a unique experience each and every time for it to be a unique, unpredictable, singular, and irreplaceable event. But at the same time, the repetition of the event must be presupposed, from the threshold [*seuil*] of the house and from the arrival of the irreplaceable. ("CIP" 235/99–100)

The lesson regarding iterability from "Signature Event Context" was thus not forgotten. Indeed it is here being repeated, if not actually radicalized, since that which opens every speech act, or indeed every sign, to repetition is precisely a relation to the future or to the other, which is, precisely, always unforeseeable and unprogrammable. That then does not mean, quite the contrary, that the supposedly singular and unrepeatable event cannot—must not—itself be repeated. How else to explain the three acts or the three iterations of Derrida in Montreal, in 1971, 1979, and 1997—the three of them now linked *in their singularity*?

Twenty-six years after "Signature Event Context," first pronounced in Montreal, Austin still seems to be in the background, animating Derrida's reference to constative and performative in relation to the event, an event that will have always been understood by Derrida in terms of an ethics of response or responsibility to context, which is to say, always in response to the other. Benoît Peeters makes this very connection in his biography on *Derrida*:

> The question of the commission (*commande*)—or rather of the demand (*demande*)—was thus fundamental to his way of working. The *responsibility* that Derrida imposed on himself was that of constantly *responding*—to the title of a conference, or to the place in which it was being held, or to the person inviting him or the circumstances of the moment. In spite of the criticism often made of him, this was anything but a rhetorical gesture. It was a way of thinking philosophy *in situ*, considering every time he spoke as a specific situation, a *here and now* that would never return and was the very thing that needed to be addressed. A conference paper by Derrida, an intervention at a meeting, was first and foremost a speech act, a performative in Austin's sense; this was a theory that he critically debated, but it was for him "one of the major bodies of thought or main theoretical events—undoubtedly one of the most fruitful—of our time." It was a matter of describing a context so as better to displace or deconstruct it, even if this meant dwelling on it at length, analyzing *by what right* people had come together, even if this ran the risk of seeming never to get to *the real issue*.[4]

It is only such a thinking of responsibility that can explain everything we have seen thus far of Derrida in Montreal, and that can explain these words from 1997 that sound so very much like what Derrida said close to three decades before in "Signature Event Context," this time, however, with iterability serving both to make the event possible and to neutralize it as an event:

> I was saying before that the saying of the event presupposes some sort of inevitable neutralization of the event by its iterability, that saying always harbors the possibility of resaying. A word is comprehensible only because it can be repeated; whenever I speak, I'm using repeatable words and uniqueness is swept into this iterability. Similarly, the event cannot appear to be an event, when it appears, unless it is already repeatable in its very uniqueness. ("CIP" 234/98)

Derrida goes on in this little text published under the title "A Certain Impossible Possibility of Saying the Event" to give us a sort of summary, one of the very best to be found anywhere in his work, of many of his published texts of the 1990s and the majority of his seminars from the same period presented under the general title "Questions of Responsibility." In each case, what is at issue is responsibility in relation to the event. In each case, one bears witness to the priority of responsibility over freedom, in part because of the notion of "capacity" or "power" that this latter almost always implies ("CIP" 237/103). For example, there is the question of the gift, the gift as what must remain beyond my powers to give, since a gift that I *can* give would be no gift at all ("CIP" 230–232/92–95); or the question of forgiveness [*le pardon*], the impossibility of forgiveness, that is, the impossibility of *me* forgiving or having the *capacity* to forgive ("CIP" 231–232/94, 237–238/103–104); or the question of invention, the event of "invention" being what is and must remain beyond my powers, beyond my ability or potentiality, and thus, in a sense, that which is and in a certain sense must remain "impossible" ("CIP" 232–233/95–96); and the question of hospitality, of hospitality as the receiving of someone unexpected, unanticipated, someone I am not prepared to receive, someone who exceeds my expectations, my horizon of expectations, and thus my "capacity to receive," hospitality, in short, as "welcoming beyond my capacity to welcome" ("CIP" 233/96–97). What is at issue in each case is the singularity of the event and its inevitable repetition, that is, its repetition *as* unique, the way a certain impossibility of the event always *haunts* the possible, just as, some twenty-six years earlier, the possibility of the speech act's failure always conditioned—or perhaps we can now say haunted—every success. It is indeed a question of power or capacity, even there where it seems that the power or capacity of a subject would have to be maintained, namely, in the decision, and especially the responsible decision, of a subject to give or to forgive, to invent or to offer hospitality. But Derrida goes on to argue here that the decision, the moment of decision, is indeed, just as he had suggested through the words of Kierkegaard way back in 1963 in "Cogito and the History of Madness," a moment of madness, a decision that is, in short, never mine but always of the other, my decision as the decision of the other, and so not that which I make but that which I undergo ("CIP" 237/102–103; see "CHM" 31/51). Gift, forgiveness, hospitality, invention, decision, and then the promise—one of Austin's primary examples of the speech act—the promise not as one speech act among others but as the very element or milieu of all language, the promise as "the basic element of language" ("CIP" 240/107), a promise that I make that is always in excess, as it were, of my capacity to make it.

Finally, Derrida speaks here, just as he did in "Signature Event Context," about possibility and the "perhaps." The reader may remember that phrase right near the end of that essay of 1971: "writing, if there is any, perhaps communicates, but does not exist, surely." Well, twenty-six years after writing those words, Derrida says this: "The history of philosophy is the history of reflections on the meaning of the *possible*, on the meaning of *being* or *being possible*" ("CIP" 236/100). Derrida had already hinted at this earlier in his remarks in one of the passages that seems to have provided the title for the entire exchange:

> a certain impossibility of saying the event or a certain impossible possibility of saying the event, forces us to rethink not only what "saying" or what "event" means, but what *possible* means in the history of philosophy. ("CIP" 227/86)

One of Derrida's great contributions to this entire history of philosophy will have thus been to rethink the impossible as that which is not *opposed* to the possible but that which *inhabits* it or *haunts* it and, in so doing, makes the possible possible. He says: "We should speak here of the im-possible event, an im-possible that is not merely impossible, that is not merely the opposite of possible, that is also the condition or chance of the possible" ("CIP" 236/101).[5]

In the case of, say, the gift, hospitality, or forgiveness, it is the necessity of a certain impossibility that makes any act of giving, of hospitality, or of forgiveness possible, "the experience of impossibility that haunts the possible" ("CIP" 234/98). For "even when something comes to pass as possible, when an event occurs as possible, the fact that it will have been impossible, that the possible invention will have been impossible, this impossibility continues to haunt the possibility" ("CIP" 234/98).

When thinking the event, then, we need to think about this relationship between impossibility and possibility, just as in "Signature Event Context" it was necessary to think perversion or failure as a structural or structuring possibility that makes possible any success, necessary to think the abnormal, the nonserious or the parasitic (as in a play, for example) not as what is opposed to the normal or the serious or the everyday but as that which first make these possible. Derrida then suggests, just as he did in 1971, that the "perhaps" or the "maybe," the "*peut-être*," is perhaps the proper modality or category to think the event, the "perhaps" as the very relationship between the possible and the impossible ("CIP" 240/106).[6] We are, it seems, back to that "*communication*" given in Montreal at the Congrès des Sociétés de Philosophie de Langue Française, as if nothing, or very little, had happened in the meantime, nothing except a long series of texts and events, of symptoms and of deaths.

Of *deaths*, it has to be said, because, for Derrida, death is always an event, perhaps the event par excellence, at once unforeseeable and exceptional, and yet always repeatable in its very unforeseeability and exceptionality, repeatable in its very singularity. After taking great issue with Jean Baudrillard's provocative claim that the First Gulf War "did not take place," Derrida affirms: "The event that is ultimately irreducible to media appropriation and digression is that thousands of people died. . . . an event that cannot be reduced to any saying. It's the unsayable: the dead, *for example*, the dead" ("CIP" 242/111).[7] As unforeseeable, an event such as death, the event death, is always beyond any horizon. Impossible to see coming, even though we "know" it will one day come, such an event, such an "absolute surprise," must thus "fall upon me" ("CIP" 233/97).

Speaking thus of death as an event, and then of the symptomatology and *verticality* of the event as what always falls upon me ("CIP" 239/105–106), unforeseen and without horizon, Derrida evokes a verticality—a coming from on high—that is different from, but not unrelated to, religious notions regarding the *arrivance* or the coming of the other. "By verticality, what I meant was that the foreigner, what is irreducibly *arrivant* in the other . . . is that which in the other gives me no advance warning and which exceeds precisely the horizontality of expectation" ("CIP" 243/111). We have thus come all of sudden, almost without warning, to the end of this text that is at the center of our third and final act of "Derrida in Montreal." Here are Derrida's concluding remarks:

> In my discourse, the idea of verticality doesn't necessarily have anymore the often religious or theological use that rises to the Most High. Maybe religion starts here. You can't talk the way I do about verticality, about absolute *arrivance*, without the act of faith having already commenced—and the act of faith is not necessarily religion, a given religion—without a certain space of faith without knowledge, faith beyond knowledge. I'd accept, therefore, that we speak of faith here [*J'accepterais donc que l'on parle de foi ici*]. ("CIP" 243/111–112)

Derrida's last public and published sentence in Montreal—at once constative and performative, it seems, there on April Fool's Day 1997, was thus this: "I'd accept, therefore, that we speak of faith here." It is all there, in a single sentence, *signature event context*: there is, first, the signature, for as Jacques Derrida writes in *The Post Card*, "*J'accepte* [I accept], this will be my signature henceforth" (*PC* 26/31). Then there is the event, a certain profession of faith, or a certain faith in profession, "I'd accept, therefore, that we *speak of faith* here."[8] And then there is the context, namely, *here*, that is, in this context, *Montreal*. "I'd accept, therefore, that we speak of faith here [*J'accepterais donc que l'on parle de foi ici*]." It is with this singular phrase, a phrase of the French language, this signature phrase, this signature event, that the curtain suddenly falls—like an event that befalls the event—on "Derrida in Montreal," the curtain falling from on high, all at once and without warning, in one fell swoop, that is, as one says in the French that was Derrida's, *d'un coup sec.*

Encore: Cocoon

> I love very much everything that I deconstruct in my own manner; the texts I want to read from the deconstructive point of view are texts I love.... They are texts whose future, I think, will not be exhausted for a long time.—Derrida at a "Roundtable on Autobiography" at the University of Montreal in October 1979

The play is thus over, the curtain has fallen, the lights have gone black, and the audience slowly begins to file out of the theater.[1] But before anyone can make it to the exit, someone suddenly calls out for what is called in perfectly good English an encore, because encore there was, and I would have never known about it—I would have perhaps myself already left the theater—were it not for an email from Ginette Michaud from Montreal. When I told her about my plans to write a work, a sort of play in three acts, about "Derrida in Montreal," she responded to tell me that after that event on April 1, 1997, what I took to be Derrida's final public event in Montreal, Derrida in effect returned to the stage the very next day, not at the Centre Canadien d'Architecture but at the old Bibliothèque Nationale de Québec, the former Bibliothèque Saint-Sulpice, in Montreal, in a large auditorium or theater, as chance would have it, where he presented "A Silkworm of One's Own," the text that would be included in *Veils*, the book he wrote with Hélène Cixous. Standing on stage with a long white raincoat draped over his shoulders because of the chill in the room, Derrida read the entirety of that text, which was still in manuscript form. It was, Ginette attested, an "unforgettable performative act," though it today figures nowhere in our bibliographical archives, nowhere perhaps but in the memory of those who attended that event—and, perhaps, *here*.

We should have thus suspected that Derrida's last words would not be his last, that other words, "written" words, would continue beyond that supposedly final event to produce an event. Instead, then, of "I'd accept, therefore, that we speak of faith here," perhaps these were Derrida's final public words in Montreal, the final words of "A Silkworm of One's Own":

> *I have promised.*
>
> *A lapse of time: it was only an interval, almost nothing, the infinite diminution of a musical interval, and what a note, what news, what music. The verdict. As if suddenly evil never, nothing evil ever, happened again. As though evil would only happen again with death—or only later, too late, so much later.* ("SOO" 92/85)

Promise, verdict—those words, spoken, as Ginette told me, by Derrida in Montreal in April 1997, those words, while not exactly citations, are nonetheless also Austin's words, performative words, event words—to say nothing of *death*—so that, once again, we are brought back to "Signature Event Context" some twenty-six years before. We are brought back to the relationship between writing and death, though we are also, with these words from "A Silkworm of One's Own," sent forward, into the future and toward the possibility of an event. For Derrida also reminded us in "Signature Event Context" that the text itself, related always to the other, has the power to break with its context, the text which is woven together by signs and marked with the point of a signature like a sort of tissue or veil or, better yet, a cocoon waiting for its event.

One might thus imagine for this encore, this curtain call, as it were, for "Derrida in Montreal," a single actor coming on stage before that closed or fallen curtain, a single actor reading those final lines from "A Silkworm of One's Own," reading them slowly, patiently, heading toward that final "so much later." And we might imagine him, as he reads, slowly shredding the curtain behind him, tearing it away piece by piece, pulling it down and wrapping himself in it like a veil or a shroud, a web or a cocoon, the actor completely concealed within it by the end of the reading, perhaps moving, perhaps not, perhaps breathing, perhaps not, because it is difficult to tell in the penumbra of the theater. But with the curtain completely down, the curtain now completely covering the actor, the audience can see that there is, to cite *Glas*, "nothing behind the curtain [*rien derrière le rideau*]" (*GL* 49a/59a),[2] nothing behind and nothing in front, except that cocoon. *Rien derrière le rideau*, say the audience members to themselves and to one another. It is a phrase that can be heard in the context of an event like this one as a constative that marks the true end of the story or the play, the final unveiling—"there is nothing behind the curtain," no author, no staging, nothing more to see or hear, time to go home, the performance is over, as are all our illusions. But that same phrase might also be read, perhaps, as a signature, *derrière le rideau* as yet another signature to be read, a signature encore, a speech act from beyond the grave, improbable and yet, *here*, irrefutable, an event if ever there was one.[3]

PART II

The Open Seminar

scolaire en particulier, ou encore que les deux codes, le génétique et le scolaire ont une xxxxxxxxxx provenance ou une appartenance commune qui devra être interrogée. Quant au mot "enseigner", le voici. Il s'agit du vieux problème de l'hérédité des caractères acquis. Jacob ne pense pas que le mot "enseigner" soit impropre en lui-même, xxxxxxxxxxxxxxx xxxxxx pour désigner l'opération par laquelle l'hérédité est transmise. Son risque, simplement, c'est de donner à penser que l'enseignement de l'hérédité est exactement identique à celui qui se donne, à travers le langage parlé, la mémoire du cerveau, etc. dans les écoles. Et ici, nous allons voir quel est le principe xxxxxxxxxxx, selon Jacob, et l'explication de ces possibilités métaphysiques. Que dit en effet le paragraphe dans lequel on lit l'expression "enseigne l'hérédité"? Il remarque d'abord qu'un organisme est la transition entre ce qui fut et qui sera. Un organisme ne se pense pas au présent, si vous voulez, il n'est pas d'abord la production d'un présent. Il est d'abord, d'avance, xxxxxxxxx ce que j'appellerai un "effet de reproduction". Ça ne commence pas par la production mais par la reproduction. "La reproduction, dit J., en constitue (de l'organisme) à la fois l'origine et la fin, la cause et le but.". Or c'est pour penser cette reproduction que s'était constitué la problématique classique de la biologie ou de la génétique, oscillant entre xxxxxxxxxxxxx finalisme et mécanisme, nécessité et hasard, fixité ou transformation. C'est précisément à la notion de programme que Jacob reconnaît le pouvoir d'effacer les xxxxxxxxxxx oppositions, voire les contradictions xxxxx qui construisent cette problématique classique, la philosophie ou la métaphysique de cette problématique classique. "Avec le xxx concept de programme appliqué à l'hérédité, dit J. disparaissent certaines des contradictions que la biologie avait résumées par une série d'oppositions: finalité et mécanisme, nécessité et contingence, stabilité et variation."

Comment Jacob conçoit-il ou construit-il ce concept de programme? Il n'y retient pas la référence qui s'y trouve faite à l'inscription, au graphique, ni au sens de l'écriture phonétique, ni au sens de l'écriture non-phonétique. Nous y reviendrons d'une autre manière tout à l'heure. Pour construire ou analyser le concept de programme tel qu'il travaille dans le champ de la génétique, Jacob retient deux prédicats essentiels, ce qu'il appelle deux notions : la mémoire et le projet. Et c'est à l'intérieur de ces deux notions, partageant et articulant chacune

---

LE DROIT A LA PHILOSOPHIE POUR TOUS

CONTRE LE PROJET HABY DANS SON ENSEMBLE
Contre la sélection sociale
l'orientation hâtive
la rentabilisation de l'enseignement

CONTRE LA LIQUIDATION DE LA PHILOSOPHIE

POUR L'EXTENSION DE L'ENSEIGNEMENT PHILOSOPHIQUE
à toutes les classes du second cycle et aux C.E.T.

le G.R.E.P.H. organise un

MEETING DE MOBILISATION

SAMEDI 19 AVRIL à 15h

fac. de Jussieu, amphi X3 (rue Guy de la Brosse)

Groupe de Recherche sur
l'Enseignement Philosophique
45, rue d'Ulm, Paris (5ème)

The Counter-Program: Syllabus

"I never liked school": that is how Derrida in the 2002 movie by Kirby Dick and Amy Ziering Kofman begins to answer a question regarding his early education. "I never liked school," he repeats, "the first years of what is called in France *la maternelle* [kindergarten] were just miserable [*c'était la tragédie*]. I cried every day."[1] Derrida goes on to recount at some length the daily "trauma" of being dropped off at school, abandoned, as it seemed to him, by his mother to a space filled with strangers, "monsters" in the form of unfamiliar teachers and administrators.

It is a strong reaction, to be sure, but not one that is especially unique to Derrida, unlike what comes next, which is somewhat more unique: "in a certain sense, this has never stopped . . . I have never liked school, at no matter what age, and even still today. . . . I have never liked educational institutions"—and then comes, as it were, the punch line—"where I have, of course, spent my entire life." The sequence concludes, "Even now when I set foot in an institution, in a university, when I enter an educational, academic, institutional space, I feel a sort of anxiety."

In spite of his early and continued fear and dislike of school, then, Derrida somehow managed to stay in school right up to the end of his life. For after surviving kindergarten he would go on to grade school and high school in Algeria, *classes préparatoires* at the Lycée Louis-le-Grand in Paris, schooling at the École Normale Supérieure, a fellowship year in the United States at Harvard University, two years of military service back in Algeria (spent mostly as a teacher and translator), and then, after all these years of schooling, he would take up a series of teaching positions back in France: a year in a lycée for boys in the city of Le Mans (1959–60), a handful of years at the Sorbonne in Paris (1960–64), two decades back at the École Normale Supérieure where he had himself been a student (1964–84), and then another two decades at the École des Hautes Études en Sciences Sociales in Paris (1984–2003). The man who never liked school would thus end up spending the better part of his first thirty years attending school and then the next forty-three as a full-time teacher or professor. And those last forty-three would be pretty much without interruption, without sabbaticals or leaves of absence or substantial periods of time outside educational institutions. In fact, when Derrida had vacation breaks from his teaching obligations in France he would often spend one or more weeks teaching abroad, and particularly in the United States, at Johns Hopkins, Yale, UC Irvine, or New York University. And all that would be in addition to the countless talks and conference presentations he would give during the academic year, the vast majority of these taking place in the very academic institutions Derrida says he always felt some anxiety entering.

Much has already been written—though much more remains to be written—about Derrida's relationship to educational institutions in France and elsewhere, not only his personal reactions to these institutions but his willingness to work with or within them for decades, his attempts to reform them and even to create new ones, and, of course, his work as a teacher, as a pedagogue, his manner of teaching and his way of teaching others to teach. Before turning, therefore, in this second part of *Class Acts* to three recently published seminars, a few comments are in order regarding Derrida as a teacher, comments derived both from what is readily available in the public record and from a more personal perspective.

For more than four decades, Derrida offered "courses" or "seminars"— either one or two a year—to students doing degrees at the Sorbonne or the École des Hautes Études (EHESS), or else to students preparing for the competitive *agrégation* exam at the École Normale Supérieure (ENS). But as Derrida began to publish more widely and his writings became better known, those courses or seminars—and in particular the "open seminar" that I mentioned in the introduction to this work—would be attended not only by the students officially enrolled in those seminars but also by intellectually curious Parisians and international students and professors who wished to hear Derrida speak in person.[2] I myself was one of these latter, having had the chance to study in France and attend two full years of what was simply referred to by the mid-1980s as "Derrida's Seminar," a seminar on "Philosophical Nationality and Nationalism" in 1986–87 and then the first year of the seminar "Politics of Friendship" in 1988–89. In addition, because the seminar was always at the same time and place, year after year, Wednesday afternoon from 5:00 to 7:00 in the Salle Dussane of the École Normale Supérieure (45, rue d'Ulm), or, later, in a large amphitheater at the École des Hautes Études (105 Boulevard Raspail, right next to the Alliance Française), I, like others, was often able to attend a session or two if I found myself in Paris for a couple of weeks at the beginning or end of an academic year.[3] It was not necessary to enroll or have a student card or do anything other than just show up, preferably fifteen to twenty minutes in advance to ensure getting a seat, for while both rooms seated more than two hundred students, there were often more students than seats, and late arrivals were condemned to sitting on the stairs or in the aisles. The only unofficial requirement for attending the "open seminar" (as opposed to the closed or "restricted seminar" for advanced students, many doing their DEA—Diplôme d'Études Approfondies—degree with Derrida) was signing an attendance notebook that was passed around at the start of every seminar session, a minimal requirement that, as I recount in the second chapter of this section, became a constant source of consternation for Derrida and a weekly amusement for his students.

A typical seminar had between ten and fourteen weekly sessions, beginning usually in mid-October and running through early June, with several sessions at the end of the year being reserved for student presentations and Derrida's often lengthy comments on them. For each of the regular sessions of a seminar Derrida would arrive in class with a prepared text of some twenty to thirty pages, a text that was more or less completely written out, in sentences and paragraphs, with transitions and notes to self about what to put on the blackboard, when to develop a point extemporaneously, when to comment on a text—or the translation of a text—being cited, even when to pause during the presentation. These texts were either handwritten (from 1960 to 1966), typed (from 1968 to 1987), or written on a word processor or computer and printed out and read in class (from 1987 to 2003).[4] Everything, then, was prepared and fully written out, with the exception of longer quotes, Derrida preferring to read from photocopied pages or else from the text itself, which meant that he would usually arrive in class for each session with half a dozen or so books to read from and comment on over the course of the two-hour session. For each yearlong seminar, then, there are in the archives at the University of California at Irvine and/or at the IMEC archives in Normandy some 200 to 400 pages, an estimated 14,000 pages for the forty-two years of seminars combined, the vast majority of these pages perfectly readable (with the exception of the handwritten seminars, which are practically indecipherable to the uninitiated) and in need of relatively little editorial work when compared with seminars given by professors working from notes or an outline. While not absolutely polished texts, these seminar sessions are nonetheless perfectly fluid and coherent, needing only the correction of typos, the insertion of those longer quotes, and the addition of bibliographical and editorial notes in order to be prepared for publication.[5]

Derrida would thus slowly read what he had prepared, commenting as he went, sometimes taking the entire two hours of a session to complete the reading of his prepared text, sometimes leaving some time at the end for questions.[6] Typically written in the days just before the seminar, these seminar presentations would often contain references to the news of the day, a way for Derrida to reframe or rethink the topic under consideration in the seminar or to put it in a more contemporary light. That was especially true when the topic was something like hospitality, or forgiveness, or the death penalty, where there were often ample material for discussion from the daily news. When Derrida felt that too many sessions had gone by without sufficient time for questions, or when current events coincided with the topic of the seminar in a particularly poignant way, half a session or occasionally an entire session would be reserved for discussion.

As for Derrida's extemporaneous comments during class, they were almost as articulate and developed as the written ones. Indeed, if one were just listening and not watching, it was not always easy to know exactly when Derrida had broken away from his text, so good was he at improvisation and extemporaneous reflection. Fortunately, many of these oral additions, additions that comment on or supplement the written text or, occasionally, take the place of the written text for those rare sessions when Derrida spoke solely on the basis of notes, have been preserved by one of the many students who, beginning in the late 1970s, recorded the sessions on cassette tapes. (Attendees of the seminars will recall the ritual of students getting up every thirty to forty-five minutes to turn over or change the tapes on their tape recorders, which were lined up across the front of Derrida's desk. A minor annoyance at the time, these recordings have become an invaluable source for anyone wanting to experience a Derrida seminar more fully and to hear Derrida himself reacting to or commenting on his own text in "real time.")

As the editors of the Seminars of Derrida have made clear from their first introduction on, we come to see in these seminars a very different Derrida from the one we have come to know only through his writings. Though the seminars were often the basis for published work, they differ in many ways from the works that would eventually come out of them. We see in the seminars an exemplary pedagogue working patiently through texts, providing greater context for them, making comparisons to other texts or thinkers or arguments, and giving examples to his students, all in an attempt to aid them in understanding his presentation.

As I will try to show in the chapters that follow, these seminars were, in their writing and thinking, places of great innovation, invention, and experimentation. They were engaging and inspiring for those attending them, even though they were principally conducted as lecture courses (what are called in French *cours magistraux*), with the vast majority of the speaking being done by the instructor, that is, by Derrida, a "teaching from the podium" (or in this case from a desk at the front of the room) that is usually not on the shortlist of today's best pedagogical practices. While time was often reserved for some questions, there was little to no student-centered learning in the way we understand it today, no flipped classrooms or breakout sessions, no audiovisual aids, no group presentations or collaborative learning, only lecturing on the one side and note-taking on the other. So while a student comment, question, or suggestion could sometimes shift or inflect the trajectory of a seminar (see, for example, the beginning of volume 2 of *The Beast and the Sovereign*, where Derrida explains that it was an American student who suggested to him a reading of Defoe's *Robinson Crusoe* [*BS 2* 14/37]), the major lines and direction of the seminar had been determined by Derrida well in advance. From this perspective, then, Derrida's seminars were, despite the originality and inventiveness of their content, decidedly traditional.

Of the forty-three years of seminars given at the Sorbonne, ENS, and EHESS, eight have been edited and published as of this writing. These are, in order of their publication: the two years of *The Beast and the Sovereign* (*La bête et le souverain*), seminars of 2001–2002 and 2002–2003 at EHESS; two years of *The Death Penalty* (*La peine de mort*), seminars of 1999–2000 and 2000–2001 at EHESS; *Heidegger: The Question of Being and History* (*Heidegger: La question de l'Être et l'Histoire*), seminar of 1964–65 at ENS; *Theory and Practice* (*Théorie et pratique*), seminar of 1976–77 at ENS; *Life Death* (*La vie la mort*), seminar of 1975–76 at ENS; and the first year of *Perjury and Pardon* (*Le parjure et le pardon*), seminar of 1997–98 at EHESS. In the three chapters that follow I concentrate on the last three of these seminars, not simply because they are the most recent to be published but also, and especially, because of the way these seminars intersect with the themes of the first part of this work. It so happens, for example, that much of the material central to Act 2 of "Derrida in Montreal," that is, Derrida's 1979 presentation of "Otobiographies" at the University of Montreal, was first presented at ENS in the 1975–76 seminar *Life Death*. The seminar that follows *Life Death*, namely, *Theory and Practice* (1976–77), then coincides almost exactly with the writing of "Limited Inc" and Derrida's debate with Searle, which explains, in part, Derrida's many references to Austin and speech act theory in that seminar. Finally, the seminar on "Perjury and Pardon," a seminar first given at EHESS as part of the longer seminar series "Questions of Responsibility," begins just months after the third and final act of "Derrida in Montreal," that is, at more or less the same time as Derrida's last important public event in Montreal, the one whose proceedings were subsequently published as "A Certain Impossible Possibility of Saying the Event." Moreover, as one might gather just from the title "Perjury and Pardon," this seminar of 1997–98 turns around the very questions of the speech act and of speech act theory that were central to the first part of this work.

But just as important as these chronological overlaps between "Derrida in Montreal" and these three recently published seminars, the two seminars from the mid-1970s that are the focus of the next two chapters coincide with and reflect Derrida's growing interest in the theme of education itself. That is, they coincide almost exactly with Derrida's first truly explicit considerations of educational institutions in France and in the history of those institutions, as well as with his first public attempts to change these institutions by intervening in contemporary debates. Indeed, the year 1975—the year in which the seminar *Life Death* begins—turns out to be a pivotal year for all these questions, since it was in that year that Minister of Education René Haby officially proposed a series of educational reforms that aimed to eliminate the philosophy requirement in the final year (what is called *terminale*) of French *lycées* or high schools. It was in large part in response to these proposed reforms, as a way of fighting back against them, that Derrida and others would form the organization GREPH (the Groupe de Recherches sur l'Enseignement Philosophique), a group of philosophy professors from both universities and high schools across France that would begin by contesting the proposed elimination of philosophy in the final year of the *lycée* but would eventually argue for the extension of the teaching of philosophy to the two preceding years and for a number of other teaching reforms regarding the training of philosophy teachers, the relationship between the teaching of philosophy and that of other disciplines, and reforms in the program of philosophy taught in high school. While organizational meetings for GREPH had been held already in 1974, the group was officially constituted on January 15, 1975, that is, the same year that Derrida would begin the *Life Death* seminar, with the École Normale Supérieure becoming the group's unofficial headquarters and Derrida its de facto head.[7]

The mid-1970s thus coincides with a sort of *prise de conscience* or awakening on Derrida's part with regard to teaching. In a text from 1976 titled

"Where a Teaching Body Begins and How It Ends," Derrida does not simply describe but testifies, as it were, to this awakening—and, first of all, to the *place* he began to see himself occupying within the French national educational system:

> Here, in the École Normale Supérieure, in the place where I, this teaching body that I call mine and that occupies a very specific function in what is called the French philosophy teaching body today, I teach. I say now that I am teaching.
>
> And where for the first time, at least in this direct form, I am getting ready to speak about the teaching of philosophy.
>
> That is to say, where, after approximately fifteen years of experience called "teaching" and twenty-three years as a civil servant [*de fonctionnariat*], I am only beginning to question, exhibit, and critique systematically. (. . . It is the *systematic* character that is important, as well as its *effectiveness*, which can never come down to the initiative of a single person. And that is why, for the first time, I am here linking my discourse to the group work engaged in under the name of GREPH.) I am beginning, then, this late, to question, exhibit, and critique systematically—in view of a transformation—the borders of that within which I have given more than one talk. (*WAP* 70/*DP* 114–115)[8]

The mid-1970s, the period at issue in the first two of the three following chapters devoted to Derrida's seminars, thus corresponds to a certain coming-to-awareness on Derrida's part with regard to his role as a teacher and to the beginning of a systematic critique of the institutions of teaching in France. This critique had been triggered or inspired, as I have just argued, by current events and proposed institutional changes in France at the time, but it will have been, at least implicitly, always on the program. As Derrida suggests just a couple of pages later in "Where a Teaching Body Begins and How It Ends," what had gone under the name deconstruction had never fit squarely within traditional educational institutions but had always worked at their margins or on their borders, criticizing and trying to transform them or at least the values associated with them from a place that is neither completely inside nor completely outside them:

> As for what I will call, to be brief, my place or my point of view, it had long been obvious that the work in which I was involved—let's name it algebraically, at the risk of new misunderstandings, the (affirmative) deconstruction of phallogocentrism as philosophy—did not belong simply to the forms of the philosophical institution. (*WAP* 71/*DPP* 117)

Whether it was through a critique of certain hierarchies in the history of philosophy, or a rethinking of various modes of authority, mastery, or sovereignty, or an interrogation of the ways in which a tradition is formed, legitimated, and passed on, the ways in which certain forms of knowledge are preserved, repeated, and transmitted, that is, certain forms and not others, deconstruction will always have had, it seems, education and, at least implicitly, the educational system in view. One could cite any number of texts from the 1960s and 1970s to make this case, whether it be Derrida's critique in "Plato's Pharmacy" of the supposed "mastery" of speech over writing (that is, the mastery and authority of Thamus, who is not only a king but a master or a teacher, over Theuth, his subject and his disciple, his pupil) or, to recall what was at issue in "Derrida in Montreal," Derrida's critique of the supposedly sovereign subject as determinative of a context in "Signature Event Context" and the question of who would become the legitimate "heir" or disciple of Austin's speech act theory in "Limited Inc." Questions of education and authority were thus always at issue in these earlier works, such that the mid-1970s marks less a change of direction than a more explicit and thematic investigation of what had always been at stake. As Derrida argues:

> Deconstruction—or at least what I have proposed under this name, which indeed is as good as another, but no better—has therefore in principle always concerned the apparatus and function of teaching in general, the apparatus and function of philosophy in particular and par excellence. Without reducing its specificity, I will say that what is underway now is but a stage to be crossed in a systematic journey. (*WAP* 73/*DPP* 118–119)

The mid-1970s thus marks a shift in Derrida's explicit thinking about education, that is, both in terms of his philosophical interests and his political commitments, beginning with GREPH and other initiatives at ENS just a year before the foundation of GREPH. What had been an implicit questioning of the values of education had become, to use Derrida's term, a "systematic journey," that is, a more organized and rigorous questioning and critique of the French educational system. Once again in "Where a Teaching Body Begins and How It Ends," Derrida recounts having initiated in 1974–75 "a sort of counter-seminar" at the recently established Research Center on the Teaching of Philosophy at ENS, a center that preceded and was distinct from GREPH, as Derrida explains, but that would end up having numerous interactions with it (*WAP* 68/*DDP* 112). The questions "on the program" for that year show to just what extent the "content" of Derrida's seminar came to coincide with questions regarding its "form" or its milieu, that is, regarding the institutions that made such a seminar possible in the first place:

> What is a teaching body—of philosophy?
>
> What do "defense" and "philosophy" mean today in the slogan "the defense of philosophy"?
>
> Ideology and the French ideologues (the analysis of the concept of ideology and of the politico-pedagogical projects of the French Ideologues at the time of the Revolution). (*WAP* 68/*DDP* 113)

What Derrida describes here as "counter-seminar" was thus not, from all appearances, an anti-seminar. It appears to have used the seminar form or format to question the institutions of teaching—and particularly of the teaching of philosophy—in France.[9]

The seminar *Life Death*, which is at the center of the following chapter, thus comes just one year after this seminar—or "counter-seminar"—that Derrida gave in 1974–75 at ENS under the hybrid title "GREPH (the concept of ideology in the French ideologues)." At the same time, then, as Derrida was reading and thinking along with his students about questions of language, translation, education, national identity, and so on, in French thinkers of the seventeenth and eighteenth centuries, and especially Étienne Bonnet de Condillac (1714–80)—a thinker whose views on writing, we recall, were treated by Derrida as indicative of the entire Western philosophical tradition in "Signature Event Context"—he was in the process of helping to found GREPH and clarify its mission and goals.

Working on both a theoretical and a practical level (assuming we can rely on such a distinction after Derrida's seminar of the following year, *Theory and Practice*), Derrida begins both to investigate and to treat the theme of education and to question the current educational institutions of philosophy in France, including his own role in those institutions. We should not be surprised, then, to find Derrida making remarks at the beginning of both *Life Death* and *Theory and Practice* about the *agrégation* exam and, especially, about the "program" of the *agrégation* for which Derrida was, in accordance with his position as *agrégé-répétiteur* at ENS, preparing his students. As Derrida recalls, yet again in 1976, this was a time when his teaching came to inform and to be informed by the critique of the educational institutions in which he found himself:

> Here in the École Normale Supérieure, which transforms itself by resisting its own transformation, here in the place where I, this

teaching body that I call mine, a very specific *topos* in body supposed to teach philosophy in France today, I teach.

In a sort of contraband between the *agrégation* and GREPH. (*WAP* 88–89/*DDP* 141)

Much more will be said about the *agrégation*—this quintessentially French institution, this exam that determines, in effect, who will and who will not have a right to teach philosophy in France—in the next chapter. For the moment, note simply that Derrida had spoken of his 1974–75 seminar as a "counter-seminar" and of his work on behalf of the French educational system (preparing students for the *agrégation*) in conjunction with his work to reform that system (through GREPH) as being related through a "sort of contraband"—two moments of "countering" that are not to be understood as a simple negation or reversal but as part of a more powerful and productive process of critique and transformation.[10]

It is this contestation of institutions from within or from their margins, this encountering or countering of institutions from their borders, this contrabanding of teaching, publication, and public engagement, that characterizes much of Derrida's work during this period.[11] This is particularly evident from the volume *Du droit à la philosophie*, which, despite having been published in 1990 and translated into English in 2002 (in the two volumes *Who's Afraid of Philosophy? Right to Philosophy 1* and *Eyes of the University, Right to Philosophy 2*), has still not drawn the critical attention it truly deserves.[12] This impressive and imposing volume of more than six hundred pages gathers together many (though not all) of Derrida's reflections about education, both theoretical and more practical, from 1975 through 1990, that is, from the time of GREPH to well after the founding of the Collège International de Philosophie in 1983, the second major public initiative that Derrida undertook in tandem with his teaching and his "research."

Du droit à la philosophie can and should be read for what it tells us about the life and work of Derrida, though it should also be read as a case study or profile in being an engaged intellectual. In addition to republishing Derrida's contributions to two important collective volumes that came out of the efforts of GREPH[13] and out of the meeting of teachers of philosophy from across France during the Estates General of Philosophy held at the Sorbonne on June 16–17, 1979,[14] the volume collects a diverse set of texts from 1975 through 1990. It combines more theoretical texts on language and translation (the relationship between French and Latin in Descartes, for example), topics that were often the focus of the series of seminars that ran under the title "Philosophical Nationality and Nationalism,"[15] with texts on the modern university and the division of faculties (in Kant, for example)[16] or on the function of philosophy in education and in the modern university (Hegel's own early philosophical education, for example, and his correspondence with Victor Cousin over questions of education)[17]—themes, topics, and questions that were all central to the work of GREPH.

The volume thus contains texts on many different topics and issues related to education, both historical and contemporary, and it contains texts with very different origins, purposes, and destinations. It combines newspaper and journal articles related to the Haby Reform and to GREPH's opposition to that reform[18] with conference presentations on education in Benin, West Africa, Toronto, Canada, and Cornell University in the United States,[19] texts originally written as prefaces to the books of others,[20] remarks made during roundtables,[21] even reports detailing the goals or demands of GREPH and two of the founding or preparatory documents for the Collège International de Philosophie.[22] This enormous collection on education even contains Derrida's remarks during his own *soutenance* or thesis "defense" at the Sorbonne in 1980 in support of his application for a Doctorat d'État,[23] a rather unique text in Derrida's corpus inasmuch as it combines, in the form of a prepared and publicly presented text, reflections about Derrida's intellectual itinerary from the 1960s onward: his early interest in literature and phenomenology; his concentration on the question of "writing"; his identification (for good or ill) with "deconstruction"; his focused works on Heidegger, Blanchot, and Levinas, among others; his attempts at a less academic, more experimental kind of writing in texts such as *Glas* and *The Post Card*; his interest in speech act theory and his debate with John Searle; his own conflicted belonging to the French university system; and, finally, his interest in questions of education and his work with GREPH. Essays, seminars, conference presentations, reports—these are, as it were, so many speech or language acts that feed off, reinforce, or contraband one another, and that give us a very different sense of Derrida's philosophical and pedagogical itinerary than the one we get simply from his other published works.

This collection of texts all related in some way to teaching and to the teaching of philosophy begins with a long introduction, "Privilege," in which Derrida tries to rethink, in effect, the status of philosophy "itself" and of philosophical institutions, along with the question of who *has* and who *should have* the "right" to philosophy, the right to study it and the right to teach it.[24] Written in July and August 1990 (that is, during *les vacances scolaires*, as they are called in France), this preface looks back over the preceding fifteen years and contextualizes Derrida's evolving interest in educational institutions, from his work on GREPH to the founding of the Collège International de Philosophie. After asking about the relationship between "right" (or law), about what institutions can and should legitimate or guarantee a certain "right to philosophy," Derrida explains that "Du droit à la philosophie" was first of all the title of a seminar given by him in January 1984 at another pivotal moment in his own teaching. He was still teaching as maître-assistant at ENS but was already preparing his move to EHESS as "directeur d'études," that is, director of studies in the area or domain of—not coincidentally—"Philosophical Institutions." Just the preceding autumn, he had helped found the Collège International de Philosophie (the official inauguration date was October 10, 1983), and he had been elected its first director. Derrida thus describes in 1990 the contents of that 1984 seminar, which looked essentially at the institutions or conventions that guarantee or feign to guarantee the right or "privilege" of philosophy and that determine or feign to determine the question of *who* has or should have this right or this privilege. Derrida's answer to this latter question will be, in short—as a flier from 1975 announcing a meeting of GREPH had once put it—"everyone"; everyone should have the right to philosophy, which means that everything needs to be done in educational institutions and beyond to guarantee that right. The example that will guide his analysis will thus be, says Derrida in "Privilege," the Collège International de Philosophie, designed to be "open," like Derrida's seminar, to anyone who wanted to attend (all that is usually required, as I can again attest, having attended several courses and events at the Collège from the late 1980s on, is a valid ID of some kind). If the mid- to late 1970s were thus concerned with issues related to GREPH (the training of teachers, the teaching of philosophy in secondary schools), the early 1980s were more concerned with establishing that new "counter-institution" called the Collège International de Philosophie, this second initiative being in many ways the natural outgrowth of the first ("ANC" 23).

From the mid-1970s up through 1990, we see Derrida thinking, writing, and speaking explicitly about various educational institutions, trying on occasion to reform those institutions, and, when possible, as with the Collège, to found other kinds of institutions. With the publication of more and more seminars—for example, that 1974–75 seminar on GREPH and the French ideologues, or the seminars of the 1980s on philosophical nationality and nationalism—this contrabanding of speech acts with founding acts will become even more apparent, and we will be able to fill out and further contextualize this important chapter in French intellectual history and in the philosophical itinerary of Derrida. We will be better able to follow and understand the shifts in Derrida's focus from protecting or even extending the teaching of philosophy in high schools and beyond to reforming the *agrégation* to rethinking the role and function of the university. We will see that long after Derrida had left the ENS and was no longer obliged to offer courses to prepare students for the *agrégation*, that is, long after having been granted at EHESS a greater freedom with regard to the kinds of courses he could offer, questions related to philosophical education and philosophical institutions would remain vital to Derrida. And this concern would continue to animate Derrida's work well beyond *Du droit à la philosophie* in 1990, as is evident from texts such as "L'autre nom du collège," a text from 1993 marking the ten-year anniversary of the founding of the Collège International de Philosophie, and "The University Without Condition" in 1999, a work that develops many of the educational questions and issues first articulated during the founding of the Collège.[25]

All these works can be read today as a sort of testament to this contrabanding of tradition and transformation, teaching and counter-teaching, to this interweaving of teaching and publications, conferences and political actions, in short, of speech acts of various kinds that all aim to articulate some aspect of what Derrida called in 1988, as we will see in a moment, a "counter-program" within existing educational institutions or some aspect of the "counter-institutions" that must be invented in the margins of those institutions. What Derrida gives us in the end is a different "model" or "figure" for education born out of his own experience teaching in French educational institutions, out of his systematic study and critique, oftentimes in his own seminars, of the history of those institutions, and, no doubt, out of his own often unhappy experience as a student within different educational institutions.

I began with Derrida's lament in the movie *Derrida* regarding his early experience in school in Algeria, the daily "trauma," as he went so far as to call it, of being abandoned by his mother in kindergarten. About fifteen years before that interview from the movie, during the time *Du droit à la philosophie* was no doubt being prepared for publication, Derrida gave an interview to the journal *Cahiers Pédagogiques* (one that would not be included in *Du droit à la philosophie*) in which he tells the very same story in almost exactly the same terms. Recalling the rampant racism and anti-Semitism in his school in an Algeria under the control of Pétain's Vichy government, Derrida again uses the term "traumatizing" to characterize this time in his life, and he again testifies to the fact that this early childhood experience was never completely overcome, even though he will have spent his entire life in the kinds of institutions in which it first took place: "I cried at the beginning of every school year up until the age of thirteen or fourteen.... I have an absolutely neurotic relation to the institution in which I have nevertheless lived my entire life; and even today, when I walk into a building like this one"—the interview took place at the Maison des Sciences de l'Homme in Paris—"I get a pit in my stomach [*ça me prend aux tripes*], I'm not exaggerating, and these are all things—one would have to analyze them—that go back to kindergarten" ("EE" 42). The interview has the colorful title, taken from Derrida's own words during the interview, "School for Me Was Hell."

But in the second part of the interview, published in the same journal, *Cahiers Pédagogiques*, a couple of months later, we hear about Derrida the teacher rather than Derrida the student, and, in the process, we hear not just about what school *was* for Derrida but what it *could be*. After a long and fascinating discussion of some of the context or root causes of GREPH, which is there identified as a distant effect of the "shock wave" that was 1968 in France,[26] Derrida returns to some of the themes we just saw developed in *Du droit à la philosophie*. He recalls, for example, having "devoted a seminar to the problem of philosophical teaching, beginning with the French ideologues of the eighteenth and nineteenth centuries, in relation to the history of French philosophical institutions" ("LC" 45), and he recalls having challenged at this same time not just Haby's proposal to eliminate philosophy in the last year of high school but ultimately the very idea of *beginning* an introduction to philosophy at age seventeen and not before. Derrida describes having himself, along with others associated with GREPH, come to the idea of a "progressive introduction" to philosophy that would begin well before the last year of high school, an extension of philosophical teaching that would require "transforming everything: the professors, the procedures, the programs" ("LC" 46), "a radical, profound transformation not only of the lycée but of society more generally," even, he says, of "the family" ("LC" 46). What is ultimately needed, he argues, is a transformation of existing institutions and practices and the "invention" of new ones, the invention of new relations to language and to philosophy, new relations between philosophy and the other disciplines.

But even this, it seems, is not quite enough, and not quite enough because it would be, perhaps, already too much. After affirming the need within education to "unleash curiosity" and "awaken desire" ("LC" 47) in view of a "true national education program," Derrida argues that even if this were to come about, even if such a program were ever to be put in place, one would still need to "continue to fight to accommodate places of nonconformity" ("LC" 47). One must thus always try, says Derrida, to work on two fronts simultaneously, on a front that tries to institute this "true educational program," that tries to create, in short, "a good school," but then also and at the same time on a front that would go "against [*contre*] this good school," a front that would not necessarily be opposed to it, Derrida clarifies, but that would be right up against it, exercising "vigilance" with regard to it. For it is "important," Derrida goes on to argue, "not to subject everything to the program of this good school, important to leave room for a counter-power," one for which philosophy would have a special role to play insofar as it would be "a place, precisely, of contestation of this educational model," "a place for the struggle to loosen up programs" ("LC" 47). And GREPH, he goes on to say in 1988, thirteen years after its founding, would have a part to play in all this: "if it has a future, it is there" ("LC" 47). While one must thus do everything possible, it seems, to create or to invent the best possible educational "program," "one must not try to program everything," since philosophy must remain, in spite of or in addition to everything that is on its programs, a "place" that facilitates the critique or the countering of those programs, in short, "a place of deprogrammation" ("LC" 47).[27]

It is with this appeal to "deprogrammation," to a sort of "counter-power" against the program, that the second part of this interview of 1988, published under the much more uplifting title "Unleashing Curiosity, Awakening Desire," ends. In accordance with Derrida's ever-present suspicions with regard to the notion and even the term "program," as well as his willingness to use and to negotiate with that notion and that term, Derrida suggests forming or creating a "program" that would be opposed to the program in place, a "program" that would try to transform or contest or, ideally, replace the traditional program. But he then goes on to suggest that philosophy become or, better, *remain* something that would oppose or run counter to the very notion of a program. Without arguing that philosophy or a philosophy seminar ever "completely abandon the transmission of knowledge" brought about through its programs ("LC" 47), without suggesting that a philosophy seminar ever become a free-for-all or a place of free play—and Derrida's own seminars, as I have tried to make clear, were anything but that—Derrida suggests that "space" be left for a counter-program within the program or right up against the program, a counter-program that would not simply be another program or curriculum (though it may also involve that) and would not simply require a transformation of the teaching body or the teaching *corps* (though it might involve that too) but that would involve or would inscribe, I would like to suggest, something like a difference in *tone* or *inflection* within pedagogy, one that could easily be mistaken or misunderstood, interpreted as too conservative or too radical, a tone or inflection that would at once present and interrupt, teach and counter-teach, transmit knowledge and somehow give access to what opened up that knowledge in the first place. While there would always be a certain tension or friction between this teaching and this counter-teaching, this program and this counter-program, the program being taught and the tone that is being struck in the teaching, the relationship between them would not be one of simple opposition.[28] This perhaps helps explain, at least in part, how the person who said he never liked schools or educational institutions allowed himself to spend the last forty years of his life working in and training others to work in those same educational institutions, the same ones but different, or at least that was the hope, the same but "open" to something different through a change in tone.

I have recounted elsewhere my own "introduction" to Derrida as a student, my own reception by him in his seminar, in a word, the *hospitality* I received from him as a teacher and as an individual, though also as a thinker who opened up the educational space in which I was received to something else.[29] As Derrida says in *A Taste for the Secret*, in a context that is not explicitly related to education but that can be heard as appealing to it: "The other may come, or he may not. I don't want to program him, but rather to leave a place for him to come if he comes. It is the ethics of hospitality" (*TS* 83). While neither of the two yearlong seminars I attended in the late 1990s were *on* hospitality (the two seminars explicitly on this theme were in 1995–96 and 1996–97), hospitality was, I would like to believe, their frame or their milieu, the "space" or "place" in which they unfolded, above and beyond, or right up against or alongside, the topics and texts that were explicitly treated.

Now one will notice that Derrida insisted in the interview quoted earlier on philosophy as a "place." What he meant by that, clearly, was not that philosophy has a particular place—like the Salle Dussane at the ENS or the large amphitheater at EHESS—but that, in giving rise to curiosity and desire, philosophy is a "place" that opens up different kinds of questions and thinking, a "place" that somehow inflects traditional spaces and turns them toward their own limit, their own conditions of possibility. I would like to believe that what one saw or heard in those lectures delivered at ENS or EHESS (and I imagine the same was true, even if different, at Yale, Hopkins, Irvine, Cornell, or NYU) was not only the rigor and power of Derrida as a reader and thinker of texts but his way of opening texts and thinkers up and putting them into conversation with one another in unexpected and often exhilarating ways, in short, his hospitality toward both the tradition and what exceeds the tradition. For in addition to seeing week after week and year after year in those seminars an erudite scholar reading texts in an informed, careful, rigorous, and inventive way, one had the impression of being witness to something else, something even more rare: someone truly thinking or, better, someone opening up a space for thinking, someone perpetually on the threshold of thought, on the brink or on the verge of something that had not yet been thought and would perhaps forever remain to be thought. While Derrida mostly read, as I have recounted, what he had prepared before coming to class, it always felt as if he were *thinking* it for the first time as he was reading it, thereby drawing his listeners along with him, drawing them into the draught of his thought or into the opening of that thought. Despite the fact that these texts were so fully written out and articulated in advance of the seminar session, despite the fact that no writing, and indeed no language, as Derrida will have taught us from at least *Of Grammatology* on, is ever completely devoid of some machine, some automaticity, Derrida's presentations always felt as if they were poised on a threshold where speaking and writing, the organic and the mechanical, the spontaneous and the rehearsed, were not yet fully distinct, a threshold that was at once the subject of the teaching and the "place" from which it came. Listening attentively for two straight hours was thus often challenging—especially in a foreign language—challenging and, truth be told, sometimes exhausting, but I would be willing to bet that the majority of Derrida's listeners found themselves riveted to the development of those lectures, to the reading of a text that was being slowly unfolded or an argument that was being carefully made, to a thinking that seemed at once accessible and profound, a thinking of and on the threshold that made one think that philosophy was truly beginning again. If one initially began attending Derrida's seminar out of simple curiosity, just to see what the founder of deconstruction was like and what he would say, one often left the room thinking that the topic that had just been treated was the most important and urgent topic in the world, and not just for philosophy but for thinking and acting more generally. In other words, one left thinking that what had been on the program was of the utmost importance and that what opened up that program, beyond any "transmission of knowledge," was something like a lesson in exercising along with Derrida, thanks to Derrida, a certain "right to philosophy."

It is unclear, of course, whether one can ever really demonstrate any of this, unclear whether that which opens up the program can even appear, in the present, in any pedagogical space. Perhaps only one's own writing or teaching can testify or bear witness to that opening, however indirectly or obliquely, a writing or teaching that somehow, in turn, transmits not only knowledge but also, in whatever way and to whatever degree this is possible, that same invitation to thinking otherwise, to thinking at the limits of thought, that same hospitality within an education program to what is always other than the program, that same invitation to remain for a time on the threshold.[30]

What follows in this second part of *Class Acts* are three modest examples of the kind of work that has been opened up or made possible by the publication of Derrida's seminars, in this case, by the last three seminars to be published. In the first chapter I look at Derrida's critique near the beginning of the 1975–76 seminar *Life Death* of the *agrégation* exam, and particularly its *program*, for which Derrida, still teaching at the École Normale Supérieure, was supposed to be preparing his students. The chapter then goes on to follow the notion of "program" as it is developed by Derrida in the seminar, in particular through his reading of the biologist François Jacob.[31] In the second chapter, I look at the way in which the recent publication of Derrida's 1976–77 seminar *Theory and Practice* should cause us to rethink Derrida's relationship to Marx and to Marxism, his treatment of questions of work and language and the relationship between theory and practice, questions, we should keep in mind, that were being treated by Derrida in the seminar at the very same time he himself, as we just saw, was rethinking and rediscovering some of the practical and theoretical underpinning of his own pedagogy. Finally, in the last chapter of this section I look at the first volume of *Perjury and Pardon*, where Derrida returns, more than a quarter of a century after "Signature Event Context," to questions of contingency and the speech act and, especially, the possibility of a speech act in writing, a speech act that would go under the name of an oeuvre or a work, a "speech act" that would thus challenge many of the assumptions of speech act theory as articulated by Austin and Searle insofar as such a work or "speech act" would be essentially detached or detachable from its context, severed right from the start from anything like the intention or the living presence—in a word, from the life—that would have supposedly produced it.

That is what is on the *program* for this second part of *Class Acts*, that is to say—even though it was not customary in French universities to hand one of these out at the beginning of a seminar, and, in this one regard at least, Derrida remained very French—on the *syllabus*.

Class 1: *Agrégations*

The Chance of Life Death *(1975–76)*

> My colleagues must have told you why they came down so hard on some of your arguments [regarding Descartes] . . . There is no question at all of your talent and, as is the case every year—such is the rule when it comes to the *agrégation*—we had to allow candidates to pass who were of a significantly lower intellectual "quality" than some who fell victim to the written or oral exams, since the former students played by the rulebook and were successful by dint of their conscientiousness and their patience. Don't forget that the "leçon" ("lecture") part of the *agrégation* isn't an exercise in pure virtuosity, but first and foremost an educational tool which pupils can follow—though this doesn't mean that, once you've rapidly dealt with the things you'd tell your class, you can't address the examiners directly.
> —Letter from Maurice de Gandillac to Jacques Derrida

The importance of the *agrégation* exam in the French educational system has long been known, especially to those who have grown up within that system. And that is particularly true in philosophy.[1] As a rule, no one is able to teach philosophy in a French university without passing that exam, and one's success in the exam, that is, one's ranking vis-à-vis other successful candidates of the same year, determines the kind of position one will receive from the National Educational System. In short, the *agrégation* makes careers in the academy and, more often than not—since only about 5 percent of those who take the exam in philosophy pass it in any given year—it breaks them.

All this is, as I say, very well known. What has been less well known, at least until relatively recently, is the role played by the *agrégation* in determining what is taught in the university philosophy classes that prepare students for the exam and, as a result, the influence of the exam on the interests and directions of philosophy itself in France. And what has gone almost completely unknown up until very recently is the influence of the *agrégation* exam on the teaching and, thus, on the work and the interests of Jacques Derrida. The aim of this chapter—this first act or class session in what I have called Derrida's "Open Seminar"—is in part to explore this influence by looking at two recently published seminars from the mid-1970s, two seminars that will show to what extent Derrida's philosophical concerns were shaped by the position he held for some twenty years at the École Normale Supérieure, that is, his position as *agrégé-répétiteur* charged with helping students prepare for that all-important exam.

But before turning to the influence of the *agrégation* on the philosophical interests of Derrida, let me begin with an anecdote as a way of thanking my friend Alan Schrift, whose work I will be relying on in what follows, and in order to show how the *agrégation* exam has very recently helped us to understand not only the content of Derrida's seminars—the figures, texts, and themes that figure in them—but the actual *dates* they were taught. For, surprising as it may seem, some of these dates have remained in question, and it is the *agrégation* exam, curiously, that has helped us to determine them. I am also beginning here because it is an anecdote about chance, about the relationship between chance or contingency and determination or programmation, notions that are at the theoretical heart of many of Derrida's seminars and that are also, as I will try to suggest, put into practice or put to the test by the recent publication and translation of these seminars.

Here, then, is the anecdote. In the summer of 2017 I was in Paris visiting Alan Schrift, professor of philosophy at Grinnell College, and I recounted to him a little conundrum those of us involved in the Derrida Seminar Translation Project were facing regarding the dates of a couple of Derrida seminars. Just a few months earlier, Éditions Galilée had published *Théorie et pratique* as the *Cours de l'ENS-ULM 1975–1976*, and the summer before that our translation group meeting at IMEC in Normandy had worked through David Wills's English translation of this same course, which we too, following the French and in keeping with all available bibliographies, assumed took place, as the Galilée edition had it, in 1975–76. Since Derrida refers in a few places in this seminar to the preceding year's seminar on the topic of "life death," we could then assume—since neither of the manuscript versions of those two seminars is dated—that that earlier seminar took place in 1974–75, dates that once again were confirmed by all the bibliographies we had consulted. So, the seminar *Life Death* (*La vie la mort*), the French edition of which Pascale-Anne Brault and Peggy Kamuf were in the process of preparing, dated from 1974–75, and *Theory and Practice* (*Théorie et Pratique*) was from 1975–76.

But as Peggy Kamuf and Pascale-Anne Brault began to edit for publication the French edition of that earlier seminar, they—and then the rest of us on the editorial and translation team along with them—began to have some doubts. Secondary texts that had not yet been published were being referred to by Derrida in the seminar as already published, and—one of the more interesting examples of academic sleuthing—Peggy noted that some of the early sessions of the *Life Death* seminar, while all undated, were typed on the back of fliers announcing a meeting of the Groupe de Recherches sur l'Enseignement Philosophique (GREPH) (a "meeting de mobilization") at the University of Paris, Jussieu, that would have taken place in April 1975.[2] It would have thus been very strange, we all thought, for Derrida in October or November 1974 to be using as scrap paper copies of a flier announcing an event that had yet to take place and, given the ad hoc nature of GREPH, even stranger for this event to have been so well planned six months in advance. We thus began to suspect, though without any definitive proof, that *Life Death*, not *Theory and Practice*, had been given in 1975–76 and that this latter was given in 1976–77.

Now what would really clinch the case, I said to Alan after recounting this long saga, would be to find the actual *agrégation* programs (*programmes*) for these years, since we know that both of these seminars were given at the École Normale Supérieure to help students prepare for the *agrégation* philosophy exam at the end of the year. Those programs would pretty much settle the matter, I said, but despite all our best efforts at both the ENS library and the Bibliothèque Nationale, they had proved elusive. Well, it was at that point in my story that Alan got up, went to his study, and came back in about sixty seconds with photocopies of the very *Programmes des Concours*, including that of the *agrégation*, that we had been looking all over Paris for. Lo and behold, the topic of the *deuxième épreuve* for the 1976 *agrégation* exam read very clearly "*La vie et la mort*," while the topic of the *deuxième épreuve* in 1977 was, just as clearly, "*Théorie et pratique*." As we had suspected, then, the seminar *La vie la mort*, which was supposed to prepare students for that spring 1976 exam, would have been given during the academic year 1975–1976, while *Theory and Practice*, intended to prepare students for the spring 1977 exam, would have been given in 1976–77, and not, as Galilée had just published it, 1975–76. It is thus that the *agrégation* exam, with the invaluable help of Alan Schrift, proved more helpful in determining the dates of Derrida's seminars than anything found in those seminars or in all our available bibliographies.

But I really should have known better—not about the dates themselves but about where to go to confirm them. For Alan Schrift is, as I well knew, the author of a 2008 article in the *Journal of the History of Philosophy* on the history of the *agrégation* exam from its inception in 1766 up to 2008 and, even more interestingly, on "the effects this history has had on philosophical practices in France."[3] Schrift there documents in great detail the wide-ranging effects of this uniquely French exam, and particularly of the program of the exam, on both the students who must study for and take the exam and the professors who must prepare their students for it. As Schrift argues, the program of the *agrégation* determines to a very large extent the future of philosophy itself in France: it determines what students study, what professors teach, that is, the themes, figures, and texts that are treated in courses designed to prepare students for the exam, and, as a result, it determines to a large extent what these same professors and sometimes students will end up publishing on in the months and years following the exam. Moreover, insofar as professors educate students not only through the figures and texts they teach for the exam but also through the style, rhetoric, and type of argumentation they believe the institutional bodies responsible for preparing and grading the exam will find legitimate or acceptable, these same professors, teaching to or for the exam in this way too, end up reinforcing very particular institutional norms or standards of philosophical writing.[4]

The exam thus preprograms, as it were, not only the canonical figures and texts that are to be taught and learned—and, in the process, which figures and texts are to be considered canonical in the first place—but also the nice, systematic, three-part essay with an introduction and a conclusion that shows one knows how to treat these texts properly. On this account, then, the *agrégation* is an enormous feedback loop of production or reproduction, a self-regulating system of self-reproduction that, in effect, determines or programs what good philosophy *has been* in the past and what it *will be* in the future in France. It determines what philosophers and philosophies will "survive" in France and what will not, which ones will be selected to live on in the academy and which ones will be selected out.[5]

Now, we know from some of Derrida's published works, for example *Du droit à la philosophie*, though also from his more recently published seminars, that no one was more aware of the constraints or limitations of such institutions of reproduction or self-reproduction within the academy than Derrida himself, who, in his capacity for many years as *agrégé-répétiteur* at the École Normale Supérieure (*caïman* in ENS slang), was charged with preparing students for the *agrégation*. Derrida writes this in 1976 about his role as *agrégé-répétiteur*, about twenty years after receiving that consoling but also no doubt somewhat discouraging letter from Maurice de Gandillac after his own failure in the exam:

A repeater, the *agrégé-répétiteur* should produce nothing, at least if to produce means to innovate, to transform, to bring about the new. He is destined to repeat and make others repeat, to reproduce and make others reproduce: forms, norms, and a content. He must assist students in the reading and comprehension of texts, help them interpret and understand what is expected of them, what they must respond to at the different stages of testing and selection, from the point of view of the contents or logico-rhetorical organization of their exercises (*explication de texte*, essays, or *leçons* [the *leçon* being, recall, one of the stumbling blocks in Derrida's own path toward passing the exam]). With his students he must therefore make himself the representative of a system of reproduction.... Or, rather, he must make himself the expert who, passing for knowing better the demand to which he first had to submit, explains it, translates it, repeats and re-presents it, therefore, to the young candidates. (*WAP* 75/*DDP* 122)[6]

We can hear quite clearly in this text of 1976 Derrida's ambivalence, if not his objections, with regard to the system of the *agrégation* and the role that he was playing in it. But with the recent publication of Derrida's seminars, we are beginning to understand how this ambivalence and these objections made themselves heard in the very seminars that had as their object the preparation of students at the ENS for the *agrégation* exam. And that is particularly true of the seminars I mentioned a moment ago, that is, those seminars of 1975–76 and 1976–77 titled *Life Death* and *Theory and Practice*. We hear Derrida at the outset of both of these seminars wondering aloud, in front of his students, how he is *both* going to respect his obligation to help students prepare for an exam that will determine whether or not they will ever be able to teach in a university or even in certain lycées or high schools *and* register his great dissatisfaction with the entire *agrégation* system. How, in short, he asks himself, is he going to "negotiate" with these diverse and sometimes conflicting obligations? How is he going to prepare students for the exam and yet still give a seminar—as Derrida liked to say—"worthy of the name [*digne de son nom*]"?

Derrida begins his seminar of 1975–76 by explaining the title he had given to his seminar, a title that suggests that it will indeed be a question of *life* and of *death*, the two topics announced for the exam that year, but not, as the *agrégation program* had prescribed it, a question of "life *and* death" (my emphasis). It is a little difference that changes just about everything. Derrida says near the beginning of the very first session of the seminar, whose title, announced in advance, is *Life Death*:

> The suspension of the *and* in my title, in the title of the seminar, constitutes a rather discreet, not terribly violent intervention, you will say, in the *agrégation* program, which this year bears, in a very traditional way, [the title] "life and death," life first, then death. Every year for a number of years now, at the beginning of each seminar, as some of you know, I explain my uneasiness in trying to adapt my work here to the *agrégation* program and the strategic decision that I make, each time, all the while fighting against the institution of the *agrégation*, elsewhere and even right here, to negotiate with it from within a given set of conditions. I am not going to repeat what I have already said and reproduce ad infinitum the same schema. I would rather, in analyzing the title of the *agrégation* program, not conform to it but make of it the object—to be deconstructed—of this seminar. (*LD* 7/25)

Derrida says this just after commenting at some length on his reappropriating transformation of the *agrégation* topic, that is, on his erasure of the "*et*," the "and," between "Life" and "Death," explaining that his focus will be "*La vie mort*," "Life Death," and not, as the *agrégation* committee had prescribed it, "La vie *et* la mort," that is, "Life *and* Death," or else, if one hears the word between "la vie" and "la mort" not as *et*, as "and," but as *est*, as "is," "Life *is* Death," as a certain Hegel would have it, life being the *truth* of death, *spiritual* life as the overcoming or the subsumption of *biological* life, and so on. If the *agrégation program* said "*La vie et la mort*," Derrida will—and this is his compromise, his negotiation—try to think "*la vie la mort*," another logic, as he calls it, of life and death, one that will take him fourteen sessions to develop through readings of Nietzsche, Heidegger, Freud—with detours through Hegel, Claude Bernard, and Georges Canguilhem—as well as the 1965 Nobel Prize–winning geneticist François Jacob.

Now, it will be in this latter, in the work of Jacob, that Derrida will find, so as then to question, the opposition between, precisely, two kinds of *program*. We will look at this opposition, or this supposed opposition, in detail a bit later, but for now it is enough to mark the fact that Derrida finds in Jacob the opposition between a genetic *program* (that is Jacob's own word), that is, the program of DNA, the program that orders and controls the reproduction of all living beings, and a human, institutional, cerebral, cultural program, one that would include, of course, institutions of human learning and pedagogy, including the university. It is an important reading for thinking the implications of deconstruction for the life sciences as well as the implications of the life sciences for deconstruction. But as we might have expected, Derrida will also go on to relate these two kinds of program and the type of reproduction they entail to the very program of the *agrégation* in order to suggest that, in the end, the *agrégation* is itself a system of reproduction that is perhaps no less rigid than that of DNA, at least as Jacob understands it, and that Jacob's optimism regarding the promise of the cultural, institutional program is far less founded than he believes.

As I suggested earlier, the system of educational reproduction that is reinforced by the *agrégation* is to be found not only in the figures, texts, and themes that are prioritized by the *agrégation* program but also in the style or rhetoric that is accredited by the *agrégation* committee. At the very end, therefore, of that same first session of *Life Death*, Derrida returns once again to the *agrégation*, speaking this time not so much of the "content" to be addressed by the exam but, precisely, of the style in which that content is to be addressed. Once again, Derrida lets his dissatisfaction be heard loud and clear. After mentioning an essay by Georges Canguilhem published under the title "The Concept and Life," Derrida first seems to make a genuine concession to the *agrégation* and a genuine recommendation for his students to follow: "I recommend that you read this article, along with the entire volume [in which it is included], as well as *La connaissance de la vie*, an earlier work. All of this will be very useful for you from the point of view of the *agrégation*" (*LD* 20–21/41). But after citing a brief passage from this essay by Canguilhem, to whom he will return in later sessions, Derrida leaves little doubt—and succeeding sessions will remove any and all doubt—about his appreciation for the kind of "*agrégation* rhetoric" he finds on display in Canguilhem:

> It is also for the sake of finding models of *agrégation* rhetoric that I recommended that you read Canguilhem in order to follow in his work, as in the works of all the epistemologists of the French school, some of the effects of the *agrégation*, the effects of French schooling. (*LD* 21/42)[7]

We find something similar at the beginning of the seminar *Theory and Practice*, a seminar given in 1976–77 in order to prepare students, as I recalled a moment ago, for an *agrégation* exam that would address the question "Theory and Practice." Instead of deforming the *agrégation* program title as he had done the year before, either through subtraction or addition or in some other way, Derrida apparently decided to accept or adopt the title as his own, but not before, as we will see in the next chapter, expressing his great dissatisfaction regarding it too.

But let us return to *Life Death*, the seminar of 1975–76, where Derrida will develop his most radical rethinking of the relationship between life and death in the Western philosophical tradition. One there sees at work an analysis that is interesting and important in its own right but one that also teaches us something crucial about Derrida's way of reading or about his argumentative strategy more generally. Through close readings of Hegel, Nietzsche, Heidegger, Freud, and—perhaps most surprisingly and interestingly, as I suggested—French geneticist François Jacob, Derrida develops what he calls a logic of *life-death* that contests both a philosophical logic of opposition (life vs. death) and a logic of subsumption (life *is* death or life is the *truth* of death). But what is equally interesting, though initially much less evident, is Derrida's attempt in this seminar to rethink traditional philosophical categories or oppositions such as contingency and teleology, chance and necessity, or freedom and determination, in relation to that notion of *program*. Sessions four through six, plus large sections of the first session (some hundred manuscript pages in all), are all concerned with François Jacob's then relatively recent book *The Logic of the Living* (*La logique du vivant*, 1970), a work that attempts to give an account of the reproduction of living beings in terms of the reproduction of the genetic code or the *program* of DNA.[8]

Now it is precisely this notion of program that explains why Derrida finds Jacob's *The Logic of the Living*, a work written by a geneticist and not a philosopher, a legitimate object of philosophical critique. The problem is not just that Jacob himself uses philosophical language to describe and interpret his own scientific project, though he certainly does that as well. The larger problem for Derrida, it seems, is that Jacob claims throughout *The Logic of the Living* that by speaking of "living beings" rather than of "life," by speaking of *le vivant* rather than *la vie*, he is able to avoid all the trappings and false problems of Western metaphysics, all the vague but enduring concepts of the metaphysical and theological tradition. Derrida will let it be heard that he does not buy any of these claims and that, in his view, Jacob not only did not avoid such a metaphysics but actually fell in line with some of the most traditional aspects of it in his reinscription of teleology, essence, and, especially, despite his claims to the contrary, *life*. Derrida is thus going to demonstrate that Jacob ended up falling prey to some of the most traditional aspects of metaphysics by repeating, reproducing, and reinscribing a notion of teleology in his conception of living beings and by projecting a problematic humanism into the hierarchization of those living beings.

It is already in the very first session of *Life Death* that Derrida, after having spoken of the *agrégation* and of its program for that year, begins his reading of Jacob. And he begins by going right to the heart of the matter, the notion of "program" in Jacob's *The Logic of the Living*, the very thing that Jacob thought spared him from this metaphysics. Derrida actually begins his critique of Jacob by referring—and this rather is rare in the seminars—to his own previous work, in this case, to his own use of the notion of "program" in *Of Grammatology*. Derrida refers to and then cites this work in this first session of the seminar:

> Some ten years ago, in *Of Grammatology*, in a chapter near the beginning that is titled (already, one might say, by coincidence, prescience, or an almost subjectless teleology) "The Program," I recalled that "the contemporary biologist speaks of writing and *pro-gram* in relation to the most elementary processes of information within the living cell." The point there was not, however, to reinvest the notion or the word *program* with the entire conceptual machine of logos and its semantics but to try to show that the appeal to a non-phonetic writing in genetics had to or should involve and incite an entire deconstruction of the logocentric machine rather than a return to Aristotle. (*LD* 23/44; see *OG* 9/19)

Derrida will arrive at this critical conclusion in the course of a long analysis of Jacob's notion of *program*, which is so central to *The Logic of the Living*. In that work, Jacob distinguishes between two programs or two kinds of program, each with its own unique form of memory. The first of these is the genetic program of DNA, a program that humans share with all other living beings. Jacob characterizes this program in terms of rigidity and inflexibility, that is, in terms of a memory that works by simple repetition or retranscription of a preestablished code. This is, of course, the encoded memory of deoxyribonucleic acid, memory in the form of the genetic code that gets passed down inflexibly from one generation to the next.

The second program, then, which is to be rigorously distinguished from the genetic program in Jacob's view, is the institutional, cultural, cerebral, mental (or nervous) program of the human, the program that has, in effect, set human beings apart from all other living beings. The memory of this program is, according to Jacob, much more flexible than the genetic program and capable of being transformed inasmuch as it, unlike the genetic program, can learn from experience and so can pass on acquired learning from one generation to the next.

There are thus two programs, one inflexible and unable to learn from experience, the other flexible and able to transmit what it learns from experience to subsequent generations. Derrida writes:

> We should thus conclude from this that the mental (institutional) program has a relation to the outside, that it learns from experience, that it lets itself be transformed, whereas the genetic program forms a closed, deaf [*sourd*] system, purely endogenous, impervious to the

kind of change that Jacob calls, with this very suspect word, "deliberate." (*LD* 18/38–39)

We can here see Derrida beginning to cast suspicion upon Jacob's use of philosophical terms and categories with a long and cumbersome tradition. According to Jacob, the institutional program is able to change because of "deliberate," by which he means free, conscious, interventions from the outside, whereas the genetic program, which is closed, "deaf," says Jacob, to everything outside it, can undergo or be struck by no such interventions. The genetic program can change through mutations, of course, but, as Derrida writes, quoting Jacob, "in no case can there be a correlation between the cause and the effect of the mutation." In short, "each individual program is the result of a cascade of *contingent events*" and "the very nature of the genetic code prevents any deliberate change in program whether through its own action or as an effect of its environment" (*LL* 3/11; cited at *LD* 18–19/39; my emphasis). Unlike the institutional, cerebral program, therefore, the genetic program, while unable to learn from experience, is able to change through mutations, which are—and this is Jacob's analogy—like unintentional copying errors that, once introduced, get faithfully transmitted from one generation to the next. To follow out the analogy, which Jacob does not, while the genetic program changes through the unintentional copying errors of a scribe, the institutional program changes through the intentional, conscious planning of a writer or, better, a speaker who innovates, invents, speaks freely, and guides the scribe who tries to get down his every word—a bit like a student listening to an *agrégé-répétiteur*.

Hence, the genetic program is characterized by contingency, by causes that come in the form of mutations in a wholly unplanned, unpredictable, nondeliberate, contingent way. It is worth noting here, then, that Jacob opposes that contingency not to necessity, since the genetic program follows a more or less necessary chain of causes and effects, but to freedom, deliberation, consciousness, and so on. Jacob thus associates the genetic program with everything that is typically identified with contingency and exteriority in the metaphysical tradition, namely, a certain automaticity, signifiers divorced from signifieds, signs divorced from their meaning, and so on.

At first glance this might appear to be an enormous break with the Western metaphysical tradition, inasmuch as Jacob appears to be identifying *life itself*—or at the very least the code or program of life, the very workings of DNA—with contingency or chance. There where philosophers and theologians had once located an ordering *logos*, a meaningful teleology, sometimes even a creative breath, Jacob will have placed—or so it seems—a certain contingency, a sort of blind chance or dumb luck. This does indeed seem to be, as Jacob had thought, a radical interruption, if not a thoroughgoing deconstruction, of the metaphysical tradition.

But let us return for a moment to the other program, that is, to the institutional or cerebral program. That is the program whereby, according to Jacob, information is passed on from one human generation to the next not in a contingent, nonintentional, blind way, as it is in the genetic program, but knowingly, deliberately, or freely through human culture and institutions. This program itself developed, of course, through a mutation in the genetic program, but that mutation was so radical that it resulted in a completely new form of memory and program, the institutional program of the human. So radical was this mutation in fact that the cerebral program has actually been able to free itself from the rigidity of the genetic program by means of institutions that can now *deliberately* and *selectively* pass on information from one generation to the next. Even more, with the discovery of the workings of DNA in the middle of the twentieth century, it even became possible to intervene in that previously blind or deaf retranscription of DNA, that is, to intervene in the very processes of heredity itself, in order to manipulate and change both mankind's own genetic program and that of other living beings. While changes have thus occurred throughout the whole evolutionary process through mutations, these have been due "entirely to chance," that is, they have come about without any deliberation or planning, without any correlation between cause and effect. The institutional program can thus be understood as the "supplement"—and this too is Jacob's word—to the genetic program that today allows humankind to alter the genetic program itself, replacing chance or contingency by deliberate human planning. Here is how Jacob, near the end of his *Logic of the Living*, envisions the possibility of mankind actually controlling evolution through the genetic program:

> With the accumulation of knowledge, man has become the first product of evolution capable of controlling evolution. . . . Perhaps one day it will become possible to intervene in the execution of the genetic program, or even in its structure, to correct some faults and slip in supplementary instructions. Perhaps it will also be possible to produce at will, and in as many copies as required, exact duplicates of individuals, a politician, for instance, an artist, a beauty queen or an athlete. There is nothing to prevent immediate application to human beings of the selection processes used for race-horses, laboratory mice or milch cows. (*LL* 322/343–344)

Jacob can thus claim that modern genetics will have, in effect, resolved the longstanding debate within biology over whether acquired traits can be inherited. The cerebral, institutional program allows humankind not only to learn from experience but also to transmit "acquired traits" to future generations. As we just heard in those final lines of *The Logic of the Living*, Jacob is not just enthusiastic but positively exuberant about this possibility, and one can only imagine what he would have thought about new gene-editing programs such as CRISPR or Prime (*LL* 3/11). Of course, one does not need to look very far into twentieth-century history to see how easily this dream of controlling the evolutionary process, of being able, for example, to select out certain debilitating diseases in men and milch cows, a development that is indeed to be celebrated, can turn just as well into a eugenics nightmare.[9]

Such a critique of Jacob can be heard in the background of Derrida's analysis, but it is far from the only one or even the most trenchant to be developed. Derrida's aim is to put into question this entire relation, or opposition, really, between the genetic program and the institutional program, that is, the opposition between a supposedly rigid, inflexible, program exposed to contingency, and a deliberate program, controlled or at least controllable by human planning. He begins this putting into question—and this is a strategy, a logic, that one can find operating in *all* of Derrida's work, from beginning to end—by asking whether the more valued of the two sides of the opposition, the side that has been traditionally elevated or celebrated, can be so readily separated from the less valued, denigrated side. In this case, he begins by asking whether the institutional program—that is, the more valued program, the human program, the supposedly deliberate program, the program that is now promising to control, manipulate, and transform the genetic program—really is as deliberate as all that, that is, whether there is not a kind of *contingency* built into it as well. Having cited Jacob on the opposition between the two programs, Derrida notes:

> In order, then, for the genetic program, when described in this way, to be opposed in a pertinent fashion to the mental, cerebral-institutional program, one would need to be certain that the same thing cannot be said about this latter. But can't the same thing be said about it? (*LD* 19/40)

He then continues—and this is, recall, written in 1975–76:

> If there is one generally accepted tenet of a certain number of theoretical breaks in what I call, just to say it quickly for now, modernity, it is that causality in the order of, let us say, "cerebral-institutional" programs (psychical, social, cultural, institutional, politico-economic, and so on) has exactly the same style, in its laws, as the causality that

> Jacob seems to want to reserve for genetic programs, namely [Derrida now quotes Jacob's words regarding the *genetic* program but applies them to the *institutional* program] "all the phenomena which contribute to variation in organisms and populations occur without any awareness of their effects." [Derrida continues:] Similarly, the heterogeneity between causes and effects, the non-deliberate character of changes in the program, in a word, everything that places subjects from within the system in a situation of being unconscious effects of causality, everything that produces effects of contingency between an action coming from the outside and the internal transformations of the system—all of this characterizes the non-genetic program as well as the genetic program. (*LD* 19–20/40)

Derrida thus suggests that, despite or in addition to all the seemingly deliberate planning, all the supposed freedom operating in the institutional, cerebral program, there are—as we have learned from psychoanalysis, sociology, economics, and so on—all kinds of nondeliberate, unconscious, that is, in Jacob's lexicon, *contingent* effects that cause the program either to repeat itself or to change in ways and according to processes that are beyond the deliberate, conscious control of any of its actors. To be clear, Derrida is not denying the role played by consciousness, intention, deliberation, and so on in the institutional, cerebral program. He is simply suggesting that this program can never *exclude* nonconscious, unplanned, contingent effects, and that since it cannot exclude them, it is from the start compromised or contaminated by them, its self-control or its mastery compromised from the very beginning.

Hence Derrida appeals to certain insights from the *social sciences* in order to question Jacob's claim about the noncontingency of the institutional program. What remains for him now is to use the insights of *philosophy* to diagnose the reasons why Jacob would make such a claim in the first case. I continue the quote:

> [But] where does Jacob get the notion that, outside the genetic system and the genetic programs, changes in program are deliberate, essentially deliberate? Where does he get this notion if not from an ideologico-metaphysical opposition that determines superior or symbolic programs (with humanity at the very summit of these) on the basis of meaning, consciousness, freedom, knowledge of the limit between the inside and the outside, objectivity and non-objectivity, etc.

Having suggested that the institutional program has a share of contingency or nondeliberation, Derrida is now arguing that there is in Jacob's work a latent or implicit metaphysical humanism in this same program. It is in fact this humanism that will have motivated Jacob to oppose the institutional, cerebral program to the genetic one on the basis of attributes such as *deliberation* and *freedom*—attributes or terms about which, let me note in passing, Derrida will himself remain skeptical throughout his entire corpus, using them sparingly and almost always strategically as a way to oppose what is rigidly predetermined.[10]

Derrida in the *Life Death* seminar thus criticizes Jacob's claim that the institutional program changes because of the free, deliberate, conscious choices or decisions of its actors. According to Derrida, the institutional program changes—mutates—not because of the fully deliberate choices or decisions of free, rational actors but, to a large degree, because of those nondeliberate, unconscious, in Jacob's words *contingent* causes that look a bit like mutations within DNA. Taking the terms of the genetic program, then—unconsciousness, nondeliberation, lack of freedom, contingency—and applying them to the institutional program, Derrida argues that the human is not the master of its own program, that is, the master of the institutional, cerebral program, despite appearances to the contrary. This does not mean, of course, as I suggested a moment ago, that we must completely abandon notions of freedom, deliberation, and so on. What it does mean is that we must use these terms with more circumspection than Jacob does. It also means that the institutional program cannot be rigorously distinguished from the genetic one on the basis of notions such as contingency and freedom. Jacob's distinction or, rather, opposition between the two programs, one characterized by contingency and the other by noncontingency, seems to be itself, on Derrida's reading, conditioned or subtended by a *generalized contingency* that marks and determines, in different ways and to varying degrees, both programs. Derrida concludes this passage:

> Here again, as you see, the opposition between the two programs cannot be rigorous, and this seems to me to be due to the fact that, for lack of reelaborating at once the general notion of program and the value of analogy, we leave these marked by a logocentric teleology and a humanist semantics, by what I will call a philosophy of life. (*LD* 20/26–27)

Now, in speaking here of a "logocentric teleology" and a "philosophy of life" Derrida seems to be suggesting yet something else, something more. What Jacob says about the genetic program—namely, that it is a program of contingency, of exteriority—seems to be contradicted by the suggestion that there is a certain *teleology* within that program as well. This teleology does not, of course, correspond to any kind of divine plan or intelligent design but it does seem to be related to a sort of *logos* that unfolds or develops in time or in history. This is, as it were, the second moment or the second gesture in Derrida's interpretative strategy. After having suggested that the institutional program is itself conditioned by nondeliberate, unconscious, contingent elements—all those things that Jacob had attributed only to the genetic program—Derrida now suggests that there is a *concealed* or *surreptitious* teleology animating Jacob's own understanding of the genetic program. It is teleological, in part, because that to which the genetic code for *all* life is compared is a human code, the human book. It is as if the coded language of the bacteria, a booklike language, were waiting for the human book to become perfected, to come into its own, as it were. Whereas Jacob's characterization of DNA as code looked like a radical break with the metaphysical tradition, it was, in the end, completely consistent with that tradition insofar as that code was understood *logocentrically*, that is, as the unfolding of a *logos* or some kind of predetermined design. Had Jacob considered the genetic code from a non-logocentric point of view, his understanding of the workings of DNA would have been very different, even more radical, perhaps, and more in line, it appears, with what the last fifty years have taught us about, for example, the role played by epigenetics in the transmission of DNA.

Derrida is thus suggesting that within even the genetic program there is, for Jacob, no real chance or contingency insofar as a surreptitious teleology has been guiding its development from the beginning, a teleology that culminates in the human. Derrida's aim in these pages of the seminar devoted to Jacob is, it seems, to expose this latent or hidden teleology and humanism in Jacob's interpretation in order to restore an element of chance or contingency both to the genetic program whose mechanisms were first revealed and explained by the likes of Jacob and to the human program that Jacob believed humans capable of controlling in a free, intentional, and deliberate way.

In the end, what Derrida finds to be surreptitiously at work in Jacob is not unlike what he finds at work in many other philosophers or philosophical texts. For example, it is not unlike what he finds operating in the speech act theory of John Austin, namely, as Derrida puts it in "Signature Event Context," "the teleological lure [*leurre*] of consciousness" ("SEC" 327/389).[11] This lure or this illusion, this *phantasm*, as Derrida will call it in later works, is inherent, it seems, in the very notion of "program" as Jacob understands it. On the side of the institutional program, it is precisely this "teleological lure of consciousness" that is at work, the lure of full, self-present consciousness. In the genetic program there is something that looks like the teleological lure of meaning, the lure of an unfolding intelligibility or meaning in human history or in the history of living beings.[12] These are all aspects of what Derrida calls "logocentrism," the logocentrism that can be found not just in a thinker of the phenomenological tradition such as Husserl or an ordinary language philosopher such as Austin but in the discourse of a biologist such as François Jacob.

The institutional, cerebral, mental program is thus not nearly as conscious or deliberate as Jacob thinks, and Jacob thinks the way he does, opposing the institutional program to the genetic program, because of a metaphysical humanism that has caused him to attribute freedom and deliberation to the institutional program and a *logos* and *telos* to the genetic program. Whereas a certain contingency or chance, as well as a certain relation to the outside, conditions, on Derrida's account, *both* the genetic program *and* the institutional program, making it impossible to distinguish the two with attributes such as contingency, on the one hand, and freedom, on the other, Jacob has infused *both* programs with the humanistic and teleological assumptions that characterize the institutional, human program.

As I suggested at the outset, Derrida's analysis is interesting and important in its own right, but it also tells us something about Derrida's strategy more generally. By localizing or identifying what has been excluded or devalued in a discourse, for example, contingency in the form of a cascade of unplanned effects, Derrida can show how this contingency marks or even conditions everything that is valued and thought to control these devalued things, for example, consciousness, freedom, deliberation, and so on. Instead of an opposition between two programs defined in terms of qualities such as rigidity, inflexibility, and contingency on the one hand, and flexibility, consciousness, and freedom on the other, Derrida suggests that both sides of these oppositions are effects of a *general* or *generalized contingency*, which itself is not unrelated to what Derrida, in many other texts from the late 1960s and 1970s, texts such as *Of Grammatology* and "Signature Event Context," to name just two, called a general iterability (or a general citationality); the fact, for example, that a letter—like a retranscription of DNA—can always *not* arrive at its destination, thereby turning contingency into something like a structuring condition.

The result of Derrida's analysis is surely not to attribute everything to mere chance or to contingency, to deny the role played by consciousness, deliberation, or freedom. It is, rather, to show that the part played by chance can never be completely excluded or ruled out of human affairs and that everything that exceeds or escapes the program by chance cannot be excluded in principle from the program. And the fact that chance cannot be excluded in principle means that it is, in a way, included in a necessary or structural way from the very beginning. It thus becomes necessary to show how, each time—and each time in a unique way—the nonprogrammable can always come to interrupt the program, always in an unforeseeable way, never completely the same.[13] It becomes necessary to show that the unprogrammable is never simply what happens to the program as an accident but that which defines or conditions the program from the very start. In other words, it becomes necessary to show that a certain chance will continue to haunt the best-laid plans and programs of mice, milch cows, and men.

How, then, to conclude, can this analysis of the two programs in Jacob help us to rethink the notion of program with which I began, that is, the program of the *agrégation*? How does Derrida's analysis of this relation between the two programs help us to rethink an institutional "program" such as the *agrégation*? To the extent that Derrida's analysis shows us that the institutional program is much less flexible, less under the control of its human actors, than Jacob tends to believe, then one can begin to understand the *agrégation* and its "program" as an enormous self-regulating system, a giant feedback loop in conformity with the analyses of Alan Schrift. In short, one can begin to understand the *agrégation* program as a system that reproduces itself with an efficacy that resembles that of the genetic code—an enormous system of self-reproduction where nothing, or very little, changes from one generation to the text, where one reads the same texts in the same way as our philosophical "ancestors."[14] It is almost as if these two programs—the program of the *agrégation* and the program of DNA—were themselves "aggregated," that is, combined, intertwined, like the two strands of DNA, or like the front and back of those pages on which Derrida typed a good part of the *Life Death* seminar, giving us—"in a sort of contraband between the *agrégation* and GREPH" (*WAP* 89/*DDP* 141)—his philosophical analysis of Jacob (among others) on the one side and, on the other, on the flip side, the announcement for an organizational meeting, a "meeting de mobilization," of GREPH.

But it can also be said, following the other side of Derrida's analysis, as it were, that it is thanks to this law of contingency that conditions at once the genetic program and the institutional program, this law of a general iterability, that the program of the *agrégation*, like every program, is essentially and not by accident open to its outside, open in its very structure to the future, open, therefore, to variation, to mutation, in a word, to novelty and surprise. It is thus perhaps not an accident—or else it is completely by accident, that is, thanks to chance—that the same student who flunked the oral part of that infamous *agrégation* competitive exam would, once he had become a professor, take such an interest in that notion of "program" in all its manifestations.[15] It is no doubt not an accident—unless it is precisely by accident—that this student, having himself become a professor, would not outright reject this notion of "program" but proceed to "negotiate" with it in order to facilitate the emergence of something unexpected or unforeseeable from within it, something that escapes the program, something that one might call an "event." One could argue that the entire work of Derrida, and all his pedagogy, beginning with *Life Death*—much of it typed on the back of old photocopies, that is, on a series of what might appear to be identical reproductions—are the trace and the proof of both that program and, through this chance, that singular event.

Class 2: Education in *Theory and Practice* (1976–77)

I would like to begin this chapter, this second class in our "Open Seminar," with yet another anecdote, this one about Jacques Derrida's teaching, or at least about his attitude with regard to teaching, his way of registering a protest against the educational system for which he was teaching and his willingness to negotiate nonetheless with that system. The anecdote has to do not with the way in which Derrida, when teaching at the École Normale Supérieure preparing students for the *agrégation* exam in philosophy, would often begin a seminar, as we saw in the previous chapter, by expressing his great frustration at having to address the topic determined by the *agrégation* program committee and, especially, at having to address it in a way that that committee would deem acceptable, thereby giving Derrida's students a fighting chance at succeeding in the exam. No, my anecdote, at once more banal but perhaps more telling, revolves around something that would happen at one point or another in almost every Derrida seminar session I attended, not only at the École Normale Supérieure but also later at the École des Hautes Études en Sciences Sociales.

The scene was repeated nearly every Wednesday afternoon, and by the time I began attending Derrida's seminar in the mid-1980s it had already taken on the air of a farce or a comedy in which everyone, students and professor alike, played their part. At the beginning of each seminar session Derrida would date and then begin circulating to the two hundred or so students in attendance a notebook—the famous "*cahier*"—that he would ask us all to sign and pass on to the person sitting next to us. The object was for the notebook to be passed down the first row, right to left, then down the second, left to right, eventually wending its way back to the final row, at which point it would be passed forward and then placed on Derrida's desk by someone in the first row. That is, at least, the way it was supposed to work, though it almost never did. For about half an hour into the seminar session, Derrida, who always followed the progress of the notebook out of the corner of his eye, would ask with some irritation what in the world had happened to his notebook, which had not yet been returned to his desk. He would say that signing and passing a notebook side to side and front to back was not such a difficult thing to do and he was at a loss as to how we had, once again, failed to measure up to that simple task. He would then explain, in a more conciliatory tone, that that notebook was the only way he could prove to the powers that be in the national education system that he had actually taught the seminar and that he had a certain number of students in attendance. It was essential that he get that notebook back and submit it to those authorities at the end of the year in order to justify his appointment. It was at that point that the notebook would mysteriously resurface somewhere in the middle of the lecture hall and continue on its perilous journey through the auditorium and, eventually, back to Derrida's desk.

Now, in order to allay any suspicions that I am unduly exaggerating Derrida's interest in this simple attendance notebook, allow me to follow the itinerary of that misbegotten notebook through just a single seminar, one that I myself did not even attend, the first year of Derrida's seminar on hospitality of 1995–96, the very same seminar I mentioned at the outset of this work when explaining Derrida's notion of "The Open Seminar." The question of the notebook there emerges, as we will see, in almost every session, and more than once in a couple of them.

Things seem to get off to a pretty good start the first week of the seminar. No notes of concern or consternation have been captured by the tape recording I have been able to consult, and Derrida simply ends that first session by saying: "Okay, that's it. Thank you. I just ask that you return the notebook to me after signing it. I hope that everyone has signed it."

It is unclear what happened in the second session—perhaps everything went as planned—but by the third session the apparent orderliness of the weekly ritual had begun to break down. About halfway through that third session of the first year of the seminar on hospitality, at minute 56:00 of the two-hour session, to be precise, Derrida apparently notices that the notebook, after an hour of circulating through the room, has somehow disappeared and has not been returned to his desk. Speaking of hospitality and its opposites, he thus cites, ironically, as a prime example of "social disorder," the "passing around of the notebook," and he enjoins the seminar participants, "You need to ask for it!" that is, ask for the notebook. I assume the notebook mysteriously reappeared at this point and continued on its journey through the room.

Two sessions later, the same disorder continues to reign. Here is Derrida, talking about Antigone and then getting distracted by the missing notebook, right at the one-hour mark in the two-hour seminar:

> She is lamenting less her father than her own mourning, if that is possible. How can one lament a mourning? How can one lament not being able to mourn? How can one mourn one's mourning? (Is it possible to attempt some sort of rationality in the circulation of that notebook? [Laughter] Has everyone signed the notebook?) That is the question that is lamented over [*se pleure*] through the tears of Antigone.

Half an hour later, Derrida's anxiety regarding the notebook has become even more acute. Now an hour and a half into the session, Derrida, in the midst of a discussion of language, nationality, and hospitality, interrupts his train of thought once again to ask, "Is the notebook getting passed around? Okay, there it is." Again there is laughter in the room. The potential catastrophe of a lost notebook has again been averted. But Derrida's reflections about the notebook have not come to an end. When the notebook is apparently returned to Derrida's desk, just three or four minutes later, after voyaging for more than ninety minutes through the seminar room, it provokes these remarks:

> As for these two extensions of language or of the tongue, I would locate very quickly two directions of investigation, two programs . . . (Thank you. Has everyone had the notebook? It is absolutely . . . until the day I retire I will never cease to be amazed by the inability of this notebook to make its way around the room. [Laughter] It must carry within it some malefic power . . .) or two problematics to be elaborated.[1]

In the sixth session, more than halfway through the seminar session, Derrida interrupts a quotation from Franz Rosenzweig's *The Star of Redemption* on the "linguistic capacities of a people" in order to ask, once again abruptly and without transition, "is the notebook getting around? I pay attention to everything. [Laughter] Has the notebook gotten to everyone? No, okay there it is. I return to my quotation."

In the seventh session, things have clearly not gotten any better. Once again, halfway through the session—and it is with this comment that I will conclude my own little tale about the famous notebook (even though Derrida will speak of it yet again in the course of the seminar)—Derrida links, and not without provoking laughter yet again from his students, his attentiveness to that ill-starred notebook to a sort of obsession. Here is Derrida, interrupting himself yet again in mid-thought:

> It is necessary to invent an imperceptible difference that will allow for a cut, and then it is necessary to deploy the obsession ad infinitum, the internal obsession . . . the way in which that notebook circulates is ultimately going to kill me [Laughter], it's incredible, incredible. I see it. . . . What is the principle of selection here? How does it all of a sudden go from there to there? . . . So, I was speaking of an internal obsession [Laughter] . . .

I begin with this anecdote not only to provide a bit of local color to the otherwise austere or abstract topic of "Derrida's pedagogy," and not only to show how a simple attendance notebook, a *cahier d'appel* or *cahier de présence*, could become for Derrida a veritable *cahier de doléances* (of Derrida's *doléances*, Derrida's grievances), but also to give some sense of how Derrida, though often somewhat irritated by the constraints imposed on him by his role as educator, was almost always willing to "negotiate" in some way with them. It shows, it seems to me, Derrida's willingness to negotiate both in theory and in practice insofar as deconstruction is itself, as I will try to argue in this chapter, a negotiation in both theory and practice, a negotiation *between* theory and practice, with all the constraints and opportunities, all the surprises and contingencies, that such negotiation entails or provokes.

"Theory and practice," I say, because it just so happens, as I recalled in the previous chapter, that Derrida once gave an entire year's seminar under that very title, and it further so happens that that very seminar is one of the most recent of Derrida's forty-two years of seminars to be published in French and translated into English. Though just recently published, that seminar was given more than four decades ago, during the academic year 1976–77, at a time when Derrida, as we have seen, held the position at the École Normale Supérieure (ENS) of an *agrégé-répétiteur*, that is, an instructor charged with preparing ENS students for the *agrégation* exam at the end of the year.[2] The theme for which Derrida was responsible for preparing his students that year was thus none other than "Theory and Practice," a prescribed theme that Derrida adopted as the title of his own seminar, electing to retain the title in its letter rather than to transform or deform it, as he had the previous year when, as we have seen, he gave a seminar titled *Life Death* to address the theme of the *agrégation* program "Life *and* Death" (my emphasis).

Derrida thus adopts the title of the *agrégation* program (a first sign of negotiation), but not without expressing his great dissatisfaction with it—as well as with a system that *imposes* such a program and that determines in large measure the kind of seminar he will be able to give. Here is how Derrida begins that seminar of 1976–77:

> Theory and practice, then [*Théorie et pratique, donc*].
> (It) must be done [*Faut le faire*].
> When I say *faut le faire* what am I doing? (*TP* 1/13)

He then goes on to comment:

> Of course, or so it would seem, I am heaving a sigh of discouragement, discouragement tinged with ironic protest at the curriculum [*programme*] that requires us to deal, in one year in the form of a seminar, with such a question, if that is what it is. As I do each year—but rest assured I won't take it any further this year[3]—I'll start by critically analyzing the situation that is imposed on us by inviting you not to be satisfied with critiquing it, in theory, but to try to transform this situation effectively, practically. (*TP* 1/13)[4]

So, theory and practice, *faut le faire*, says Derrida, a phrase that can be heard in a couple of different ways. It can be heard, first, as simply repeating an imperative coming from the *agrégation* committee, that is, the program or curriculum committee for that year: "theory and practice," *faut le faire*, "this is what has to be done, this is what you, what we, what all of us together, must do; that is what has been prescribed to you, and thus me, to us, as our program for the year, and so that is what we must do, and not just in theory but in practice, right here in this seminar." Teaching a seminar on "theory and practice," the topic of the *agrégation* exam—"that is what has to be done," one can hear Derrida arguing, just as the attendance notebook has to be filled out during every seminar session.

But Derrida's phrase is not, notice, "il *faut le faire*," that is, "it must be done," but, more idiomatically, and again through subtraction (as in "life death" rather than "life and death"), "*faut le faire*," a phrase often used to characterize a sort of chutzpah, nerve, cheek, or impudence on someone's part. Taken in this way, Derrida's phrase can be heard as an ironic commentary on the cheek or audacity of an *agrégation* committee that would propose such a topic. Speaking no longer in the name of the *agrégation* program committee, that is, as its representative or its mouthpiece, but rather *to* it or *against* it, in his own name this time, though also, it would seem, in the name of his students with whom he is sympathizing, Derrida seems to be registering an ironic protest against the *agrégation* itself. He can be heard as saying something like: "Theory and practice. *Faut le faire*—Now that really takes some doing; can you believe the nerve or the audacity of these people, setting a topic for the exam that is so broad, so inclusive, so ill-defined, that one would really have to study the entire history of philosophy, from Plato's *Republic* and *Laws* to Aristotle's *Politics* and *Ethics* to the major works of Kant, Hegel, Marx, and Heidegger, and that's just the beginning, because the topic is not just theory and practice in, say, political philosophy—that would be bad enough—but theory and practice in philosophy in general, theory and practice in theory since Plato and Aristotle and theory and practice as it has been practiced since Plato and Aristotle. And, oh yes, to top it all off, we will have nine two-hour sessions to cover it all and prepare for the exam. *Faut le faire*."

But here is where the relationship between the program and contingency or chance, something, in short, that breaks with the program, enters the picture in a new way—a chance that Derrida was able to foresee and think from the very beginning in theory but one whose consequences in practice would remain forever impossible to predict. I am referring to the rather simple fact that, as Derrida often said, a letter or a message or, why not, a seminar *may not* always reach its destination, or—a consequence of the same law—it may someday reach another, unintended, radically unknown destination. For that seminar of 1976–77, originally addressed to a select audience of students, the *normaliens*, as they are called, a seminar originally programmed to reach only them, has been readdressed or repurposed, as any piece of writing might be, for a radically unknown audience some forty years in the future. We are thus now forced, because of this contingency, to think and read this seminar in a very different historical, philosophical, and pedagogical context, and to rethink and reread what we thought we knew about Derrida and his work in light of it. What has happened, in short, is that the "laws" of iterability that were at the center of Derrida's work from the beginning have caused this text to resist the program that had initially determined it, or seemed to determine it, opening up new possibilities for reading and thinking.

For example—and again, the point is at once banal and profound in its consequences—we cannot today read Derrida without taking into account the fact that, some sixteen years before his first and really only book on Marx, Derrida had *already* given a seminar that was devoted in large part to Marx, and to Marx on precisely the question of the relationship between theory and practice. Even if programmed, even if provoked or caused or determined by that *agrégation* program, this fact now escapes that program and, in truth, it will have always escaped it, of necessity, though that necessity has become so much more apparent in the intervening years. We thus need to reread or reinterpret what we think we know or have known about, say, Derrida and Marx or Derrida and Althusser before *Specters of Marx*, and what terms like "theory" and "practice," for example, mean in Derrida's work.[5]

Now one might recall that when Derrida published *Spectres de Marx* in French in 1993 many of his critics and detractors said, either privately or publicly, and almost always with a smile of indulgence or a smirk of condescension, that Derrida had come rather late to the party—and one can understand "party" however one wants here. Though he had been in Paris, an intellectual atmosphere permeated by Marxist ideology, since the early 1950s, though he was a student and then a friend and colleague at ENS of Althusser's, he had, these critics were suggesting, taken his own sweet time getting around to taking Marx seriously and, when he finally did, the party was over and the meeting hall was empty.[6] As for those more predisposed to Derrida and his work, they tended to look at the publication of *Specters of Marx* with a certain puzzled admiration, a first book on Marx *after* the fall of the Berlin wall and *after* the breakup of the Soviet Union, *after* the death of Althusser and *after* the vast majority of French intellectuals had either abandoned Marx or stopped writing about him. To begin concentrating on Marx and the political and socioeconomic questions that concerned him right at the moment Marx seemed most passé or irrelevant seemed like a rather daring and quixotic venture. A first book on Marx in 1993—*faut le faire*, they might have said: *that* takes some doing.

But, of course, neither side really needed to read beyond the title of that work in order to think that something else must be going on with this gesture. The "specters" of Marx that Derrida was referring to would no doubt include, it was reasonable to assume, not just that famous specter of communism that was haunting Europe in the middle of the nineteenth century, and not just the specters of capitalist speculation and exchange, but the specter or phantom or ghost of Marx himself, which would return, it could be thought, after Marx's death or after his disappearance, after his seeming irrelevance, therefore, and so at times we might least expect it.[7] It took only the title to think that Derrida might well have been playing with and against just these expectations so as to suggest that perhaps, just perhaps, it is when Marx seems most irrelevant and most dead that we need to consider the possibility of his spectral return.[8]

With the publication in 2017 of *Theory and Practice* in French and, in 2019, in English, the whole scenario I just described will have to be rethought yet again. For, as we see in this seminar of 1976–77, Derrida may not have been publishing on Marx or on Althusser (not to mention Croce or Gramsci), but he was obviously reading them, thinking about them, and teaching them.[9]

As a result of this seminar, therefore, one will have to think Derrida differently in the future, in relation now to Heidegger *and* Marx, Heidegger *and* Marx *and* Althusser. One would not want to exaggerate the interest Derrida takes here in these latter, for it is hardly unconditional—and it has been in part programmed, as I have suggested, by the *agrégation* program—but it is not simply perfunctory either, merely the result of an *il faut le faire*. What should be of interest to us, then, will be exactly what in Heidegger and Marx and Althusser interested Derrida and what did not, what about their theory, what about their practice, what about the relationship between theory and practice within them, and what about theory and practice in deconstruction and in Derrida's thinking, work, and pedagogy.

One perfectly good and necessary strategy will be to look for places of coincidence, intersection, or overlap, as well as sites of difference and deviation, among *Theory and Practice* and Derrida's already published works and his still unpublished seminars, whether before or after this seminar of 1976–77. While most will be rather minor, others will be more significant and, it could be argued, revelatory not just of a movement within Derrida's thinking and writing but, much more important, of the essential *historicity* of deconstruction and the unique theory and practice that that historicity calls for and inscribes. In other words, some of these shifts in theme or figure, in emphasis or vocabulary, will be revelatory of the very *non-contemporaneity* of writing—or of pedagogy—with itself, revelatory, therefore, of a very different way of thinking the relationship between theory and practice in general and in education in particular. Let me very quickly name six places of overlap or intersection, all of them having to do, in one way or another, with questions of theory and practice:

(1) The question of language and of the idiom, beginning with that opening phrase of the seminar: *faut le faire* (*TP* 1/13). Such a gesture can easily appear—and often does appear to many—essentially unrelated to theory or to what is actually being argued by Derrida in a text. It thus sometimes appears to be a rather gratuitous gesture, the rhetorical *flair* of this *faut le faire* being just one of Derrida's many flagrant transgressions of good pedagogical prose. But when Derrida says or announces later in the seminar that there is no metalanguage—one of the tenets, it could be argued, of deconstruction—then one can see how the question of the idiom, the question of the use of a particular language or idiom, the question of a *material* practice of language, will become absolutely crucial and unavoidable in a seminar on the relationship between theory and practice (see *TP* 29/48).[10]

The fact that the idiom in question at the outset, *faut le faire*, is a thing of language that is nonetheless also *doing* something, inevitably leads to the question of speech act theory, that is, to the question of *doing* things with language or with words (see *TP* 2/14, 6/19). As we will have also seen, the question of the speech act eventually leads to the question of the event, to the way in which speech acts produce events (*TP* 6/18–19). As we recalled in the first part of this work, the French translation of Austin's famous work on speech act theory was published just a few years before, in 1970, under the title *Quand dire, c'est faire*, and Derrida explicitly refers on at least two occasions to Austin's notion of the "performative" and the "speech act" in this 1976–77 seminar. In the first of these references, Derrida says that in their selective consideration of the relationship between theory and practice they must leave aside "the whole problematic—let's call it Anglo-Saxon—of the 'performative' and of *speech acts*" (this latter phrase in English in Derrida's original), that is, he goes on to say, the question of

> what a discourse of this or that types *does* (for example, the type that Austin has in mind when he uses the name "performative") when it consists in doing, when it is in itself an act, such as when I say—these are now routine examples—"I open this session," "I name you knight of the Legion of Honor," "I commit to doing this or that," utterances that don't describe anything, that provide nothing that can be stated or known but do something and constitute events. (*TP* 6/18–19)

Much later in the seminar, Derrida returns to Austin and speech act theory in order to speak of the way certain institutions—he is here talking about the psychoanalytic institution—attempt to create, inaugurate, or institute their own conventions or conventionality, relying upon a sort of "performative" that "doesn't conform to a context of existing conventions as does the performative according to Austin" (*TP* 120/168). This will become a constant preoccupation in Derrida's work: whenever Derrida turns to psychoanalysis, he will be interested not just in the questions, terms, claims, and procedures of psychoanalytic theory and practice but also in the *institution* of certain practices and the founding, establishment, and legitimation of psychoanalytic institutions. And he will then ask, of course, about the relationship between those processes or practices of establishing and legitimating, or self-legitimating, psychoanalytic institutions and the very theory and practice within those institutions that are being established and legitimated. This question of the instituting performatives of psychoanalysis, always in conjunction with a rethinking of psychoanalytic theory itself, will be central for Derrida right up through his 1995 work *Archive Fever* and his 2001 "Psychoanalysis Searches the States of its Soul."[11]

(2) These questions of language acts or speech acts lead to the question of act and action in general, act and action in theory and in practice, a theme that is central to one of the most recent seminars to appear, the second volume

of *The Death Penalty*, where Derrida asks who was crueler in the end, Robespierre or Kant, the one who acted during his pro–death penalty phase or the one who did not act but theorized so rigorously about the death penalty. The question of action in these two seminars would then take us to the question of responsibility, in short, the question *que faire?*, what must be done? (*TP* 3/16), a question that animates all of Derrida's seminars of the 1990s, on the secret, testimony, hospitality, perjury and pardon, the death penalty, and so on, seminars all taught under the general title "Questions of Responsibility," all the way up to the 2000 essay "Psychoanalysis Searches the States of Its Soul," where Derrida returns yet again to this question of Lenin's.[12]

(3) This then leads to the question of *historicity*, a question that is central to almost all of Derrida's early texts. Derrida recalls in *Theory and Practice*, just as he did in the Heidegger seminar of 1964–65, the importance of *historicity* for Marxist philosophy, and in particular for Althusser's "discourse and practice," which, in 1976, was still *en cours*, in process, not simply because Althusser was still alive and writing but because, says Derrida, a philosophy is in process or in progress "almost by definition when it comes to a Marxist philosophical practice" (*TP* 53/81). This emphasis on historicity is often animated by Derrida's interest in and admiration for Heidegger on this subject, something we see very clearly in that 1964–65 seminar. Though Derrida in *Theory and Practice* refers to Heidegger's claim that "the Marxist concept of history is unique in modern times as it allows one to recognize the essentiality of historicity in being itself" (*TP* 60/90), Derrida himself claims in his seminar on Heidegger that it was really Heidegger, not Marx, who understood most radically the relationship between being and history.

(4) These questions of history, of production, and of work in Marx lead to the more general question of the relationship between the human and the animal on the basis of practice or technology or work, all of which, in the philosophical tradition that runs from Plato and Aristotle to Heidegger, would be the privilege of the human alone (*TP* 59/88–89). Derrida recalls in *Theory and Practice*, for example, how Aristotle relates *technē* to *logos*, and *logos* to the human, thereby effectively restricting *technē* to man (*TP* 115/160). As a result, only man or the human has praxis (*TP* 80/116), and only man *works* (*TP* 84/122), an essentially "anthropological" determination of practice and of work, as Derrida labels it here (*TP* 82/118). This is a theme that can obviously be found in many Derrida texts, from *Of Spirit* to *The Animal That Therefore I Am* to the second year of *The Beast and the Sovereign*. But it is developed in a particularly interesting way here in *Theory and Practice*, a decade before the first of these other texts, and it is even initiated the year

before in *Life Death* when Derrida comments on Marx's theory of labor as an exclusively *human* form of labor (see *LD* 100–104/137–143).

(5) As always, a special place has to be reserved for Heidegger in Derrida's work. Indeed it is always interesting to see how Derrida treats or evaluates Heidegger in a particular text or seminar by comparing the tone, intensity, and frequency of his praise and/or criticism with that found in previous and future readings. Hence there are already—or yet again—recognizable places of difference or contestation in *Theory and Practice*. In addition to what we just saw regarding an anthropocentric bias in Heidegger, Derrida questions, first, the value Heidegger places on *Versammlung* as gathering and the related question of the unity and continuity of philosophy and the philosophical tradition (*TP* 78/122), a theme that is already in evidence in the Heidegger seminar of 1964–65 and that will return regularly in Derrida's work right up to *Of Spirit* and *The Beast and the Sovereign*. It is in part on the basis of this theme that Derrida will then also question in Heidegger the traditional philosophical privileging of speech over writing, that is, speech as what is more closely linked to the task of *thinking*.[13] This then leads, of course, to the question of all those things that Heidegger ignores or *avoids*. *Of Spirit* begins, one will recall, "What does it mean to avoid?" Derrida suggests throughout *Theory and Practice* that Heidegger avoids everything from a certain notion of alterity in Aristotle to the practice of psychoanalysis (while Heidegger speaks of psychiatry, Derrida recalls, he remains silent about psychoanalysis) to a consideration of sexual practice, not just one practice or praxis among others in the life of your everyday Dasein.[14]

But then there are, in addition to these questions or reservations, all those things that Derrida seems to find sympathetic in Heidegger—questions, gestures, ways of reading, beginning with Heidegger's practice of questioning itself, his way of turning what would seem to be a "solution" or a "response" into "a set of questions" (*TP* 91/131), though also Heidegger's eye or ear for modalities of language that precede the question, an originary engagement or responsibility before the question, a theme that is central to *Of Spirit* and other texts (*TP* 102/145, 107/151). Then there is Heidegger's emphasis on a sort of originary violence—unavoidable and irremediable—which Derrida, already in *Theory and Practice*, tracks through Heidegger's use of the verb *walten*, one of the major motifs of Derrida's final seminar *The Beast and the Sovereign* (see *TP* 90/131, 111/156).

But what are perhaps most striking are Derrida's descriptions of Heidegger's attempts to go back *before* or *behind* inherited conceptual oppositions. Derrida writes, for example: "What happens in *physis* (upsurge, growth, power, production, etc,) is also *thesis*. Heidegger takes us back to the eve of the opposition that, as he sees it, arrives late, supervenes, that between *physis* and *thesis*, an opposition that dominates the whole of philosophy to come, from Plato on" (*TP* 91/132). It is a gesture that Derrida finds so significant in Heidegger that he, Derrida, will himself repeat it, more or less in his own name, in various forms throughout his work, for example, in *Rogues* (2003), where he speaks, in a context where Heidegger is in the background but is not the object of his commentary, of the self's return to itself "before any distinction between *physis* and *technē*, *physis* and *nomos*, *physis* and *thesis*, and so on," or, later, of "the self's return to itself . . . before the separation of *physis* from its others, such as *technē*, *nomos*, and *thesis*" (*R* 10/29, 109/154). Or immediately thereafter in *Rogues*, in a line that seems to echo not only *Theory and Practice* from 1976–77 but *Life Death* from the year before: "What applies here to *physis*, to *phuein*, applies also to life, understood before any opposition between life (*bios* or *zōē*) and its others (spirit, culture, the symbolic, the specter, or death)" (*R* 109/154–155).[15]

(6) Finally, there is Marx, Marx after Heidegger or Marx with Heidegger, since Derrida's reading of Heidegger in the later sessions of the seminar seems to come out of his earlier reading of Marx, a serious reading of Marx that precedes by many years, as I said, *Specters of Marx*. Of course, it might always be argued that this is, in the end, just another *reading* of Marx, that is, just another reading in another seminar, and, as a result, just another *betrayal* of the *true* Marx, a betrayal, it would be thought, of everything that is most promising and most radical in Marx. For insofar as the main focus of *Theory and Practice* seems to be the *philosophical* implications and status of Marxism *as* philosophy and the notion of theory *in* philosophy, Derrida's critics and detractors can always argue that this seminar demonstrates even more clearly that Derrida, "always the philosopher," was really only interested, to echo the famous line from the "Theses on Feuerbach," in interpreting the world rather than trying to change it. In short, Derrida's interest in Marx and Althusser was simply academic, merely theoretical and not at all practical.

But one does not need to read very far into *Theory and Practice* to see that Derrida is concerned in this seminar with nothing other than just this *relationship* between theory and practice, the *relationship* between philosophy and a philosophical and/or political practice, with all the questions and difficulties that this relationship raises. That is why Derrida places at the very center of this seminar *Theory and Practice* that very same line from "Theses on Feuerbach," namely, "Philosophers have only *interpreted* the world, in various ways; what is important is to transform it" (*TP* 8/21)[16]—a line that, curiously, and this too could have never been predicted, has returned of late to our political discourses and our college campuses and perhaps calls for just the rereading and rethinking that Derrida suggests in 1976–77. It is, to be sure, an accident, but it is an interesting if not a happy accident, for if this seminar bears the traces of its historical epoch, the mid-1970s in France, it also echoes, and somewhat uncannily, what is happening today in the United States in what is being called the *new activism* on college campuses and beyond, an activism that had its contemporary roots in the Occupy movement but has branched out to Black Lives Matter, environmental activism, the Sanders campaigns of 2016 and 2020, and debates about "socialism" in anticipation of the 2020 presidential election. And it is an activism that seems particularly acute and developed, as I can attest, in departments of philosophy. Though Marx is obviously not always being cited, and obviously not his eleventh thesis on Feuerbach (though I *have* heard it on occasion!), there are many things about, say, curricula and the place of philosophy in today's American university that seem to have been spoken in its spirit, as if the spirit of Marx or a certain specter of Marx had returned yet again. A "certain specter" of Marx, I say, because Derrida in *Theory and Practice* will read that thesis on Feuerbach in a way that complicates its most common interpretation and use. To avoid the accusation of misappropriating and misinterpreting this thesis from a non-Marxist theoretical perspective, Derrida uses none other than Althusser to show that this thesis does not advance an anti-philosophical claim, a claim to the end of philosophy in action or in practice, but a claim about a certain way of *doing* philosophy.

Derrida's seminar of 1976–77 can thus seem oddly contemporary in places, or at least able to address the contemporary, and it can, perhaps, be read as a warning to all those who think they know what theory is and that it is, in short, a bad or ineffective thing, and that what we must do is to go beyond philosophy and theory in order to change the world through political action and practice. And so here we are, almost 175 years after the theses on Feuerbach were first written, more than twenty-five years after *Specters of Marx*, faced with the question of what to do, what we must do, *que faire*, in general, but also what philosophy can do—with regard, say, to the economy or the environment—and what falls into our laps or leaps into our hands is this strange and unexpected artifact from the archive, the typescript of a seminar from 1976–77, this strange pedagogical object called *Theory and Practice*.

Finally, then, one will have to read this seminar and ask how Derrida or deconstruction approaches these questions of language, of the speech act, of action, of historicity, of the difference between the human and the animal in Marx, Heidegger, and others, in order to rethink the question of theory and practice in philosophy, but then also the question of whether deconstruction itself is theory and/or practice, whether it is itself still philosophy or something that goes beyond philosophy, falls short of philosophy, or signals the end of philosophy in its own way. Obviously, there will be no simple or single answer to these questions, but it is hard not to think that when Derrida asks in this seminar about how a Marxist discourse treats the theory/practice distinction and about whether Marxism is a philosophy properly speaking, or when he poses similar questions to or about Heidegger, he is not also implicitly posing these questions to himself and to deconstruction. In other words, it is hard not to want to ask how Derrida's questions with regard to Marx and Heidegger, in relation to both theory and practice, reflect upon Derrida's own "theory" and "practice," a theory and practice that would at once use, mention, and call into question the pertinence of all these terms and distinctions (see TP 4/16–17, 6/18, 47/71).

According to Derrida in *Theory and Practice*, who seems to be on the whole in agreement with Althusser and Gramsci (as opposed to Croce), Marx is calling for a theoretical practice that would still be philosophy (*TP* 13–14/29).[17] He is thus not calling for the "end of philosophy," even though there are many Marxists who have ceded to this temptation to see such an end of philosophy in practice or in action. As Derrida concludes at one point in reference to Althusser, with whom he seems to have a certain affinity here: "Contrary to those who might have thought that the primacy of practice is what distinguishes Marxist philosophy from every other philosophy," Althusser "finds the very *distinction* of Marxism in the theoretical" (*TP* 51/77–78). When Derrida thus reads Althusser arguing against those who celebrate the end of philosophy in action and arguing against a certain naive pragmatism (though not at all against *theoretical practice*), one has to wonder whether Derrida does not share this view to some extent (*TP* 40–41/63). If so, it might help explain Derrida's hesitation with regard to a certain militant or dogmatic Marxism (the kind that touts a sort of messianicity *with* messianism) or his refusal to join the Communist Party in France, or his near total lack of interest in *merely* pragmatic or utilitarian arguments within his own discourse.[18] So, on the one hand, it would be hard to argue that Derrida thought deconstruction not to be philosophy and that he did not consider himself, perhaps above all, a philosopher. Derrida is interested, for example, in the fact that philosophy is able to institute itself, interested, as he says speaking of Althusser, in "the gesture of philosophy speaking of itself and positing itself as philosophy" (*TP* 50/76), interested in the way philosophy takes itself as its own object (*TP* 51/77), interested, even, in the philosophical tradition's privileging of theory over practice (see *TP* 4/16–17, 47/71).

And yet, throughout the seminar, we also see Derrida's hesitation or criticism with regard to many of these same gestures. He is, for example, critical of the way theory is privileged in philosophy, critical, it seems, of the tendency to unify reason, to unify, for example, theoretical and practical reason, a tendency he finds in various forms in Aristotle, Kant, Marx, and Husserl. Derrida will thus go on to question these philosophical gestures by, as he says, "deconstructing the oppositional (that is to say, philosophical) logic in the case of 'theory and practice'" (*TP* 4/16–17), or by trying to show how the practice of language in philosophy and of a certain action in philosophy complicates this distinction. He does this by evoking throughout an otherness or an alterity that seems to resist or to contest the supposed unity of reason, an otherness that may go by the name of the unconscious or *différance* or *physis* (*TP* 109–110/154), an alterity that seems to resist, I think we could say, any program (including that of the *agrégation*). He does this throughout the seminar by questioning the unity of the philosophical tradition itself and, by implication, the unity, self-identity, self-presence, contemporaneity, of the texts and figures considered to be *within* it.

What Derrida thus says about Althusser in 1976–77 sounds very much like what he, Derrida, will undertake some twenty years later in *Specters of Marx*, namely, "not to think the end or death of philosophy otherwise, but to reconfigure Marxist philosophy *itself*, and not even to re-configure it, but to configure it, for it is still to come" (*TP* 44/68). This promissory note is fulfilled, at least in part, in *Specters of Marx*. It is fulfilled in a contingent and accidental way, for it could always have *not* happened, it could have always been otherwise. But it is also fulfilled because of the structural law that dictates that no text is ever self-identical or contemporaneous with itself, that every text can return from time to time—like a specter. Every text can return like a specter because no text has ever fully arrived. That is true of the texts of Marx and, of course, it is true of Derrida's, for example, the text or the *seminar* titled *Theory and Practice*, a seminar of 1976–77 that has reemerged from the archives in 2017, and in English in 2019, in order to put into question everything we thought we knew about Derrida and Marx, theory and practice. Hence Derrida's theoretical point regarding the nature of the text is being put to the test yet again by a certain reading practice. For any text, even one programmed by the institution of the *agrégation*, is never one with itself and is never exhausted in its destination. This would be the last point of contact, the last point of aggregation or disaggregation, between, say, Derrida's *Theory and Practice* and his other works: the essential and irreducible *noncontemporaneity* or noncoincidence of a text or of a seminar, of a *pedagogical practice*, with itself.

As Derrida said in English—in Shakespeare's English—at the beginning of the French version of his very first book on Marx in 1993, "the time is out of joint." As teacher or pedagogue, Derrida also knew that a seminar—a pedagogical practice—is always out of joint. It is never completely clear when it begins, and it is certainly never clear when it ends—in either theory or practice. This may simply sound like a plea for Derrida's continuing *relevance* to contemporary thought, the continuing relevance of Derrida's published work as well as of his teaching, his seminars. But it is first and foremost an argument for the structural *revenance* that Derrida will have theorized and practiced and undergone and *taught* from the very beginning under the name or in the guise—*faut le faire*—of deconstruction, or else, in order to recall that a *seminar* may not always reach its destination, *dissemination*.

That the seminar *Theory and Practice* of 1976–77 is now able to speak to us and our sociopolitical situation after Derrida's death and so without his calculations in a way that *Specters of Marx* was able to address the political situation of 1993 *with* his guidance and his calculations, well, that takes some doing, *faut le faire*. Unless it takes no *doing* at all, since it would be a doing that obviously comes from beyond consciousness or conscious intention or even action, indeed beyond anything that can even be called *life*. One could always simply chalk it up to coincidence, because it is also a coincidence, but the essential noncoincidence or noncontemporaneity of writing or of pedagogy with itself is precisely Derrida's theoretical point in works such as "Plato's Pharmacy" and *Of Grammatology* right up to *Specters of Marx* and beyond. In other words, "the time is out of joint" essentially or by definition and not occasionally or accidentally. While there was no reason to expect or to predict that this seminar of 1976–77 would speak to us as it does "today," there is nothing beyond the destruction of the archives that would ensure that it would not, in other words, that it would not make its spectral return. The fact that a seminar *may not* reach its destination is thus not just the inevitable, and often regrettable, fate of all teaching. It is also its necessary and irreducible chance—a bit like that notebook that always risked never making it back to the front of the class, that risked being forever lost and completely forgotten, or else simply led astray and taken elsewhere so as to circulate in other classrooms and inform other pedagogies.

Class 3: Grace and the Machine

Perjury and Pardon *(1997–98)*

In this final chapter or class session of what I have imagined to be an "Open Seminar," an open seminar on the ongoing series of Derrida's seminars being published with Éditions du Seuil, I would like to focus on the latest seminar to appear, *Le parjure et le pardon*, *Perjury and Pardon*, Derrida's seminar of 1997–98, the first year in a two-year seminar devoted to these topics.[1] I turn to this seminar for reasons of timeliness, of actuality, but also, and especially, because it just so happens that this seminar, while treating, of course, the themes of perjury and of pardon, of foreswearing and forgiving, becomes itself a seminar about the speech act, about the accident or the accidental, about the accident in relationship not just to the unforgiveable but also to the unforeseeable, to what might be called a moment of unexpected grace in relation to the highly foreseeable and dangerously predictable machine. As we will see, this seminar will bring us back, as if by accident, to the heart of many of the questions that have been central to this work from the very beginning, that is, from the very first act of "Derrida in Montreal," questions of act and accident, of possibility and impossibility, of success and failure, all in relation to the speech act.

Let us begin, then, with the French title of this seminar of 1997–98, *Le parjure et le pardon*, which is notable for the way it pairs two words that appear to be on rather different linguistic levels. One, *pardon*, is very common in French—even if it is not, as the seminar will make clear, very well understood—while the other, *parjure*, is not only not well understood but is also not very common in everyday French. Indeed, a relatively educated

French person could pass his or her entire life never hearing, let alone using, the word *parjure*. Derrida explains in the first session of the first year of what will turn out to be a two-year exploration of the topic:

> I am using this example of precomprehension in the everyday usage of the word *pardon* (forgiveness) (an everyday and ordinary usage, which is not the case for *parjure*, which is already learned; if you do a statistical survey, in France or in a francophone country, you know in advance that the number of people who think they understand the word *pardon* is much greater than those who understand, let alone use, the word *parjure*—and this difference indexes a very serious problem). (*PP 1* 108)

Given this peculiarity, this dissymmetry, this *problem*, as Derrida calls it, we should probably ask why Derrida would have chosen this uncommon word, *parjure*, and not, say, *le mensonge*, that is, lie or lying, or *le faux témoignage*, false testimony, or *le faux serment*, the false oath, or simply *la faute* to set in relation to *pardon*. In other words, why would Derrida insist on *this* word? What resources does he find in it that would outweigh the obvious disadvantages of using a word that uncommon? As I would like to argue here, what initially appears to be a fairly specific, restricted, and rather uncommon term having to do with not telling the truth in a court of law, that is, *parjure* understood as *perjury*, will end up having much broader implications not only for Derrida's argument in the seminar but also for his understanding, in many other texts, for example in "Faith and Knowledge," of oaths and promises and faith more generally, and so for Derrida's rethinking of speech act theory beginning in the early 1970s and continuing right up through the 1990s.

That the speech act would become central to this seminar of 1997–98 should come as little surprise insofar as the question of forgiveness immediately raises the question of whether or in what way forgiveness must be granted in speech, not simply thought or spoken in one's heart but also expressed in some way to the aggrieved party. But something else will also be at work in this extraordinary seminar. As Derrida himself notes, the seminar *Perjury and Pardon* will turn out to be not just another Derrida work on the speech act, on speech act theory, but a work that is itself a speech act, a performative in its own right, from the oral presentation of the seminar to the enduring trace of it in writing, which today remains, as we will see at the end of our analysis, a kind of machine or testament to be read, an oeuvre open to rereading, interpretation, and, of course, to translation. As Derrida himself writes: "Such a seminar is not a constative but a performative—in the most obscurely abyssal sense of this word *performative*—experience of *parjure* to forgive or to be forgiven" (*PP 1* 118). In the end, we will see that *parjure* can and must be thought in relation to the speech act and, in the end, to the work of deconstruction itself.

So, to begin, the noun *le parjure*, like the English *perjury*, refers, in a first moment, to the lying of a witness, the giving of false testimony, a breach in one's oath or promise to tell the truth, the whole truth, and nothing but the truth in a court of law. This notion of a *breach* of oath or promise in an essentially legal context leads to the notion of a betrayal or transgression more generally, the violation of *any* oath or the breaking of *any* promise, whether explicit, as in a sworn testimony, or merely implicit. There is thus a narrower and a wider sense of *parjure*. Speaking in the eighth session of the first year of the seminar on Rousseau's famous theft of a ribbon and his lying about that theft, Derrida contrasts, on the one hand, the theft itself, "which is already—like every failure of presumed duty and of the implicit promise or implicit commitment that relates to it—*parjure* in the broad sense," and, on the other, "the lie of a witness," that is, "*perjury* [*parjure*] in the strict, narrow sense" (*PP 1* 321). Hence, Derrida uses the term *parjure* to speak not only of an explicit breach of oath, of *perjury*, in the narrow sense, but of a more general breaking or breaching of pretty much any oath, duty, promise, or commitment, whether explicit or implicit, in a court of law or not. This is confirmed by something Derrida says earlier in the seminar when he contrasts "a layer of implicitness, a foreswearing, a *parjure*, and a *foi jurée*, a sworn faith, *implicit* in every misdeed, in every wrong," with "the explicit and determinate figures of what appears explicitly as *parjure* and is expressly called such" (*PP 1* 117). This first reference to *la foi jurée*, that is, to an implicit *foi jurée*, an implied "sworn faith," will prove to be critical, as we will see, to Derrida's use of the word *parjure*. The word *parjure* thus means at once perjury, in the narrow sense, and perfidy, to use an equally uncommon English word, that is, lying, betrayal, infidelity, in its widest, most general sense. That is what allows Derrida to say that "every misdeed, every wrong to be forgiven, is at heart a *parjure*" (*PP 1* 116).

Still taken as a noun, *parjure* can also name not just the *thing* someone does or commits, the breach or transgression, the act, but also the *person* who does or commits the act, the actor. The novel by Henri Thomas, *Le parjure*, which Derrida comments on at length in the eighth and final session of the second year of the seminar, seems to play on the ambiguity in this word, oscillating between thing and person, act and actor.[2] Derrida uses this latter sense of *parjure* when he personifies the various traditions or heritages he is deconstructing in order to say that they are, in a sense, deconstructing themselves, and that what he, Derrida, is trying to do is "bring to light at the same time the undecidability, the contradiction, the *double bind* that works over each and all of these heritages, to oppose them as it were to themselves in the name of themselves, to show them to be as it were at fault, faulty on the inside of themselves, perjurers of themselves [*parjures d'eux-mêmes*], a *parjure* into which they draw us with them from birth" (*PP 1* 118). Here we see Derrida not only using *parjure* as a noun that would identify persons or actors rather than acts or actions but also suggesting that deconstruction is itself in some sense coextensive with this internal *parjure*, with the way in which a tradition or a heritage is always a *parjure* to or of itself, that is, always in internal contradiction with itself, undecidable in its supposedly stable concepts, oppositions, and so on. *Parjure* would thus name the way in which traditions or discourses betray or deconstruct themselves not just eventually, in the long term or long run, at some point in time, as if by accident, but, as Derrida says, *from birth*, that is, from the origin, as we will see in a moment. Hence, Derrida seems to have considered deconstruction itself to be the act or activity of a *parjure*, the process that a tradition or a text undergoes, breaching itself, being unfaithful to itself from the beginning out of a kind of fidelity. A *parjure* is thus a traitor or betrayer from the beginning, that is, to introduce the verbal form, someone defined by his or her activity of *parjurer*, someone who *parjure*s from birth or from the origin, which is why Derrida will later say in the first session of the seminar: "I always betray one for the other, I perjure myself like I breathe" (*PP 1* 74), a play on the well-known French expression "*il ment comme il respire*," that is, "he lies as easily as he breathes." (We could cite here any number of places in Derrida's corpus where he says something to the effect that he is faithful by being unfaithful to a discourse or a tradition, unfaithful out of an extreme fidelity.)

Finally, as an adjective, *parjure* is used to characterize or depict someone who has violated his or her oath or committed some other kind of betrayal or breach of faith or trust, some act of perfidy. It is in this sense that we can talk about *un homme parjure* or *une femme parjure* or, indeed, of *la ville parjure*, the title of Hélène Cixous's play about the contaminated blood scandal in France, first performed at the Théâtre du Soleil in May 1994, three years before Derrida's seminar was given in Paris.[3]

So, *parjure* as noun, verb, or adjective suggests some kind of breach of trust or faith, some breach of sworn faith, some infraction of *la foi jurée*, of sworn faith, one that can extend beyond an individual act to characterize the individual himself, someone who would thus be not just a *perjurer*, characterized by what could be a single act of perjury, but a *traitor* or a *betrayer* or an *infidel* more generally, someone who breaks their *foi jurée* as easily as they breathe.

Now, it is this reference to *la foi jurée*, as I suggested a moment ago, that is no doubt the primary reason Derrida chose *parjure* over, for example, *le faux serment, le faux témoignange*, or *la faute*. For one hears in *parjure* the *foi jurée* that, for Derrida, is to be found not simply in the law court when we swear to tell the truth and so swear not to perjure ourselves in the restricted sense of the term but in the sworn faith at the origin of every oath, promise, or speech act. As Derrida says in the first session of the *Perjury and Pardon* seminar, in what was published separately as an essay under the title "To Forgive": "every fault, every wrong, is first a perjury [*un parjure*], namely the breach of some promise (implicit or explicit), the breach of some engagement, of some responsibility before a law one has sworn to respect, that one is supposed to have sworn to respect" (*PP 1* 73). In other words, every transgression for which forgiveness might be asked is a sort of *parjure* insofar as one is breaking or breaching that explicit or implicit promise to keep one's word, to abide by one's oath to follow the law or the norm or the custom or simply one's promise to do what one said one would. And so, Derrida can say, "forgiveness always concerns a perjury [*le pardon concerne toujours un parjure*]" (*PP 1* 73); that is, to parse it further, pardon always concerns some perfidy, forgiveness some foreswearing, some breach of trust or oath, a foreswearing that would require some forgiveness or some asking for forgiveness. Derrida thus seems to have settled on pairing *pardon* with *parjure* not just because both begin with *par*, because, to paraphrase Ponge, "*Par* le mot *par* commencent ces deux mots," but because the word *parjure* evokes at once the act of faith, implicit or explicit, *and* the breach of that act, that is, both the *foi jurée* of every speech act and, through the addition of *par* to *jure*, the breaking or breaching of that speech act.⁴

There is thus the *foi jurée*, the sworn faith, the oath or the commitment to do something or to obey some law, norm, or custom, and then there is the *parjure*, the breaking or breaching of that sworn faith. But then what is the *relationship* between these two aspects or these two moments?⁵ Is the latter simply a possibility that *might* befall the former, or is it in fact something like a structural possibility or structural condition of the former? In order to answer this question we will need to venture beyond a merely linguistic analysis.

In many of Derrida's works, though especially, as we saw in the first part of this work, those on speech acts, from "Signature Event Context" through "Limited Inc" and beyond, Derrida suggests that we need to rethink the very nature of possibility such that the positive or successful possibility of something, of a speech act, for example, always includes—or at least *cannot exclude* and so therefore includes in some way—its negative possibility. That is why Derrida suggests near the end of the first session of the *Pardon and Perjury* seminar:

> Perjury [or perfidy] is not an accident [*le parjure n'est pas un accident*]; it is not an event that happens or does not happen to a promise or to a prior oath. Perjury [or perfidy] is inscribed in advance, as its destiny, its fatality, its inexpiable destination, in the structure of the promise and the oath, in the word of honor, in justice, in the desire for justice. As if the oath were already a perjury (something of which the Greeks, as we will see, had more than a premonition). (*PP I* 73)

How are we to understand this? Well, the rest of the seminar will attempt to develop this relationship between sworn oaths or sworn faith and the perjury or the *parjure* that appears to be part of its structure, the perjury or the *parjure* that cannot simply be an accident that supervenes upon the sworn faith, a *parjure* that is inscribed in the very "structure" of the promise and that is actually related, says Derrida, to the "desire for justice," an ambitious claim that would require more than a single seminar to justify. Interestingly, Derrida says something very similar about perjury or *parjure* in another text from around this same time, that is, in April 1997, in those improvised comments given at a conference at the Centre Canadien d'Architecture in Montreal, comments that were at the center of Act 3 of the first part of this work. Derrida there says:

> justice itself must be affected or haunted by its opposite, by perjury [*parjure*], for it to be justice. . . . There is no simple opposition between perjury and justice, a solemn vow, commitment, or an oath. Perjury has to be at the heart of the oath for the oath to be truly possible. It must be at the heart of justice in an irremovable way, not as a passing attribute or an accident that can be erased. The possibility of evil, or of perjury, must be intrinsic to good or to justice for either to be possible. And so the impossible must be at the heart of possible. ("CIP" 242/110)[6]

The word *parjure* thus appears to be no accident in Derrida's discourse, and it is itself fundamentally related to the very notion of an accident, not to mention possibility. But to understand that claim we need to ask along with Derrida what an accident *is* exactly, giving precedence here, for reasons of coherence, to Derrida's works on the speech act. So, what is an accident? What is an accident in the tradition and what is an accident for Derrida? And what is the relationship between essence and accident? What is, we might ask, the essence of an accident?

Derrida appears to be working with and condensing at least three different senses of accident, all of which are rather common in philosophy or everyday discourse. First, the accident is something that is secondary, opposed to the essential or the primary. While extension, for example, might be considered an essential property of all finite bodies, the color of any particular finite body could be considered a secondary or accidental property. The second sense, not unrelated to the first, opposes the accidental not to the essential or to the primary but to the necessary. In this sense, things that happen by accident are things that happen by chance, without planning or intention, as opposed to what happens by necessity or by design. And this leads, of course, to the notion of accident as an unexpected harm or injury that arrives unforeseeably or unexpectedly to a presumably intact thing—a person, a car, a state of affairs.

It could be said, then, that, as generally or traditionally understood, an essence is, in its essence, indifferent or impervious to the accident in all three of these senses. An essence can have or receive accidental or supplemental qualities, but it is in no way determined by those qualities. In other words, those qualities, like supplements, do not broach or breach the essence itself. If the essence is thus necessary and the accident or the accidental is not, then that is because the accident always comes *after* the essence, after and from the *outside*. According to this presumption or this prejudice, then, the essence, like an origin, always comes first, before, and in essence it always excludes everything that might come from the outside, like an accident, to compromise, contaminate, or corrupt it. The essence thus remains necessarily opposed to the accident, protected, or seemingly protected, indemnified, safe and sound, to use the vocabulary of "Faith and Knowledge," from all accident.

This is the traditional nature of essence that Derrida will try to question, to deconstruct, as it were, by showing that this philosophical conception of essence and accident is itself, perhaps, an accident and not at all essential or necessary, since there are perhaps other ways of thinking the relationship between essence and accident, other possible relationships between essence and accident that do not presuppose the simple *opposition* between inside and outside, before and after, actuality and possibility, and so on.[7] In other words, on Derrida's reading, there is nothing absolutely essential about this relationship between accident and essence, and the metaphysical understanding of essence and accident may well be itself an accident.

This questioning or deconstruction of accident and essence can be found more or less everywhere in Derrida, but it is especially prominent in works on or related to speech act theory. All the way back in 1971 in "Signature

Event Context," the reader will recall, we find Derrida arguing in the context of a reading of Condillac that "all philosophy . . . presupposes the simplicity of the origin and the continuity of every derivation, every production, every analysis, the homogeneity of all orders"—in other words, the simplicity of an origin that would come *before* and that would initially *exclude* or at least consign to the outside anything that might supervene upon it in order to compromise or contaminate it, for example, looking forward toward our seminar, a *parjure* that would come to breach or broach from the outside a supposedly original and pure *foi jurée* ("SEC" 311/370). In "Limited Inc," which, as we also saw in Part I of this work, follows up this theory of the speech act from "Signature Event Context," Derrida develops this notion of origin even further, arguing that "metaphysics in its most traditional form" is, and I quote at length one of the most succinct and powerful portrayals of the metaphysical tradition anywhere in Derrida,

> the enterprise of returning "strategically," ideally, to an origin or to a "priority" held to be simple, intact, normal, pure, standard, self-identical, in order *then* to think in terms of derivation, complication, deterioration, accident, etc. All metaphysicians, from Plato to Rousseau, Descartes to Husserl, have proceeded in this way, conceiving good to be before evil, the positive before the negative, the pure before the impure, the simple before the complex, the essential before the accidental, the imitated before the imitation, etc. And this is not just *one* metaphysical gesture among others, it is *the* metaphysical exigency, that which has been the most constant, most profound and most potent. ("LI" 93/173–174)

This is, recall, the place where Derrida's debate with J. L. Austin, as well as John Searle, begins. While Derrida will credit Austin with recognizing that speech acts are always open, in their structure, to going wrong, to failing, to what Austin calls *infelicities*, he will go on to argue that Austin does not see the radicality of his own insight, relying on these same traditional notions of origin and accident to couch this otherwise so original thought. So while Austin had the merit of understanding infelicity to be a "structural possibility" of every speech act, he also, writes Derrida, "with an almost *immediately simultaneous* gesture made in the name of a kind of ideal regulation"—the kind of regulation made by metaphysics in its most traditional form—posits "an exclusion of this risk as an accidental, exterior one that teaches us nothing about the language phenomenon under consideration" ("SEC" 323/385). This is a crucial moment in Derrida's reading of Austin and, as a result, a crucial moment for understanding Derrida and his rethinking of possibility. The suggestion here is that the negative of a phenomenon is always a "structural possibility" or an "essential risk" that can never simply be excluded from the positive version or possibility of that phenomenon. Indeed, the possibility of the negative or of the unsuccessful *conditions*, contrary to the traditional view, even the positive or the successful phenomenon and so is essential, in Derrida's view, to understanding that positive or successful phenomenon. As Derrida argues, "What is at stake here is an analysis that can account for *structural possibilities*" ("LI" 57/112). And "inasmuch as it is essential and structural," he will argue, "this possibility is always at work marking *all the facts*, all the events, even those which appear to disguise it" ("LI" 48/97). In the end, everything, every fact, as we saw in the "play" of Part I, is "marked in advance by the possibility of fiction" ("LI" 100/185), such that "everything is possible except for an exhaustive typology that would claim to limit the powers of graft or of fiction by and within an analytical logic of distinction" ("LI" 100/185). It is, as we also saw earlier, the power of repetition or iterability that makes all this possible.

To put this in terms developed by Derrida in "Signature Event Context" with regard to speech and writing, speech being the positive phenomenon and writing the negative one, it is writing, a notion of general writing, with its difference, deferral, lack of presence, and so on that *conditions* or that *structures* all speech, including so-called live, present speech, which then becomes a sort of species of that general writing rather than a prior origin that is subsequently compromised by writing. Similarly, then, on Derrida's account, the successful performative becomes a species, as it were, of a generalized failure or infelicity—of a generalized *parjure*, we might be tempted to say, as if *parjure* were Derrida's later, radicalized reinscription of Austin's notion of "infelicity." Indeed, it is if the *parjure*, the negative phenomenon, were just as primary, just as originary, as *la foi jurée*, that is, the positive phenomenon, the breach of faith actually making possible anything like a successful *foi jurée* or sworn faith. Again, the negative is not the opposite of the positive, an opposite that can be excluded from it, a possibility that would simply befall it, like an accident, but an "ever-present" possibility that structures or conditions the positive. That also explains why, elsewhere in Derrida, the positive notion of *pharmakon* can never exclude the negative, why perfectibility can never exclude, as its ever-present possibility, pervertibility, and so on. Hence the successful speech act depends upon a possible failure, the standard act upon a possible simulation or parasitism. As Derrida writes, "This *possibility* is part of the so-called 'standard case.' It is an essential, internal, and permanent part" ("LI" 89/167).

So while Austin recognizes the possibility of failure, of the speech act being *open* to failure, open to the contingency of failure, open to accident, he does not see failure as "an essential predicate or *law*" ("SEC" 324/385). As a result, he does not ask himself, "what is a success when the possibility of failure continues to constitute its structure?" ("SEC" 324/385) In other words, as we saw in "Derrida in Montreal," he "does not ask himself what consequences derive from the fact that something possible—a possible risk—is *always* possible, is somehow a necessary possibility" ("SEC" 324/385). This is, as we said, the core of Derrida's critique of Austin, and it will be in the background of all of Derrida's works on speech acts, including the seminar *Le parjure et le pardon*. As Derrida writes in "Limited Inc":

> A corruption that is "always possible" cannot be a mere extrinsic accident supervening on a structure that is original and pure, one that can be purged of what thus happens to it. The purportedly "ideal" structure must necessarily be such that this corruption will be "always possible." This *possibility* constitutes part of the *necessary* traits of the purportedly ideal structure. ("LI" 77/146)

What Derrida says here about infelicity and the speech act has consequences not just for Derrida's reading of Austin, and particularly Austin's notion of context, but also for the way the linguistic sign in general is to be understood. For if a sign does not consist in some stable, indivisible, *original* meaning that *then* gets repeated accidentally or incidentally, that is, if the sign has meaning only because of its *irreducible* iterability, its irreducible openness to variation, to reinscription, to citation and parasitism, open, therefore, to other contexts, to the other in general, then the sign is from the beginning open to its outside, and so to difference, absence, and, therefore, to the accident.

This emphasis on the accident also helps explain Derrida's "methodology," the fact that he often begins in the margins, with what appears to be excluded or what is claimed to be secondary. Derrida was quite clear about this in "Limited Inc." Whereas the tradition tends to concentrate on the successful or the central, Derrida does the opposite. "I deconcentrate," he says, "and it is the secondary, eccentric, lateral, marginal, parasitic, borderline cases which are 'important' to me and are a source of many things, such as pleasure, but also insight into the general functioning of a textual system" ("LI" 44/90). This is precisely what Searle did not do: "In passing I note with astonishment that Searle chooses to ignore 'marginal, fringe' cases. For these always constitute the most certain and most decisive indices wherever essential conditions are to be grasped" ("LI" 70/134).

Every speech act, then—including the oath and the promise—would thus be intrinsically open not just to success but to failure, and so not just, we might say, to the sworn faith or *foi jurée* that makes it possible but to its betrayal, its breach, its *parjure*. Beginning with the very specific speech act of perjury or *parjure*, we come to see a structure that characterizes all speech acts, and that thus compromises—like a *parjure*—some of the most traditional categories of Western philosophy that typically support or undergird a thinking of speech acts, everything from essence and accident to possibility and actuality to, as it was suggested earlier, justice and desire. In the end, almost nothing remains untouched at the most basic level by this rethinking or reinscription of the word *parjure*.

Let me take just a moment to juxtapose this analysis with a passage from another very recently published work, *Geschlecht 3*. I do so because this work contains one of the clearest and most provocative accounts of this deconstructive strategy and logic in all of Derrida's work. Though the text, excised from a seminar of 1984–85, is essentially a long analysis of Heidegger's essay of 1953, "Language in the Poem," on the work of Georg Trakl, this passage, which falls almost squarely in the center of the work, can be read somewhat independently of its context. For in this dense but extremely suggestive passage right smack in the midst of a very specific, determined reading of Heidegger on Trakl, Derrida gives us what seems to be something like a structural law regarding deconstruction and the deconstructable, a law that will have everything to do with the nature of possibility and of accident. Derrida in fact announces it in just this way: "We're touching here on what, metaphorically or ironically, I will call the great logic of the relations between deconstruction and the deconstructable" (*G 3* 80/106).

The context here is Heidegger's famous emphasis on *gathering*, in this case a gathering of possibilities in the *Ort*, the place, the tip of the spear, and the question of whether division or divisibility happens in this place of gathering as some ill or some evil, some *mal*, that affects or corrupts the place from the outside, after the fact, corrupting an intact and indivisible gathering that would precede it, or whether it is a question, as Derrida says, of "something else entirely." Considering everything said in this work thus far, one can imagine that Derrida will lean toward this latter.

Speaking of "the fact, the factum or fatality"—that is, once again, the necessity, the inevitability, the destiny but also the downfall—"of division being able [*pouvoir*] to happen [*arriver*], the fact of this possibility . . . implies that the structure of that to which this can happen be such that this can happen to it." The fact that this can happen to its structure means that the structure is, therefore, "essentially not indivisible but divisible" and that "this divisibility must not be merely an accident." Derrida then goes on to argue in one diabolically condensed and untranslatable sentence: "If the essence is accidentable, it is *a priori* accidented [*Si l'essence est accidentable, elle est a priori accidentée*]," that is, we could say, if the essence is susceptible to accident, if it is *accidentable*, liable to being in an accident, if it is accident-prone, it has been *a priori* subject to accident, that is, *accidentée*, already in an accident, already compromised, already harmed (*G 3* 81/106). If the essence is subject to accident, if it is accident-prone, then it is *a priori* or from the beginning or even of necessity the victim of an accident, from the beginning injured or compromised, that is, *accidentée*. For an accident does not or cannot happen, in the end, if the essence cannot be affected by such an accident. This then allows Derrida to argue—and you will hear him linking once again accident to desire: "This accident—here, divisibility—is not an evil, a simple evil. There would be no place, desire, or movement toward or from the place of gathering if this divisibility was excluded or extrinsic" (*G 3* 81/106).

Again, the accident is not simply the possibility of an ill that *may* befall the good from the outside, some good that would be intact, like an origin, before the accident, but the possibility of there being any good or ill, any good or evil, in the first place. Everything Derrida says elsewhere about an originary violence, or about radical evil, that is, an *ineradicable* evil, in "Faith and Knowledge," everything he says about an origin or source of religion that wants to remain indemnified, safe and sound, but that is always open in its very attempt to indemnify itself against this corruption or this contamination, needs to be thought in these terms (see "FK" §§ 14, 36–38, 50–51). Without the accident, without this *mal* from the outside, without this *parjure*, we might say, there would be no desire, no *foi jurée*, no difference and no repetition, no dissemination, and so something even worse than the negative as a constitutive moment or feature of the positive. Derrida goes on to argue: "It [this divisibility] is, then, the essential condition of possibility and impossibility for desire and for place," for if the letter were indivisible—it is the same argument we saw in "Signature Event Context"—there would be no iterability, no opening to the other, and so, writes Derrida, "the forces of death would prevail even more certainly." That is to say, "if there were only gathering, sameness, oneness, place without path [*chemin*], that would be death, *la mort sans phrase*" (*G 3* 81/106), in other words, a death that would not await other words, a death that would be immediate and without appeal.

Derrida in *Geschlecht 3* thus evokes the same language of essence and accident that we have been following here, going on to speak, he says "ironically," of a "great logic" at work in Heidegger, that is,

> the most continuous great logic of philosophy, the one that presupposes an exteriority between essence and accident, pure and impure, the proper and the improper, good and evil, [a] great logic [that] remains

at work in Heidegger (see what he says about logos as gathering), in spite of everything, in spite of powerful deconstructive movements in Heidegger against the great logic of Hegel. (*G 3* 82/107)[8]

So there you have it yet again, a rethinking of essence and accident not simply in Derrida's reading of speech act theory but in his reading of Heidegger. It is in the end nothing other than the other—a relation to the other—that motivates this whole movement or play, just as, already back in "Signature Event Context," it was the relation to the other or to an outside, to a new and unexpected context, that motivated the movement of iterability and the possibilities of citationality and parasitism that this implies.

Before returning to *Perjury and Pardon*, it is worth mentioning that, in addition to this analysis, which is so strikingly similar to what we find in Derrida's works devoted to speech act theory, there is also in *Geschlecht 3* a brief mention of speech act theory and a hypothesis regarding what Heidegger would have thought about it. Derrida speaks of the "performative of a promise," which "provides one of the privileged examples of utterances known as performative," and he then adds:

> One can easily imagine all the objections Heidegger would have raised against "speech act" [in English in the original] theory and, especially, against applying it to his text or the texts he questions. Nonetheless, I believe there would be much to be done and said *between* the two styles of thinking and the two approaches. (*G 3* 112/133–134)[9]

Let me add here one more attempt on Derrida's part to rethink the relation between essence and accident, a passage from a very different text, "Aphorism Countertime" (1986), an essay that was written not long after *Geschlecht 3* and that echoes much of its language. In the midst of a reading of Shakespeare's *Romeo and Juliet*, Derrida recalls the way in which the undelivered letter from Friar Laurence to Romeo telling Romeo about Juliet's (fake) death sets everything in motion. As Derrida there makes clear, this possibility of a letter not arriving at its destination does not simply supervene upon the fates of Romeo and Juliet from the outside, as an accident, though it is indeed also an accident. It reveals the structural law of the letter and of the accident itself. Moreover, this *fatalité* or necessity, the necessity of the accident, of the letter *not* arriving at its destination, of the sign being lost, misappropriated, or misread, is the beginning not only of tragedy but also, yet again, of the possibility of desire, of justice (just as it was in *Geschlecht 3*), and, here, of love. Derrida thus begins by speaking of "the failed rendezvous, the unfortunate accident, the letter that does not arrive at its destination, the time of the detour prolonged for a purloined letter, the remedy that transforms itself into poison," and so on, as so many traditional ways of reading the play that suggest that an accident supervenes upon the destinies of Romeo and Juliet as if from the outside. Derrida then goes on:

> This representation is not false. But if this drama has thus been imprinted, superimprinted on the memory of Europe, text upon text, this is because the anachronous accident comes to illustrate an essential possibility. It confounds a philosophical logic that would like accidents to remain what they are, accidental. ("AC" 130/134)

Yet again, the very possibility of the letter *not* arriving at its destination belongs to the structure of the letter itself, so that what happens to Romeo and Juliet accidentally belongs in some sense to the essence of letters. As in *Geschlecht 3*, this fatality—this destiny—of the letter is not simply some possible ill that might one day, possibly, eventually, supervene upon the successful possibility, the successful relation between Romeo and Juliet, in order to ruin, disrupt, frustrate, or corrupt it from without. As Derrida argues:

> What happens to Romeo and Juliet, and remains in fact an accident whose aleatory and unforeseeable appearance cannot be effaced, at the crossing of several series and beyond common sense, can only be what it is, accidental, insofar as it has *already* happened, in essence, before it happens. The desire of Romeo and Juliet did not encounter the poison, the contretemps, or the detour of the letter by chance. In order for this encounter to take place, there must *already* have been instituted a system of marks (names, hours, maps of places, dates, and supposedly "objective" place names) to thwart, as it were, the dispersion of interior and heterogeneous durations, to frame, organize, put in order, render possible a rendezvous: in other words to deny, while taking note of it, noncoincidence, the separation of monads, infinite distance, the disconnection of experiences, the multiplicity of worlds, everything that renders possible a contretemps of the irremediable detour of a letter. ("AC" 130/134)

The accidental contretemps is thus the possibility of tragedy, but also, the very "birth of desire"—as well as love: for "I love because the other is the other, because his or her time will never be mine" ("AC" 131/134). That is what the fate of Romeo and Juliet teaches us: the accident that leads to their tragedy exposes the structural law that determines the love, the desire, at the heart and origin of their relationship. Derrida continues, with the same clarity and synthetic force we just saw in *Geschlecht 3*, "The desire of Romeo and Juliet is born in the heart of this possibility. There would have been no love, the pledge [*le serment*] would not have taken place"—Derrida could have said the *foi jurée* would not have been taken—"nor time, nor its theater, without discordance" ("AC" 131/134). And then Derrida gives us once again, in another formulation arising out of a reading of another text, the law of the accident, here rethought in terms of a law of the contretemps:

> The accidental contretemps comes to *remark* the essential contretemps. Which is as much as to say that it is not accidental. It does not, for all that, have the signification of an essence or of a formal structure. It is not the abstract condition of possibility, a universal form of the relation to the other in general, a dialectic of desire or consciousness. Rather the singularity of an imminence whose "cutting point" spurs desire at its birth—the very birth of desire. ("AC" 131/134)

He continues, in what is one of Derrida's longest and most powerful meditations on love, a love that, like friendship in *Politics of Friendship*, is born not of possession but separation, not intimacy but distance, not synchrony but anachrony, a love that is thus not unrelated, perhaps unsurprisingly, to spacing—as we saw already in part one of this work—as well as to theater:

> I love because the other is the other, because his or her time will never be mine. The living duration, the presence of the other's love remains infinitely distant from mine, distant from itself in what stretches it toward mine and even in what one might want to describe as amorous euphoria, ecstatic communion, mystical intuition. I can love the other only in the passion of this aphorism. Which does not happen, does not come about like misfortune, bad luck, or negativity. It has the form of the most loving affirmation—it is the chance of desire. And it not only cuts into the fabric of durations, it spaces. Contretemps says something about topology or the visible; it opens theater. ("AC" 131/134)

To return to *Perjury and Pardon* after these detours through *Geschlecht 3* and "Aphorism Countertime," without the possibility of a *parjure* there would be no *foi jurée*, the breach of faith or the possibility of the breach of faith being essential to the oath in the first place.[10] But we now need to ask just what it is in the *parjure* that compromises or undermines the sworn faith, the *foi jurée*, so that pardon or forgiveness, asking for forgiveness, becomes necessary. I have been talking here about "structural" possibilities or "conditions," but we need to be even more specific. It is obviously much more than simply promising to tell the truth, the whole truth, and nothing but the truth, but then lying on the stand, perjuring oneself, knowingly concealing the truth, or what one believes to be the truth, and putting a nontruth in its place. If *parjure* is to be thought not just as a contingent or accidental incursion upon the *foi jurée* but as a structuring possibility of it, then the *parjure* must be something other than simply lying, other than mere perjury, other than the "knowing lie." The *parjure* would seem to compromise the *foi jurée* in an even more essential way. It would have to be, as it were, something like an *intrinsic* possibility of accident at the origin, bringing along with it everything that would compromise a putatively pure or original or indemnified oath or faith.

Let me now name, then, some of these intrinsic, essential possibilities of the accident. The first is, very simply, the necessity of repetition, of iterability, and thus the divisibility of the letter or the sign and the lack of presence that this entails. As we learned already from "Signature Event Context," it is the necessity of repetition, the necessary lack of presence in the sign, or else in consciousness, in intention, that compromises from the beginning the presence to itself of any sign or the presence to itself of any intention in consciousness. As we heard Derrida argue in *Geschlecht 3*, it is this divisibility of the *foi jurée* that makes it repeatable, iterable, a divisibility that divides the *foi jurée* from itself, compromising it and yet making it understandable in the first place. It is this divisibility within a supposedly or putatively indivisible sworn faith or *foi jurée* that thus makes for both the uniqueness of the event of the speech act *and* its inevitable repetition, the one and the other. Every speech act in the so-called present, every *foi jurée*, every promise, depends upon past and future iterations, that is, to speak phenomenologically, upon a series of protentive and retentive iterations of the promise, on a renewal of the *foi jurée*, on the promise or the oath to repeat in the future what was once promised or sworn to in the past. From this perspective, the promise or the *foi jurée* is not one speech act among others but an exemplary or even originary speech act, one that conditions all speech acts with a promise or an oath to *continue* to promise and swear allegiance in the future. But that then means that the promise can never exclude the possibility of the promise becoming a threat, or the *foi jurée* a *parjure*, or the gift as a boon or a good, the gift as poison or an evil, and so on.[11] Repetition or iterability, then, compromises every speech act or sworn faith from the beginning, at the same time as it makes possible any successful speech act or sworn faith. The very thing that makes it effective, the promise to repeat that sworn faith, to repeat the oath, is thus also that which begins to erode it, and from the very beginning. It is thus the possibility of *parjure* that opens up the space—the theater, as it were—for any "successful" sworn faith to take place, just as the possibility of iteration, the essential possibility of iteration, which means the essential possibility of the accident, opens up the possibility for the so-called successful performative.

What else compromises sworn faith? We have already named it implicitly when speaking of a lack or lack of presence within consciousness, namely, the unconscious, the possibility not just of one's tongue saying one thing and one's heart another, that is, the possibility of a lie, of a knowing falsehood, but also the possibility of one's conscious intention swearing one thing, if we can say this, and one's unconscious foreswearing it or else swearing another. From this perspective, every testimony is open to being foresworn or breached or betrayed, every testimony a "perjury trap," where one risks betraying oneself even when one has gotten one's story perfectly straight.

Next—and all these things are obviously related—is forgetting. Derrida recalls early on in the seminar the relationship between forgiving and forgetting, the fact that one often says, in English, "I forgive but I don't forget" (*PP 1* 104). But we also talk about "forgiving and forgetting," forgiving and then forgetting, or forgiving so as to forget. So either one forgives but does not forget, or else one forgives and then automatically forgets, forgives in or while forgetting. Derrida suggests that inasmuch as forgiveness repeats the act but does not coincide with it, precisely because it is being recalled at some later point in time, forgiveness is itself, in this repetition, always *already* a forgetting. Hence the purity and rigor of the distinction between forgiving and forgetting, a distinction that must nonetheless be maintained, is compromised from the beginning in its very structure.[12] As Derrida writes, making reference to the notion of accident that we have been following, "what compromises that rigor in this way is not an empirical accident that could always befall it, or not, in a contingent way, from the outside" (*PP 1* 223). In other words, forgetting is not an accident that might arrive to forgiving to compromise it in its purity. There is always *some* forgetting in every forgiving, always some self-forgetting, that is, "an essential displacement, a distancing of the self [that] has taken place, in the very heart of the heart of forgiveness, of mercy" (*PP 1* 224). Just as iterability and the possibility of citation or parasitism compromise from the very beginning the successful speech act, making it, in essence, a species of the failed speech act, so, Derrida suggests, all forgiveness is compromised, and possibly even counterfeited, by the possibility of forgetting on the side of both the one forgiving and the one being forgiven. For if, as Derrida writes,

> counterfeit pardon or forgiving is able to fall within the ambit of the unconscious, or indeed lodge itself in the very structure of forgiveness

we call "authentic"—that is said to be free of forgery or counterfeiting—then the very idea of authentic forgiveness becomes highly problematic and perhaps deserves to be abandoned, or in any case conceived of differently. (*PP 1* 104)

"Authentic" forgiveness would thus suffer the same fate as the supposedly successful speech act, the fully present experience or intention, the genuine promise, the purity of a sworn faith, and so on.

Finally, and not unrelated to the unconscious and forgetting, there is the *machine*. This notion of the machine returns regularly in the seminar *Perjury and Pardon*—often in relationship to questions of *faith* and *knowledge*. Derrida writes:

> It is that machine, that *mēchanē*, which we are going to see in operation, always stronger, like law itself, a law above the laws of faith and knowledge, laws of determinism and freedom, like the law itself that uncompromisingly requires the distinction between excusing and forgiveness at the very moment when it . . . contaminates them, has them infected by one another. (*PP 1* 228)[13]

Speaking of a "fatal law," that is, once again, of an inevitable, implacable law, of an automatic repetition of signs and so of speech acts, of phrases of excuse and excusing, of apology and forgiveness, of excusing oneself or another, of the "machine of excuse, in relation to forgiveness and foreswearing," the automatic response of the "no harm done," *y a pas de mal*, but then also of the "I forgive you" (*PP 1* 198), Derrida writes:

> This fatal law is also that of a mechanism, an automatism, or even a *deus ex machina* that reproduces, implacably and without mercy, the evil and the forgiveness. I insist strongly on this expression, at least on the word "machine," for reasons that will emerge later. (*PP 1* 180)

Derrida insists on the machine and its automaticity as what would oppose the supposedly pure, spontaneous origin of a speech act or a sworn faith that would supposedly come before all repetition and would treat all repetition as an accident that may or may not befall the original speech act of forgiveness. He continues:

> There is the machine of forgiveness, and yet there is in the absolute vocation of forgiveness the demand not to cede in any circumstances to a machinal calculation, not to any technique, to be the pure spontaneous movement of the heart, of the soul's intention, before and outside any technical repetition. (*PP 1* 180–181)

Here is a relation or an opposition that goes back to at least "Plato's Pharmacy," that between a supposedly spontaneous movement and its machinic repetition, two forms of repetition, one interior and natural, the other exterior and machinic or artificial.[14] The speech act that grants forgiveness thus cannot simply *exclude* the merely mechanical or automatic, that is, as Derrida might have said following "Signature Event Context," the merely "citational" or "parasitic," "I forgive you," at the same time as it obviously cannot simply be reduced to this. Hence Derrida writes, bringing together the so-called positive phenomenon with the negative, the good repetition with the bad, the authenticity of the heart—*cordia*—with the recording machine:

> The best is here closest to the worst, to its opposite, *perhaps* as always, and the most alive speech is closest to the immaculate silence, that of absolute muteness or automatic grammar—or the recording of a message machine—or the machinic trace—or the *record* of a CD. Subtitle of the seminar perhaps: what is the heart? Record and *misericord*, memory (*recordation*), trace of evil and evil of the trace, the forgiveness of the heart and the archival machine. (*PP 1* 220)

Misericordia is thus inseparable from memory, the heart, the *cor*, inseparable from the recording, *cordia* inseparable from the CD—just as the *foi jurée* is inseparable from the *parjure*.

It is thus nothing other than the metaphysics we saw earlier, that so-called metaphysics of presence, as Derrida would characterize it, that is compromised by this rethinking of the *parjure* in relation to repetition, forgetting, the unconscious, and, finally, the machine. It is nothing other than the supposedly full presence of a speech act that is compromised by all these things, a displacement of the self that comes about like an originary *parjure*, beyond all presence and thus, just as in "Signature Event Context," beyond life or beyond the power or capacity of a so-called living subject to initiate or to be at the origin of a trace or a work or a speech act, to be, as we say, its actor or its agent, to be fully responsible for either an act of *parjure* or an act of *pardon* (see *PP 1* 119 for this rethinking of "power"). Derrida thus speaks, or writes, in *Le parjure et le pardon* of

> what remains, the remaining trace, precarious, finite but surviving, the text that, automatically, like a quasi-machine, can reproduce forgiveness where neither the blameworthy one to be forgiven nor the forgiving victim are there any longer, presently living, are no longer "being-there" in the Living Present. (*PP 1* 175)

There is thus some machine at the origin, as opposed to some intact presence, a machine that, as machine, repeats itself, and so can never function as an origin at all. If Derrida could thus say that he *parjures* as he breathes, even this breath must now be understood as a sort of mechanical process, the living breath itself made possible, as it were, by artificial lungs.

The machine is thus what compromises the *foi jurée* and yet, at the same stroke, makes possible a trace that will remain. The machine of forgiveness and foreswearing, of *pardon* and *parjure*, is the same machine that leaves a *testamentary* trace. Derrida writes, or rather wrote, and we now read some twenty years hence, as if to demonstrate or to perform another thinking of the testamentary remainder:

> You can easily see that what matters to me and guides me in this barely preliminary phase of this introduction is already the history of forgiveness, I mean the testamentary text, the archival remaining [*restance*] of the text that, notably in the figure of the literary, of the becoming literary of poetic fiction, diverts and at the same time gathers together the biblical inheritance, assuring it of a mechanical remaining, a mechanization, a textual automatization. (*PP 1* 189)

A bit later in the seminar, Derrida speaks in similar terms of *prayer* in relation to the machine, "the prayer that requests the gift of knowledge, that asks to know whether the hymn's prayer or praise is primary, that prayer has already begun in the very request." As Derrida goes on to comment, "The machine is already on, it works all by itself" (*PP 1* 190), the good and the bad as close as possible to one another, like two repetitions.

But these references to prayer and the machine, to prayer in Augustine and others (*PP 1* 194), should make us, as readers of Derrida, recall that famous prayer of Pascal that Derrida speaks of at some length during the second year of *The Beast and the Sovereign* seminar, his final seminar, that prayer written on a piece of parchment and sewn into Pascal's garment and then discovered only after his death (*BS 2* 212/297). It is a stunning example of Derrida's rethinking of essence and accident, an empirical accident that remarks in a particularly powerful and poignant way the accidental nature or essence of the trace in general, the trace as *always* and *essentially* testamentary, a testamentary trace—a sort of machine—that would now be at the origin, that would take the place, as it were, of that putatively intact origin of metaphysics.

That which compromises the supposedly original self-presence of the origin or the essence, safe and sound, indemnified, protected from all accident or contamination, is thus also, to repeat that semantic schema from "Faith and Knowledge," that which allows the trace to live on, to survive, as testament or as archive, or, here in *Perjury and Pardon*, as a work, as an oeuvre. Just as *parjure*, as I have argued, might be read as Derrida's latter-day remarking or reinscription of Austin's infelicity, so the oeuvre, the written oeuvre, "written" in the sense that Derrida gives to that term from *Of Grammatology* onward, might be thought of as Derrida's reinscription of the speech *act*, a speech act that is now untethered from the life or living presence of any first-person present indicative active voice, this untethering then being the very condition, as we will see, of any grace. But before grace, before Derrida says grace, listen to the way he here associates trace, machine, work, and act:

> Forgiving is an action and a work, it changes things and initiates a history ["Cogito and the history of forgiveness," Derrida might have said]; and, given that, it operates its oeuvre, its *opus*, its work and the remainder of its work as *opus* that continues to work, to work all by itself, like a machine beyond the first moment of its advent or its decision, such that this first instant gains its sense as first instant only retrospectively, by the force of repetition that takes it beyond that first instant, which is to say also beyond its origin or its author, its signatory. (*PP 1* 233)[15]

A testamentary trace, then, that works all by itself, like a machine, beyond the living present and thus beyond the life of the author or the signatory—just as Derrida laid it out in "Signature Event Context" and then signed and countersigned it at the end of that essay. Here is how Derrida characterizes this same thing, same but different, some twenty-six years later in *Perjury and Pardon*, this time by means of a reference, an association, to grace and the machine, to *grace* not just as elegance but as forgiveness or as pardon, something given beyond all responsibility and received beyond all desert. Derrida evokes

> a work that will operate by itself, that will accomplish its work of working beyond, and without the living assistance of its signatory, and taking whatever time will be needed . . . operates all by itself, almost like a machine and so without any labor by the author, as though, contrary to what one often thinks, there were a secret affinity between grace and the machine, between the heart and the automatism of the puppet, as though the excusing, exculpating machine were working all by itself. (*PP 1* 267)

Grace and the machine, says Derrida, another way of saying, perhaps, event and machine, as the final phrase of Session 8 of this first year of the *Perjury and Pardon* seminar would lead us to think: "As a last word for today, how can one think together the machine *and* the event, a machinal repetition *and* what occurs [*arrive*: happens, comes about]" (*PP 1* 327).

We are talking about a speech act, then, that works or acts all by itself, in the absence of its actors or its programmers, beyond their power or capacity, beyond them even when these so-called actors are, as we say, *right there*. All this thus poses, says Derrida, "the question of the testament, of spectrality, of the trace, and especially of the becoming-literary or poetic of this testamentary and textual trace that seems to function all on its own, by itself, in the absence of its producers, like a machine" (*PP 1* 175). The textual trace as a machine, working all by itself: that is what compromises, in the end, the purity of any kind of full, assured, successful speech act, at the same time as it releases language from its attachment to every supposedly present subject or speaker, releases it from its meaning-to-say or its *vouloir dire*, from its supposed origin, in order to open it up to the accidental or fortuitous encounter.[16] Like a machine, says Derrida, but then also—for this is the chance, the accident, and the grace—like a seminar, ready for publication and distribution, for translation and interpretation, for commentary and conferences, a seminar that, as we have seen, is always accidental, always surprising, and, this time, already ripe, primed, for dissemination.

Conclusion: *Actes de naissance*

> The mother is the faceless figure of a *figurant*, an extra. She gives rise to all the figures by losing herself in the background of the scene like an anonymous persona. Everything comes back to her, beginning with life.
> —Jacques Derrida, *Otobiographies*

As we have seen, Derrida pursued some of the fundamental questions of speech act theory, questions of the relationship between speech and act, word and deed, language and the event, from at least the time of "Signature Event Context" right up through his seminar *Perjury and Pardon*. But Derrida's engagement with speech act theory would not end there. For example, in the second year of the seminar that would follow *Perjury and Pardon*, that is, *The Death Penalty*, Derrida would return yet again to the question of act, again in relation to questions of possibility and impossibility, actuality, and virtuality. After beginning by suggesting that his seminar will revolve around three questions: "What is an act? What is an age? What is a desire?" (*DP2* 3/22), Derrida continues:

> The first of these three questions ("What is an act?") reverberates like a great and precisely ageless question, a question in the great ontological tradition. What is an act, in the sense of action (with everything that can be opposed to it: passion—action/passion—theory or thought, speculation, language, acting instead of theorizing, of thinking, speculating, or even speaking, etc.), but also what is an act in the sense of act understood as *energeia* ("in actuality," with its Latin pseudoequivalent, its problematic translation as *actus*, which one blithely opposes to *dynamis*, power or potential being, or even matter, *possibilitas*, virtuality, etc.)? (*DP 2* 4–5/23–24)

Derrida thus returns here to the question of the nature of acts and of action, the question that he had been pursuing in the context of speech act theory since as early as 1971 in "Signature Event Context." But then, right on cue, Derrida refers, in words that should remind us of many of the things regarding possibility and impossibility that we saw in Act 3 of "Derrida in Montreal," to the way in which the question of act has caused him to rethink the very relationship between possibility and impossibility. He reminds us of his previous attempts to rethink the negative or a negative possibility (here called the im-possible) in both his written works, and particularly those on speech act theory, and his seminars, which can now be read as a single "open seminar" that ran over some three to four decades. Continuing to speak here of that seemingly simple question "what is an act?" which he would now like to pose in the context of his seminar on *The Death Penalty*, Derrida continues:

> An enormous problem that touches not only on the difference between agent and patient, act and passion, act and potential or possibility, form and matter, in particular and par excellence in the discourse of Aristotle, with its entire filiation (which is enormous), but also at the same time on everything that we are meditating upon or have been premeditating here for years regarding the thinking of the possible and the impossible, of an im-possible that would not be negative, of an im-possible that would escape the alternative been the possible and the actual, or even the active, etc. (*DP 2* 5/24)

After thus recalling that his seminar will have been pursuing for many years, in different contexts and with regard to diverse topics, this question of an im-possible that would not simply be the opposite of the possible or the actual, an im-possible that would continue to haunt the possible even when some possibility will have been "realized" or "actualized" (just as the possibility of failure continued to haunt even the "successful" performative in "Signature Event Context"), Derrida goes on to relate this thinking of action to the specific object of the seminar:

> It is usually thought, according to good, common sense, that the death penalty is an act, a real, concrete [*effectif*], irreversible act, one that seals the irreversible, the irrevisable, precisely because it is an act, because it is supposed to be the most active and the most actual, the most concrete, the most real of acts, the most undeniable of acts, an acting out that also claims to penalize an actual, concrete, real act, one or more real and concrete murders, for example, and not only intentions or desires that would not have been acted upon and which

basically do not belong to the time or age of the act (of the act that consists in the death penalty or in the criminal act that it claims to sanction). The death penalty would thus be an act that claims to sanction what is only an act, a concrete, real act, in actuality, and not simply what is possible, an intention, a virtuality, a desire (conscious or unconscious). (*DP 2* 5/24)

Hence the death penalty, according to good common sense, would be an act that claims to respond to another act, an act for an act, as it were, the act of the penalty for the act of the crime. Two acts, the giving of death from within the law as a response to, for example, the giving of death outside or beyond the law. Derrida will, of course, go in the seminar to call this commonsense way of thinking action into question, along with all the traditional attributes that would seem to subtend it, beginning with activity, actuality, and reality.

But then what about death itself in this rethinking of the death penalty? Would anyone ever call it an act? Unlike most other acts during a lifetime, it would seem to be an act or an action, a process or an event, that must be undergone rather than undertaken. Even in suicide, whether physician-assisted or not, one must relinquish the phantasm of actually bringing death about rather than enacting or committing it activity, consciously, presently, of one's own free will.

And yet there is something in French called an *acte de décès*, that is, an "act of death," that can perhaps tell us something crucial about the act more generally in Derrida. Commonly translated "death certificate," an *acte de décès* is an official document usually issued by the state and certified by some authority verifying the death of someone in the state. It is an *acte* that, like its prequel, the *acte de naissance*, which we will turn to in a minute, seems to waver between the constative ("X is dead") and the performative ("We declare X dead"). It is also an *acte* that, like its prequel, is always spoken or written or performed by *another* after the fact, by some authority who could never be the same as the self in question, that is, the same individual whose death or birth is being certified by the *acte*. It is an *acte* that, again according to good common sense, certifies but does not perform or bring about the death or the birth that is being certified, death or birth being an event within the world that is stated or constated or declared rather than performed or enacted. In neither case does the legitimating authority, even when there is a first-person singular or plural behind the act, bring about the death or the birth that they are simply noting or certifying on behalf of the state.

As we recall from Part I of this work, Austin does not really treat such *actes* or certificates, that is, such *written* acts, in *How to Do Things with Words* because they do not quite fit his paradigm of acts *spoken* in the first-person present active indicative. There is some kind of attestation on the part of a hospital, city, or state, an attestation that is typically marked by some sort of seal and perhaps even an accompanying signature, some equivalent of the "hereby [*par les presents*]" that we saw earlier, but there is no real first-person speaker behind such an act.

But as one may recall from Act 1 of "Derrida in Montreal," Austin does mention early on in *How to Do Things with Words* the speech act of a Last Will and Testament: "'I give and bequeath my watch to my brother'—as occurring in a will" (*HDT* 5). Austin uses this as an example because there is indeed here a first-person subject speaking (or rather writing) in the present active indicative, and Austin takes it for granted that the signature at the end of the testament will "tether" the written act to the past presence of the signer, thereby giving it the status of a speech act in the fuller sense of the term. Hence Austin evokes the Last Will and Testament signed by a living I, in the present, in the kind of time that might be noted or confirmed by the very watch that is being bequeathed from one brother to another.

Derrida, curiously, does not mention Austin's example of the Last Will and Testament, even though the focus of "Signature Event Context" is the role played by writing and the signature in Austin's text, a focus that, as we saw, takes Austin's notion of the speech act in the direction, precisely, of death, linking the speech act in general to all those attributes commonly associated with writing—distance, asynchrony, lack of presence and power, absence of intention and consciousness, the death of the addressor and addressee, and so on. Derrida then uses the very theory of the speech act and of writing developed in "Signature Event Context" and elsewhere to rethink, at once with Austin and against him, questions of death, mourning, survival, the work, the archive, and so on. It is thus that he begins to link the speech act itself, the speech act in general, and not just some speech act called "A Last Will and Testament," to the notions of the testament and the testamentary. It is a connection that Derrida would continue to develop right up through the seminar *Perjury and Pardon*, indeed right up to "Learning to Live Finally," what would turn out to be Derrida's last published interview, given to *Le Monde* in the summer of 2004, just a couple of months before his death. He there says, recalling some of the tenets of a generalized writing that he had articulated some three decades earlier in that essay of 1971 first presented in Montreal:

> The trace I leave signifies to me at once my death, either to come or already come upon me, and the hope that this trace survives me. This is not a striving for immortality; it's something structural. I leave a

piece of paper behind, I go away, I die: it is impossible to escape this structure, it is the unchanging form of my life. Each time I let something go, each time some trace leaves me, "proceeds" from me, unable to be reappropriated, I live my death in writing. It's the ultimate test: one expropriates oneself without knowing exactly who is being entrusted with what is left behind. Who is going to inherit, and how? Will there even be any heirs? (*LLF* 32–33/33–34)

As we saw at the end of the preceding chapter, Derrida thinks the speech act in relation to a testamentary trace that goes beyond the presence and authority of a subject who himself or herself bequeaths, in the present, to the future. Derrida thereby follows the notion of speech act as Austin developed it but then rethinks it in terms of a new notion of "writing" and a new notion of "act" that condition both speech and writing and so is not incompatible with an act of speech. Even more, Derrida extends or displaces Austin's notion of the speech act well beyond its original limits in order to think something like an *event*, something that happens in speech or in writing that goes well beyond the expectations or powers of any individual speaker or actor. It was, it seems, as Derrida testified on numerous occasions, something within Austin that will have provoked this, something within Austin's "fecund" text, something within his work, his oeuvre, that opened up a future beyond anything Austin or his text could have intended or taught.[1] In other words, Derrida takes Austin's notion of speech act—the act or action of a speaker—and develops it in the direction of acts such as the "birth act" or "death act" that exceed the subject, that is, in the direction not just of the written certification but of the *event*, the event of birth or of death, acts that go beyond not only the individual but, now, individual or discrete generations.

So what, then, of birth? What of the act or the *acte* of birth? Not just the act or *acte* that certifies, marks, or announces a birth but the act or the *acte* of giving birth or of being born? It is, as we said above, common to speak in French of an *acte de naissance* as well as an *acte de décès*: it is a term that pretty much anyone born in France or in a francophone country would have occasion to use from time to time. The phrase names, simply, a "birth certificate," the kind of official document one gets—or that one's parents get—when one is born, the kind of document one usually needs when applying for some other official document, like a passport, a visa, or a marriage certificate. It is, as it were, the first *acte*, the first attestation by a state, often the first of many such *actes* in a list that commonly goes all the way up or down to that *acte de décès*, a document that the child or the heir, that is, that the *next* generation, typically gets in order to settle the affairs of the preceding one.

Acte de naissance, then, "birth certificate," though, sometimes, especially in Quebec—for we have returned, as chance would have it, to Quebec—the term is translated as "act of birth," and *acte de décès* as "act of death." And so, after all of Derrida's references to the testamentary in relation to the speech act, it should perhaps come as some surprise that, in Derrida's very final seminar, in his very last evocation of the performative and of speech act theory in his more than forty-year "open seminar," the second and final year of *The Beast and the Sovereign*, Derrida would recall something like an *acte de naissance* or an "act of birth" that would be related not to the past but to the promise of a future.[2] The reference occurs in the context of Derrida's reading of the phrase of Paul Celan, "*Die Welt ist fort, ich muss dich tragen*," a phrase that Derrida tries to read as the conjunction or combination of a constative and a performative, or, rather, as the enfolding or enveloping of a performative within a constative. Derrida there suggests that among all the different ways of understanding this phrase, among all its different registers, one might hear it as a "double proposition," both parts of the proposition being marked by speech act theory:

> one of which seems to be constative (this is how things are, from now on, isn't it, *Die Welt ist fort*, the world is going to hell), and the other of which, performative rather, *ich muss dich tragen*, seems to sign a commitment, a promise, an oath, a duty, like the seal of a love that, at the moment of good-bye, of good-bye to the world, salutes or swears to work for your safety [*salut*], to save you without salvation—among all the imports, then, which accord between them a constative proposition and a performative proposition, each held to the other in their radical heterogeneity (for how on earth could you deduce, and by what right, from the fact that *Die Welt ist fort*, the obligation to carry you? What demonstrable link between them? . . . (*BS 2* 258/357–358)

Let me here interrupt Derrida in midsentence, and in midparenthesis within the sentence—because we are only about a third of the way through what is, in French as well as English, a *single* sentence—in order to recall the context for this session of Derrida's seminar. It is March 23, 2003—just three days after the beginning of the American invasion of Iraq—and the world could not have felt more far away or more threatened, more in the process of "going to hell," especially for the tens of thousands of Iraqi civilians who would be killed in the weeks and months following the invasion. It is in that context that Derrida is reading Celan, thinking about death, the absence or end of the world, and, somewhat surprisingly, somewhat hopefully, the possibility of birth within that end of the world. I continue the quote, that is, the single sentence we find in Derrida's seminar, written, clearly, in the days just before it was read aloud in the seminar:

> Why should I still carry you, if the world is going away?)—among all the imports which place side by side or accord between them a performative proposition *and* a constative proposition which is not just any constative proposition (since it concerns nothing less than the world itself, the totality of what is and that is called the world), a constatation that, moreover, presupposes at least that the addressee and the signatory of the statement share a language and the comprehension of what "world" means, inhabit the same world enough to be able to hear with one and the same ear and say with one and the same voice *Die Welt ist fort*, so that at the moment at which this phrase is spoken the world is still there, perhaps not here but still there, and the two supposed partners, interlocutors, even lovers in the poem cohabit the same world, precisely this world that is going away, which is getting ever more distant . . . this world which at bottom comes or advenes only by going away, the world as it goes—well, still beyond all the imports I've already tried to count here or there of this unheard-of double proposition, of this performative lodged like a pearl in the oyster of a constative, like a still unborn child, to be born, to be carried to term in the uterus of the origin of the world as it is, there would be today the import of a declaration of love or of peace at the moment of a declaration of war. (*BS 2* 258–259/358)[3]

At the end, then, of this long, winding, extraordinarily convoluted or involuted sentence, Derrida says he has begun to hear in that double proposition of Celan a performative pearl (I must carry you) lodged within the constative claim (the world is gone), like a still unborn child awaiting its *acte de naissance*, as it were. Though the performative is attached here to an "I," to the first-person singular active indicative ("I must"), Derrida compares it not to the oyster, to that which "produces" the pearl, but to the pearl itself, and so not to the living being that produces the pearl but to the thing produced by it. The performative is compared to a pearl inside the constative, inside the oyster or the world, a performative that seems to promise a new world or a radically new relation to the world, a pearl that is produced within the oyster not autonomously, by the oyster alone, but, as always with a pearl, as a reaction to something that has come into the oyster from the *outside* and that has acted as an irritant or incitement. No spontaneous generation, then, but a performative that acts in response or as a response to the outside, an oyster that forms a pearl in all its perfection thanks to a flaw or an intrusion, an accident or an infelicity, as it were, within the oyster.

. . . (Hence the *perle*, in French, as both a thing and a thing of language, an image of perfection and distortion, a gemstone and an unwitting deformation within language, a doing things with words that works only because some rule of grammar or some law of the lexicon has been broken in an amusing way, producing what we might call a real doozy or, better, a real "gem."[4])

The performative pearl, like an unborn child awaiting its *acte de naissance*, its birth act, is thus linked not to the present but to the future, not to the generation of the one who will have pronounced it but to the next generation, to a declaration of love or of peace that will not simply affirm what already is the case but that will bring it about, an act of love or of peace within a declaration of war, a performative pearl waiting for its time, for a future that may not ever simply be affirmed in a present. The pearl inside the oyster, like the performer in our "encore" for "Derrida in Montreal," enveloped in his or her cocoon, waiting for his or her time. A pearl, an unborn child—"I must carry you," "I must bear you," as a declaration of love or of peace in a time of war, a performative pearl that promises peace coiled up inside what is also a testamentary goodbye in Derrida's final seminar, a performative within the world that somehow goes beyond the world in which it is spoken—or written—a performative pearl that would also be a work, or a lesson, waiting for its time. For what we have come to learn is that a work, untethered from the present, from action, from all present actors, a work, an oeuvre, is never synchronous with its own time. We can thus never know with any certainty when a work or a seminar will have arrived at its destination, when a work or a seminar, a speech act or an act of pedagogy, has begun or ended. We may have thus gone there, gone to the seminar, to gather pearls of wisdom from the master's lips, but the real pearl was perhaps something else altogether, some performative lodged within, a declaration of love or of peace that is still waiting for its time.

Acknowledgments

This is a work about Jacques Derrida's engagement with speech act theory and pedagogy in two rather different but related settings: Derrida's public presentations and his seminars from the early 1970s through 2004. True to that double theme or source, this work was itself inspired by two different events, one having to do with a public presentation and the other a seminar. The first part of this work grew out of an invitation by Ginette Michaud to give a lecture at the University of Montreal in October 2018 to mark the fourteenth anniversary of Derrida's death. It was that invitation that eventually led to the publication of *Derrida à Montréal: Une pièce en trois actes* (Presses de l'Université de Montréal, 2019), which has been translated and rewritten for the first part of the present work. Let me thank here publicly Ginette Michaud for her generous invitation to present and publish that work and for her invaluable help with the French-language edition of that text. I am also very grateful to Ginette's colleagues at the University of Montreal, and especially to Georges Leroux, who paid me the extreme honor of writing an afterword to that Quebecois edition.

The second event at the origin of this work was a twenty-week graduate seminar in 2018–19 on the theme of "Derrida and Speech Act Theory" that I taught at DePaul University with my colleague Elizabeth Rottenberg. Many of the ideas of this work had their first airing during that seminar and were subsequently refined thanks to the comments and suggestions of my colleague and the dozen or so students who participated in the seminar.

A few pages from the first part of this work were originally published in the fiftieth-anniversary issue of *Research in Phenomenology* in 2020. I would like to thank here John Sallis and Jim Risser for granting me permission to publish a revised version of those pages. The first chapter of the second part of this work was first published in French in the journal *Philosophiques* in a special issue entitled *Derrida en cours* (Montréal, 2019), under the title "*L'agrégation, le programme: La chance de* La vie la mort." I thank Nicholas Cotton and Maxime Plante, editors of that special issue and, as chance would have it, students of Ginette Michaud, for the invitation to contribute to that issue and for their help with the rewriting and editing of my contribution. A few pages from this chapter on Derrida's reading of Jacob were also rewritten with an eye toward the more general question of contingency and included in the essay "Dumb Luck: Jacques Derrida and the Problem of Contingency," in *Throwing the Moral Dice: Ethics and the Problem of Contingency*, edited by Thomas Claviez and Viola Marchi (Fordham University Press, 2021). Early versions of this chapter were presented at the University of Toronto, thanks to an invitation from Owen Ware, and at the University of Michigan at a conference devoted to *Life Death* organized by Sergio Villalobos Ruminott. I am grateful to Owen, Sergio, and the faculty and students at both institutions for their questions, comments, and suggestions. An early version of the second chapter of the second part of this work was published in spring 2020 in *Studies in Philosophy and Education* in a special issue on *Derrida and Education Today*. My thanks to the journal and to the editor of that special issue, Emile Bojesen, for allowing me to publish a revised version of that essay here. Finally, an early version of the third chapter was first presented at the University of Vienna at the invitation of Jason Wesley Alvis and Michael Staudigl. I thank them and their colleagues for their generous invitation and their many helpful comments on this work.

Notes

Introduction: The Program

1. Austin's title plays, obviously, on the American tradition of the "self-help" book, such as Dale Carnegie's *How to Win Friends and Influence People* (1936).

2. In the beginning of "Ulysses Gramophone" Derrida evokes the distinction between *use* and *mention* in the context of the double valence of the "yes, yes [*oui, oui*]" with which he begins the essay: "In the first case, I affirm, acquiesce, subscribe to, approve, reply, or make a promise; at any rate, I commit myself and I sign: to take up again the old speech act theory distinction, which is useful up to a certain point, between *use* and *mention*, the use of *oui* is always implicated in the moment of a signature. In the second case, I would, rather, have quoted or mentioned the *oui, oui*" ("UG" 256–257/58).

3. As a sign of just one of the many overlaps between Derrida's public presentations and his teaching, this lecture on Nietzsche was initially presented in Paris in 1975 in one of the opening sessions of the seminar *Life Death*, one of the three seminars that will be at the center of the second part of this work.

Act 1: The Context (1971)

1. For a lucid and philosophically astute account of the event, see Luce Fontaine-De Visscher and Christian Wenin, "Le XVe Congrès des Sociétés de philosophe de langue française," *Revue Philosophique de Louvain* 69, no. 4 (1971): 572–577.

2. The conference took place from August 29 to September 2, 1971. Benoît Peeters tells us in his biography *Derrida* that "Paul Ricoeur gave the inaugural lecture. Derrida spoke just afterwards, giving the paper 'Signature Event Context,' a reading of Austin that would give rise, a few years later, to a polemic with John R. Searle that would create many ripples. But for now, it was with Ricoeur that

159

Derrida had a long and lively [*vive*] discussion that subsequently continued through their respective writings." See Benoît Peeters, *Derrida: A Biography*, trans. Andrew Brown (Cambridge: Polity Press, 2013), 226.

All this seems to be confirmed by Derrida in a footnote apparently added after the fact to an interview in 1972: "'Signature Event Context' analyzes the metaphysical premises of the Anglo-Saxon—and fundamentally moralistic—theory of the performative, of speech acts or discursive events. In France, it seems to me that these premises underlie the hermeneutics of Ricoeur and the archaeology of Foucault." "Avoir l'oreille de la philosophie," in an interview with Lucette Finas in *Écarts: Quatres essays à propos de Jacques Derrida*, by Lucette Finas, Sarah Kofman, Roger Laporte, and Jean-Michel Rey (Paris: Fayard, 1973), 309; originally published in *La Quinzaine littéraire*, November 16–30, 1972; cited by Derrida himself at "LI" 39/80. Luce Fontaine-De Visscher and Christian Wenin describe the debate between Ricoeur and Derrida during colloquium in this way: "MM. Ricoeur and Derrida engaged in a friendly sparring match that turned out to be highlight of the session for many of those attending the congress. The exchange of views allowed everyone to get a clearer sense of what distinguishes these two modes of thought" ("Le XVe Congrès des Sociétés de Philosophie de Langue Française," 573–574).

3. "Communication" might thus not have been, in this case, the best translation of the French "*communication*"; "lecture" or "talk" might have been more accurate. And yet any translation other than "communication" would have obscured the relationship between Derrida's talk and the topic of the colloquium; in short, any other translation would have led to even greater problems of "communication."

4. This reading of Condillac would be developed, as we know, two years later in Derrida's *Archaeology of the Frivolous*. But it has recently come to light that Derrida planned to publish yet another book on Condillac right around this same time, a book in two columns, like *Glas*, with a reading of Condillac on questions of philosophical method, and particularly the relationship between philosophy and rhetoric, in the left column and a reading of Condillac in conjunction with Freud's *Beyond the Pleasure Principle* in the right column. The text was apparently never completed, and the project was abandoned, but the seventy or so pages of the manuscript have recently been edited and presented by Geoffrey Bennington and Katie Chenoweth under the title *Le calcul des langues: Distyle* (Paris: Editions du Seuil, 2020). The following passage from *Du droit à la philosophie*, which I will turn to in some detail in the introduction to the second part of this work, could function as an epigraph to Derrida's reading in *Le calcul des langues* of Condillac—one of the French "ideologues" who wished to rethink the teaching and discipline of philosophy in France: "What has been called 'deconstruction' is also the *exposure* of this institutional identity of the discipline of philosophy: what is irreducible about it must be exposed as such, that is to say, shown, watched over, laid claim to, but in that which opens it and ex-appropriates it, as what is proper in its properness distances itself from itself in order to relate to itself—first of all, in the least of its questions about itself" (*WAP* 9/*DDP* 22). This alone is perhaps enough to explain the form of Derrida's own text from 1973, its doubled columns, its inserts

and detours, its questioning of the supposed method of philosophy (as opposed to rhetoric) and of the institutional identity of philosophy, its interrogation of the proper form for philosophy to be practiced (the treatise or the book) and its juxtaposition of Condillac with Freud's *Beyond the Pleasure Principle* on questions of method and *pleasure* (questions that will return just a couple of years later in *Life Death* in an even more in-depth reading of Freud's 1920 text).

5. Derrida had already anticipated this earlier in passing when he suggested that while Condillac defines writing in relation to the absence of the addressee, he is silent about the absence of the addressor or the sender: "The absence of the sender, the addressor, from the marks that he abandons, which are cut off from him and continue to produce effects beyond his presence, and beyond the present actuality of his meaning, that is, beyond his life itself, this absence, which however belongs to the structure of all writing—and I will add, further on, of all language in general—the absence is never examined by Condillac" ("SEC" 313/372).

6. Derrida speaks in a similar way in "Limited Inc" of "a certain legibility that is operative beyond the disappearance or demise of the presumed author" ("LI" 62/121), and he recalls his own analysis in *Spurs* of all the possible ways of taking Nietzsche's "I forgot my umbrella" ("LI" 62–63/121–122).

7. Derrida writes just after that: "I will extend this law [the law of iterability] even to all 'experience' in general, if it is granted that there is no experience of *pure* presence, but only chains of differential marks" ("SEC" 318/378).

8. As Derrida affirms in "Limited Inc," "the structure of iteration . . . implies *both* identity *and* difference" ("LI" 53/105).

9. In "Signature Event Context" Derrida recalls that "across empirical variations of tone, of voice, etc. . . . one must be able to recognize the identity, shall we say, of a signifying form" ("SEC" 318/378). And in "Limited Inc" he speaks of iterability as what "ruins (even ideally) the very identity it renders possible" ("LI" 76/144).

10. For this notion of *remains* (*reste, restance*), "Limited Inc" is again extremely helpful: "The rest of the trace, its remains [*restance*], are neither present nor absent" ("LI" 83/156–157). For the difference between these remains or this remaining and Searle's notion of "permanence," the so-called permanence of writing, see "LI" 51–54/102–107.

11. Derrida thus says about a statement such as "the sky is blue," "the structure of possibility of this statement includes the capability of being formed [*de pouvoir être formé*] and of functioning [*et de pouvoir fonctionner*] either as an empty reference, or cut off from its referent" ("SEC" 318–319/379).

12. For example, some three decades later, during the second year of his seminar on *The Death Penalty*, Derrida returns to the question of capacity and the speech act, linking it, this time, to sovereignty, to the sovereign power to decide. Speaking of the supposedly "performative 'I can' of decision" and of the "sovereign 'I' in general," Derrida remarks: "An 'I' itself never decides anything. Precisely because it can. The consequences of these statements are formidable" (*DP2* 127/175; see also 87/126).

13. The title is a play on the title of Descartes's "Fifth Meditation," "Concerning the Essence of Material Things, and Again Concerning God, That He Exists" (see "LI" 82/154–155).

14. John L. Austin, *Quand dire, c'est faire*, trans. Gilles Lane (Paris: Éditions du Seuil, 1970).

15. Austin adds at this point, "this is not, if you come to think of it, a large claim" (*HDT* 3–4), since there have been, if I understand Austin's irony correctly here, so few revolutions in philosophy.

16. In addition to all the well-known points of common interest for Derrida and Austin (the emphasis on *force* as well as *meaning*, on juridical performances such as perjury and pardoning, and, especially, on promising, and on a sort of implicit or originary performative that conditions even the constative—a "yes" or an "I believe" or an "I ask you to believe me when I tell you" that would precede every constative), there are other points of convergence that are less well known. For example, *cats*, not the musical but the animal. Cats are often mixed in as a bit of spice in Austin's English humor, as when he says, for example, "There are more ways of killing a cat than drowning it in butter" (*HDT* 48). And Austin's favorite example of a constative is none other than "the cat is on the mat." Derrida uses cats in neither of these ways, but in *The Animal That Therefore I Am* it is a cat in the bathroom (perhaps on a mat, we are not told) staring at Derrida naked that seems to motivate many of Derrida's reflections on animals in general.

But then there is this extremely odd connection between Derrida and Austin: both of them would have produced or would have worked on major works revolving around the "phonestheme" *gl*. For Derrida, that would be *Glas* (1974), while for Austin it would be the work he was writing at the time of his death. I cite the end of the Wikipedia entry on the life of J. L. Austin:

Austin died at the age of 48 of lung cancer. At the time, he was developing a semantic theory based on sound symbolism, using the English gl-words as data. For example, the English phonestheme "gl-" occurs in a large number of words relating to light or vision, like "glitter," "glisten," "glow," "gleam," "glare," "glint," "glimmer," "gloss," and so on; yet, despite this, the remainder of each word is not itself a phonestheme (i.e., a pairing of form and meaning); i.e., "-isten," "-ow," and "-eam" do not make meaningful contributions to "glisten," "glow," and "gleam." See https://en.wikipedia.org/wiki/J._L._Austin.

17. Derrida clarifies in "Limited Inc": "*Sec never said* that this absence is *necessary*, but only that it is *possible* . . . and that this possibility must therefore be taken into account: it pertains, *qua possibility*, to the structure of the mark as such" ("LI" 47/95).

18. Of course, the reasons for this lack of purity will be different for Austin and Derrida: whereas, for Austin, the performative is not pure because it can never be completely distinguished from the constative, for Derrida it is this general citationality that makes it impossible to distinguish the serious, successful performative from the nonserious or unsuccessful one, a general citationality, itself based on a general iterability, which introduces difference, absence, and so on, into every mark,

every utterance, every convention, every speech act. For Austin, the pure performative remains an ideal or an abstraction that certain utterances can approach but never achieve. For Derrida, every successful or normal performative is necessarily impure, necessarily caught up in iterability and parasitism ("SEC" 325/388; see 328–329/391–392).

19. This will not mean, as Searle will claim, that Derrida thinks Austin thinks that parasitical uses of language—in a poem or on a stage—are not part of "ordinary language." They certainly are, but in such a way that they transform our very understanding of what "normal" or "ordinary" language is. As Derrida writes in "Limited Inc": "the logic of parasitism is not a logic of distinction or of opposition" ("LI" 96/177–178; see 90/167–168, 99–100/184–185, 103/190–191), for "you cannot root-out the 'parasite' without rooting-out the 'standard' [*le 'propre*'] at the same time. What is at work here is a *different* logic of mimesis" ("LI" 90/168). Derrida returns at some length to these arguments in "Afterword: Toward An Ethic of Discussion" (see especially "ATE" 127–131/230–237).

20. Derrida makes this even clearer in "Limited Inc" when he writes, for example, "*at no time* does *Sec* invoke the *absence*, pure and simple, of intentionality" ("LI" 56/110). "What the text questions is not intention or intentionality but their *telos*, which orients and organizes the movement and the possibility of a fulfillment, realization, and *actualization* in a plenitude that would be *present* to and identical with itself" ("LI" 56/110). That is, "what is limited by iterability is not intentionality in general, but its character of being conscious or present to itself (actualized, fulfilled, and adequate), the simplicity of its features, its *undividedness*" ("LI" 105/194). Hence Derrida is very clear in about his intentions *not* to do away with the category of intention but to question the terms in which it has traditionally been understood. He writes, for example, "Intention is a priori (at once) *différante*: differing and deferring, in its inception . . . It is divided and deported in advance, by its iterability, towards others, removed in advance from itself" ("LI" 56/111). And it is nothing other than "the structure of the mark" that "always divides or removes intention, preventing it from being fully present to itself in the actuality of its aim, or of its meaning (i.e., what it means-to-say [*vouloir-dire*])" ("LI" 57/113). Hence it is not the category itself that is in question but, as Derrida goes on to argue, "the plenitude of intentional meaning [*vouloir-dire*], and all of the other values—of consciousness, presence, and originary intuition—which organize phenomenology" ("LI" 58/114). Derrida insists on this because it is one of the major points of contention with Searle: "I repeat that *Sec never* adduced, from the possibility of this 'break,' the pure and simple absence of all intentionality in the functioning of the mark that remains; rather, what it calls into question is the presence of a fulfilled and actualized intentionality, adequate to itself and to its contents" ("LI" 64/124).

21. The language of psychoanalysis can be found throughout "Limited Inc," everything from "incorporation" ("LI" 77/146, 84–85/158, 102/190; Derrida mentions *Glas* and *Fors*) to "pleasure" ("LI" 37/77–78, 44/90), "delight [*jouissance*]" ("LI" 72/137), pleasure in relation to "repetition" ("LI" 35/73–74), the possibility

of "unconscious pleasure" ("LI" 75/143), to, finally, the "unconscious," a "structural unconscious" ("LI" 73/139), and "the Unconscious . . . as the great Parasite of every ideal model of a speech act (simple, serious, literal, strict, etc.)" ("LI" 74/140). It is this latter notion that helps explain, at least in part, how, for Derrida, every promise is haunted (perhaps unconsciously) by a threat ("LI" 74–75/141–142).

22. Derrida here writes, in a passage that will greatly exercise Searle: "Is it that in excluding the general theory of this structural parasitism, Austin, who nevertheless pretends to describe the facts and events of ordinary language, makes us accept as ordinary a teleological and ethical determination (the univocality of the statement . . . the self-presence of a total context, the transparency of intentions, the presence of meaning for the absolutely singular oneness of a speech act, etc.)?" ("SEC" 325/387) In other words, Austin appears to be asking us to take what *ought to be* for what *is*. Derrida recalls in "Limited Inc" his emphasis in "Signature Event Context" on "the ethical and teleological discourse of consciousness" ("LI" 76–77/145), on "the teleological lure [*leurre*] of consciousness" ("SEC" 327/389).

23. Let me underscore here that this difference between speech and writing in terms of the relative detachment from the origin or the source is Austin's. When Searle thus says in his "Reply" that the real difference between speech and writing is the relative permanence of the latter, he is not defending Austin but deviating from him.

24. This is true notwithstanding Searle's claim, which we will look at later, that I am "present" to my writing when I carry around the shopping list I made out earlier or when I write notes to a friend sitting beside me at a conference or a concert. It is hard to know whether to take Searle seriously here. Sure, the writer is "present" in some sense in the supermarket with his list, or "present" in the lecture hall with his note, but he is hardly present in or to the writing itself, and the mere fact that that list can be lost or misplaced in the store and those notes taken by someone else in the lecture hall should be enough to prove that.

25. Derrida writes, "the word 'improbable,' in the first (French) version of the text, which was published *without* the handwritten signature in the Proceedings of the Colloquium (*La communication*, Montréal, 1973), is the next to the last word of the text. The last one, which is not my signature, is 'signature': 'the most improbable signature'" ("LI" 34/72–73). So the essay was published in 1971 without the signature (or signatures) and then with it (or them) when it was published in 1972 in *Marges de la philosophie*.

Intermission 1: Glyph 1

1. Derrida raises at several different moments these personal or rather autobiographical aspects of Searle's text. He says, for example, that Searle presents himself as the "self-proclaimed heir (especially when the father has died too young, at the age of 48!)" ("LI" 42/85); "he alone shall have the right of criticizing or correcting his teacher, defending him before the others at the very moment of murderous identification, of parricide" ("LI" 42/86). "Thus, Sarl would like to be Austin's sole legitimate heir *and* his sole critic" ("LI" 42/86).

2. For a clear and balanced analysis of the debate, see Raoul Moati's *Derrida/Searle: Deconstruction and Ordinary Language*, trans. Timothy Attanucci and Maureen Chun (New York: Columbia University Press, 2014).

3. Derrida's argument here is utterly convincing: "The 'shopping list for myself' would be neither producible nor utilizable, it would not be what it is nor could it even exist, were it not possible for it to function, from the very beginning, in the absence of sender and of receiver" ("LI" 49/98). Hence "the sender of the shopping list is not the same as the receiver, even if they bear the same name and are endowed with the identity of a single ego" ("LI" 49/98).

4. Hence, as Derrida asserts, "the possibility of a *certain* absence (even a relative one) must then be conceded and the consequences must be drawn" ("LI" 57/113).

5. As Derrida argues in "Limited Inc": "These notes are only legible or writable to the extent that my neighbor can do without my being present in order to read whatever I could write without his being present" ("LI" 50/99–100).

Act 2: The Signature (1979)

1. Derrida writes all this, one must not forget, in late 1976 or early 1977, at the age of forty-six, and he wrote those pages on Nietzsche's *Ecce Homo* in *Otobiographies* in 1975, at the age of forty-five, the very age that Nietzsche himself speaks of at the beginning of *Ecce Homo* ("I buried my forty-fourth year today . . .").

2. The question first arose, Derrida says, during a discussion the preceding day at McGill University: "Yesterday, during a session at McGill University, someone asked me a question about the word 'deconstruction.' I said that when I made use of this word (rarely, very rarely in the beginning . . .), I had the impression that it was a word among many others, a secondary word in the text which would fade or which in any case would assume a non-dominant place in a system" (*EO* 85–86/ *OA* 117).

3. "By going around the table, we could remark the fact that not one of us is like a fish in water in the language he or she is speaking. Unless I am mistaken, not one of the subjects at this table speaks French as his or her maternal tongue, except perhaps two of us. And, even then, you [Péraldi] are French; I'm not. I come from Algeria. I have therefore still another relation to the French tongue" (*EO* 146/ *OA* 192).

4. See "Déclarations d'indépendance," in *Otobiographies: L'enseignement de Nietzsche et la politique du nom propre* (Paris: Éditions Galilée, 1984), 11–32. This volume is accompanied by the following note: "Complete text of a lecture given in French at the University of Virginia (Charlottesville) in 1976. Until now it had been published only in German. . . . A part of the same lecture was delivered a second time at the University of Montreal in 1979 during a colloquium and round table whose proceedings were published in Canada in 1982 (*The Ear of the Other: Otobiography, Transference, Translation*, Texts and Discussions with Jacques Derrida under the direction of Claude Lévesque and Christie V. McDonald)" (my translation). It is clear from this note that Derrida read *all* of *Otobiographies* at the University of Virginia and that when he presented it again at the University of Montreal he left out the chapter "Declarations of Independence."

5. In "Limited Inc" Derrida recalls this phrase from near the end of "Signature Event Context," "to conclude this very *dry* discussion [*Pour conclure ce propos très sec*]," and then comments: "*Sec* is set there—in a manner which, you may take my word for it, was hardly fortuitous—in italics. Three points follow, which lead to the apparent simulacrum of 'my' signatures, of my seal in bits and pieces, divided, multiplied. . . . *Signature Event Context* might also lend credence to the parasite of a 'true' dependent proposition: 'signature event that one texts' [*signature événement qu'on texte*]. Concerning the calculated necessity of this neological usage of the verb *text* [*texter*], cf. '*Having the Ear of Philosophy*' [*Avoir l'oreille de la philosophie*], Conversation with Lucette Finas, reprinted in *Écarts, Quatre essais à propos de Jacques Derrida* (Paris, 1973)" ("LI" 108n1/67n1). Let me say here in passing that when Derrida uses "*texter*" as a verb he was obviously not talking in 1971 about what we today call "texting," though the phenomenon would have hardly surprised him, and one could imagine an abbreviation or acronym such as SEC, with or without emoji, becoming a staple of texting culture.

Intermission 2: Glyph 2

1. First published in *Glyph 2* (1977): 162–254, and translated by Samuel Weber, the essay "Limited Inc a b c . . ." was later published in the volume *Limited Inc* (Evanston, IL: Northwestern University Press, 1988), 29–110. This volume also includes "Signature Event Context," trans. Samuel Weber and Jeffrey Mehlman, 1–23; Gerald Graff's "Summary of 'Reiterating the Differences,'" 25–27; and "Afterword: Toward An Ethic of Discussion," trans. Samuel Weber, 111–154. "Limited Inc a b c . . ." was first published in French in a special "supplement" to *Glyph 2*, and then in *Limited Inc* (Paris: Éditions Galilée, 1990), 61–197, which also includes "Signature événement contexte," 15–51; "Réitération des différences: Réponse à Derrida," by John R. Searle, Summary by Gerald Graff, 53–59; and "Postface: Vers une éthique de la discussion," 199–285. Given that the intention of the volume *Limited Inc* was obviously to gather together in one place all the elements of the debate between Derrida and Searle, one would expect the latter's "Reply" to be included. But Benoît Peeters recalls that the debate became so acrimonious that "Searle would refuse to allow his text to be reprinted next to Derrida's in the volume *Limited Inc.*" Peeters, *Derrida: A Biography*, trans. Andrew Brown (Cambridge: Polity Press, 2013), 327; see also the Editor's Foreword to *Limited Inc*, vii/14.

As for the title "Limited Inc," the incorporation into a single phrase of two corporate designations, one English and the other American, also leads, of course, to the virtual sentence: "There is limited ink," "I have limited ink," which suggests that, at a certain point—it will take eighty-five pages—Derrida's pen or printer will run dry (*sec*). But the title also gestures toward Austin's posthumously published "Three Ways of Spilling Ink" (see "LI" 73/139, 109n3/90–91n1). As for the "a b c" of the title, Derrida is referring both to the twenty-four letters of the French alphabet that will structure his text and to Searle's unvoiced assumptions regarding phonetic writing: "Sarl adheres to a narrow definition of writing as the *transcription* or *representation* of speech. He thereby adheres to a certain interpretation of phonetic writing, indeed to the alphabetic model, to the *a b c*'s of logo-phonocentrism" ("LI" 79/149; see also 45/90 and 86/162).

Derrida says in "Limited Inc" that he received Searle's reply before Christmas 1976 ("LI" 30/64). This would have thus been approximately six months after the end of the *Life Death* seminar (1975–76), just five months after "Declarations of Independence," and a couple of months after the beginning of his seminar *Theory and Practice* (1976–77).

2. Does the debate "take place"? Derrida asks throughout "Limited Inc" whether one can really know "what it means for events taking the form of apparently written speech acts to take place or not to take place" ("LI" 35–36/75; see 107/197).

3. In addition to Searle and Sarl there is "*sceau*," seal, as in "Sarl's seal" ("LI" 57/112), *sceau* being already a word from *sec* ("LI" 31/66). It is almost as if Searle had been designated or set up from the start to be the one to respond to "Signature Event Context."

4. Derrida goes on in this text to comment explicitly on this -ability, this being-possible, which must be distinguished from every power on the part of a subject: "What must be included in the description, i.e., in *what* is described, but also in the practical discourse, in the *writing that describes*, is not merely the factual reality of corruption and of alteration [*de l'écart*] . . . but corrupt*ability* . . . and . . . dissocia*bility*, traits tied to iter*ability*, which SEC proposes to account for. That can only be done if the '-bility' (and not the lability) is recognized from the *inception* on [dès *l'entame*] as broached and breached [*entamée*] in its origin by iter*ability*" ("LI" 78/146–147).

5. Searle has the odd habit of claiming something that Derrida also claims and then objecting to the fact that Derrida himself does not claim it. Derrida can hardly get over the gesture: "It is strange that, after having recalled that *Sec* analyzed the characteristics *common* both to writing and speech, the *objection* is made that, from the standpoint of iterability, there is no difference: precisely the thesis of *Sec*, if there is one" ("LI" 46/93). Derrida returns to this bizarre argumentative "strategy" in several places (see "LI" 47/94, 55/109, 77/146, and 105/194).

6. Derrida wishes to show that "the exclusions practiced by Austin," exclusions that "*present themselves as* procedures of strategic or methodological suspension," are all part of a strategy that is "fraught with metaphysical presuppositions" ("LI" 85/160; see 93/173).

Act 3: The Event (1997)

1. The scholars in question are Gad Soussana, a young philosopher who at the time was completing his thesis on the question of the event in Hegel, and Alexis Nouss (Nuselovici), a professor in the Department of Linguistics and Translation at the University of Montreal.

2. Derrida also writes in these same pages: "At the very moment when someone would like to say or to write, 'On the twentieth . . . etc.,' the very factor that will permit the mark (be it psychic, oral, graphic) to function beyond this moment—namely the possibility of its being repeated *another* time—breaches, divides,

expropriates the 'ideal' plenitude or self-presence of intention, of meaning (to say) and, a fortiori, of all adequation between meaning and saying" ("LI" 62/120). In other words, Derrida continues, "the graphics of iterability inscribes alteration irreducibly in repetition" ("LI" 62/120). For Derrida's reading of "the date" in Celan, see *Shibboleth* (in *SQ* 1–64).

3. René Lévesque (1922–87) was a reporter, a minister of the government of Quebec, the founder of the Parti Québécois, and the twenty-third premier of Quebec.

4. Benoît Peeters, *Derrida: A Biography*, trans. Andrew Brown (Cambridge: Polity Press, 2013), 431; the reference here is to "Marx & Sons" ("MS" 224/27).

5. Derrida argues in "Limited Inc" that we must distinguish between *possibilité* and *éventualité*, a distinction that, Derrida is well aware, is difficult to render in English. He writes, for example: "*Sec* distinguishes clearly between *possibility* [*possibilité*] and *eventuality* [*éventualité*] . . . it is regrettable that the distinction made in *Sec* between *possibility* and *eventuality* was not rendered in the English translation" ("LI" 86–87/162; Bass's translation does, in fact, distinguish between the two). Just a few pages later, he writes: "A standard act depends as much upon the possibility being repeated, and thus potentially [*éventuellement*] of being mimed, feigned, cited, played, simulated, parasited, etc." ("LI" 91–92/171; see also 57/112 and 88/164).

6. Derrida writes of this "perhaps" in "Limited Inc": "In leaving the existence of writing undecidable, the 'perhaps' marks the fact that the 'possibility' of graphematics places writing (and the rest) outside the authority of ontological discourse" ("LI" 83/156).

7. These comments are echoed several years later in a public debate with Jean Baudrillard held just weeks before the American invasion of Iraq in March 2003 (see *PG* 37–38).

8. See my comments on the notion of an originary or elementary faith in *Miracle and Machine: Jacques Derrida and the Two Sources of Religion, Science, and the Media* (New York: Fordham University Press, 2012), especially 75–76.

Encore: Cocoon

1. See *EO* 87 and Peggy Kamuf's comments on the epigraph to this "Encore" in her *Book of Addresses* (Stanford, CA: Stanford University Press, 2005), 26–27.

2. Elsewhere in *Glas* we read: "Derrière, behind, isn't it always already behind a curtain, a veil, a weaving. A fleecing text. [*Derrière n'est-ce pas toujours déjà derrière un rideau, un voile, un tisage. Un texte toisonnant*]" (68bi/80bi); "In Algeria, in the middle of a mosque the colonists would have transformed into a synagogue, the Torah, brought forth from behind the curtains [*En Algérie, au milieu d'une mosquée que les colons auraient transformée en synagogue, une fois sortie de derrière les rideaux, la Thora*]" (240bi/268bi).

3. During one of the roundtables in 1979, Claude Lévesque brings up this notion of the *rideau* and the phrase *derrière le rideau* as a signature of Derrida, who responds: "I agree entirely with what you said . . . about the disseminated name

'*derrière le rideau*,' which, already in *Glas*, was the object of a certain amount of work. And you're right, playing with one's own name, putting it in play, is, in effect, what is always going on and what I have tried to do in a somewhat more explicit or systematic manner for some time now and in certain texts. But obviously this is not something that one can decide: one doesn't disseminate or play with one's name. The very structure of the proper name sets this process in motion. That's what the proper name is for. . . . So now every time you utter the word '*derrière*,' you'll be paying a tax to my name, settling up what you owe" (*EO* 76–77/*OA* 104–105).

The Counter-Program: Syllabus

1. This scene is actually one of the Derrida interview "outtakes" included in the DVD version of the film.

2. Among the many "faithful" who attended Derrida's seminar year after year were Marguerite Derrida, Hélène Cixous, Marie-Louise Mallet, and the unforgettable Georges Comtesse. A Lacanian analyst and fixture on the French intellectual scene from the 1960s to 1990s, Comtesse regularly attended for decades both Derrida's and Deleuze's seminars. In Derrida's seminar, at least, he was regularly the first person to ask a question, or to try to do so, when Derrida opened up the floor. Those who attended Derrida's seminar will recall the intense, animated tone of those questions, which invariably tried to relate the subject of the seminar—whatever it was—to questions of madness. I once asked Derrida in the spring of 1991 about Comtesse, and he said: "This is very interesting. You know that he has been my student for thirty-one years now; from the very beginning he has been there. He got his diploma long ago and he teaches but he still comes. For thirty-one years he has been coming to my seminar and he never agrees with me. He always speaks in the name of madness or paranoia, and he always contests what I say. But this is really the very image of fidelity, and it is probably because of this that I have grown really to love him. He is the most faithful of all my students even though he seems never to agree with anything I say." Knowing, I have to think, that the second year of *The Beast and the Sovereign* would be his last seminar, Derrida pays Comtesse a fitting tribute in the middle of the fifth session of the seminar, inscribing his name into the record as it were. Not simply mentioning Comtesse in an oral aside in the midst of the seminar but reminding himself to mention him in the written version of the seminar, Derrida says: "An article communicated to me (and I thank him for it) by our friend Comtesse rightly insists . . ." (*BS 2* 133/196).

3. For whatever reason, Derrida continued to give his seminar in the Salle Dussane of the École Normale Supérieure into the 1990s, well after his official move from ENS to the École des Hautes Études en Sciences Sociales in 1984.

4. There are, apparently, no seminar materials, whether handwritten or typed, in the archives for the academic years 1966–67 and 1967–68.

5. It was in large part the completed nature of these texts that convinced those close to Derrida to publish the seminars. See the Editors' General Introductions to the seminars (for example, *La vie la mort*, 7–9/*Life Death*, ix–x).

6. This was the case as well for Derrida's presentation of many of these same sessions in the United States. Derrida taught mostly in French in the early days at Yale and Hopkins, but at Irvine he would often either read an English translation that had been prepared for him (often by Peggy Kamuf) or else improvise a translation on the spot.

7. For a more complete and sophisticated account of the events that led to the creation of GREPH, see Vivienne Orchard's masterful account in *Jacques Derrida and the Institution of French Philosophy* (London: Legenda, 2011). Others, such as Canadian researcher Nicholas Cotton, are currently in the process of working through Derrida's vast corpus on the themes of education. This work will eventually give us an even clearer and fuller picture of Derrida's own pedagogy and his parallel interest in questions of pedagogy.

8. This text first appeared in the collective volume *Politiques de la philosophie*, with texts by François Châtelet, Michel Foucault, Jean-François Lyotard, and Michel Serres (Paris: Grasset, 1976).

9. One will notice here Derrida's use of the word "program," a word that is constantly submitted to critique by Derrida but will never be completely abandoned by him. Monographs remain to be written about Derrida's use of this term in its biological, cybernetic, educational, and even ethical context, the way in which, for example, Derrida will frequently suggest that a genuinely ethical decision (if there is one, as Derrida always hastens to add) must always exceed any kind of program or programmation, that is, any kind of machinal or automatic deployment of a prior set of rules or procedures.

10. As Vivienne Orchard argues, while "GREPH cannot simply be subsumed into Derrida's oeuvre without remainder," "his role and involvement were crucial, and his participation is significant within the trajectory of his work in general" (*Jacques Derrida*, 2). The text "Where a Teaching Body Begins and How It Ends," a text that, as Derrida says at the outset, is little more than a series of notes and was not initially intended for publication, helps confirm this when it lists at the conclusion GREPH's provisional administrative address as the École Normale Supérieure (rue d'Ulm, 75005) and Derrida as the person to whom all correspondence should be addressed. All this confirms Orchard's claim that while Derrida was hardly alone in founding of GREPH he was "the key figure of the group, its public figure-head," its "soul," even, as Vladimir Jankélévitch would put it (see *Jacques Derrida*, 2).

11. This is the theme of Simon Morgan Wortham's excellent study *Counter-Institutions: Jacques Derrida and the Question of the University* (New York: Fordham University Press, 2006), still one of the only works to date to treat in any detail Derrida's engagement with educational institutions from a philosophical as well as a historical perspective. See especially chapter 1, "Counter-Institution, Counter-Deconstruction," 25–43.

12. The single volume *Du droit à la philosophie* (Paris: Galilée, 1990) was thus published in two separate volumes in English translation. The first, *Who's Afraid of Philosophy? Right to Philosophy 1*, trans. Jan Plug (Stanford, CA: Stanford University Press, 2002), contains Derrida's long preface and the first of the French edition's

four parts. The title of the English edition is the title of that first part. The second English volume, *Eyes of the University, Right to Philosophy 2*, trans. Jan Plug and others (Stanford, CA: Stanford University Press, 2004), contains parts II–IV of the French edition, the third of which gives its title to the English edition. Though there are a few texts that complicate such a simple division, most of the texts in *Who's Afraid of Philosophy? Right to Philosophy 1* address questions of the teaching of philosophy in high school and the attempts by GREPH to extend that teaching to lower grades, while *The Eyes of the University* essentially addresses, as its title indicates, the teaching of philosophy in the "university," with several texts devoted to the founding of the Collège International de Philosophie.

13. The first of these, *Qui a peur de la philosophie?* (Who's Afraid of Philosophy) (Paris: Flammarion, 1977), contains three essays about education, educational reform, and GREPH's role in confronting these reforms: "The Age of Hegel," "Philosophy and Its Classes," and "Divided Bodies: Reponses to *La Nouvelle Critique*." In addition to the three contributions by Derrida, there are essays by Sylviane Agacinski, Michel Bel Lassen, Roland Brunet, Michel Cresta, Alain Delormes, Claude Dis, Bernadette Gromer, Jean-Pierre Hédoin, Sarah Kofman, Michèle Le Doeuff, Jean-Pierre Lefebvre, Martine Meskel, Jean-Luc Nancy, Bernard Pautrat, Hélène Politis, and Michael Ryan.

14. This second collective volume, *États Généraux de la Philosophie* (Paris: Flammarion, 1979), includes Derrida's "Philosophie des États Généraux," 27–44, along with an introductory essay by Vladimir Jankélévitch, transcriptions of some of the discussions of participants at the Sorbonne during the Estates General, which drew more than 1,200 people, and then reports by various working groups on the Haby reforms, on redesigning the "programs" in philosophy, on the "extension" of teaching and research in philosophy, on the training of philosophy professors, on teaching and the media, and on women in philosophy, to name just a few. The beginning of the volume lists those who were part of the organizing committee, a veritable who's who of philosophers in France at the time: R. Brunet, D. Cahen, F. Châtelet, J. Colombel, C. Coutel, G. Deleuze, J. Derrida, J.-T. Desanti, E. de Fontenay, F. Godet, B. Graciet, M. Hocquet-Tessard, V. Jankélévitch, H. Joly, G. Kaléka, G. Labica, Ph. Lacoue-Labarthe, M.-L. Mallet, J.-L. Nancy, P. Ricoeur, and H. Védrine.

15. The second part of *Du droit à la philosophie* begins with two essays from 1984 addressing questions of the "language and institutions of philosophy," taking as their central example the relationship between French and Latin and the place of translation in sixteenth and seventeenth French philosophy, and particularly in Descartes. As Derrida recalls in a footnote, "The question of the idiom was at the center of a seminar I gave over several years on Philosophical Nationality and Nationalism, which was the necessary development of the 1983–84 seminar (Right to Philosophy) whose outline or schema I follow here. I hope to be able to prepare the seminar for publication later" (*WAP* 197n20/*DDP* 53n1). Two texts from the following year ("Theology of Translation" and "Vacant Chair") address, again, philosophical and theological questions of translation, in Kant, Schelling, and

Benjamin, but also the question of the division or conflict between the "faculties" in Kant and Heidegger's interpretation of the principle of reason.

16. See "Mochlos, or The Conflict of the Faculties," a text of 1980 that looks at questions of philosophy and the disciplines in Kant's 1789 *The Conflict of the Faculties*.

17. Derrida mentions in a footnote (*WAP* 204n4/*DP* 185–186) his treatment of Cousin in "works [*travaux*]," presumably the seminar of 1974–75, on "Ideology and the French Ideologues," as well as his treatment in 1975–76 of Nietzsche's *Ecce Homo* and *The Future of Our Educational Institutions* on the question of education. For the importance of Cousin in the debate over the role of philosophy in France, see Orchard, *Jacques Derrida*, 27–32.

18. "In Praise of Philosophy" (1981), for example, is an interview of 1981, first published in the newspaper *Libération*, while "Philosophy and Its Classes" from 1975 first appeared in *Le Monde de l'éducation*, and "Divided Bodies," an essay that explains and defends the project of GREPH and the place of philosophy in education, appeared in *La Nouvelle Critique* 84 (May 1975) and 85 (June 1975).

19. Three years later, in 1978, in "The Crisis in Teaching," an essay first delivered at a conference in Benin, Derrida talks about the development of philosophy in Africa, the heterogeneity of deconstruction, the Haby Reform of 1975, and, of course, of GREPH's opposition to this reform.

20. Such is the case for both "The Antinomies of the Philosophical Discipline," which originally appeared as the preface to the volume *La grève des philosophes: École et philosophie* (Paris: Osiris, 1986), and "Popularities: On the Right to the Philosophy of Right," originally published as the preface to *Les sauvages dans la cité: Auto-émancipation du peuple et instruction des prolétaires au XIXe siècle* (Seyssel: Éditions du Champ Vallon, 1985).

21. "Who's Afraid of Philosophy?" from 1980 is a series of remarks first given during a roundtable following the Estates General of Philosophy in 1979, where Derrida returns once again to the Haby Reform and the work of GREPH.

22. The first of these two works, "Titles (for the Collège international de philosophie)," was written by all the members of the commission charged with forming the Collège (François Châtelet, Jacques Derrida, Jean-Pierre Faye, and Dominique Lecourt), while the second, "Sendoffs (for the Collège international de philosophie)," was written by Derrida alone. Both texts were later published in *Le rapport bleu: Les sources historiques et théoriques du Collège international de philosophie* (Paris: Presses Universitaires de France, 1998), 19–45, 91–129, a collective work that documents the founding of the Collège International de Philosophie.

23. See "Punctuations: The Time of a Thesis." Almost fifty at the time, and already the author of more than a dozen books, some, such as *Of Grammatology*, *Writing and Difference*, *Margins of Philosophy*, and *Glas*, already acknowledged classics in Continental Philosophy, Derrida was able to apply for a Doctorat d'État on the basis of already published work. As a defense of sorts, "Punctuations" is addressed ostensibly to Derrida's committee or "jury," which consisted of Pierre Aubenque, Jean-Toussaint Desanti (Derrida's thesis supervisor), Maurice

de Gandillac (head of the jury), Henri Joly, Gilbert Lascault, and Emmanuel Levinas. Derrida here recounts in some detail his own intellectual itinerary from the 1960s onward; his early interest in literature and in phenomenology; his concentration on the question of "writing"; his identification with "deconstruction"; his focused writings on Heidegger, Blanchot, and Levinas, among others, his attempts at a less academic, more experimental kind of writing in texts such as *Glas* and *The Post Card*; and—to recall themes central to the first part of this work—his interest in speech act theory and his debate with John Searle (see *EU* 125/*DP* 455).

24. In this long preface of 1990, Derrida returns on a couple of occasions to questions that were central to "Signature Event Context" and "Limited Inc," though also, and perhaps more importantly, since Derrida would have just completed writing this text, to "Afterword: Toward An Ethic of Discussion," published in 1990 in *Limited Inc* as the last sustained contribution by Derrida to the "debate" with Searle. Derrida recalls, for example, the way in which "the *law of iterability* . . . limits (structurally and definitively) the pertinence of such a concept of the origin and of technique" (*WAP* 27/*DDP* 49) and he refers the reader in a note to both "Signature Event Context" and *Limited Inc* (*WAP* 197n16/*DDP* 49n1). A few pages later in the same essay he refers to Austin himself, who "reminds us that a word never has meaning by itself, but only in a sentence" (*WAP* 42/*DDP* 71).

25. Published by Éditions Galilée in 2001, *L'université sans condition* was first delivered in English at Stanford University on April 15, 1999 (not 1998, as a note in the Galilée edition has it).

26. See, again, Orchard, *Jacques Derrida*, 46.

27. In a public conversation with Hélène Cixous from March 2003; Derrida pushes this desire to the point of *jouissance*. He asks: "How is one to institute, in as refined a way as possible, the perverse polymorph that we all repress, in the university? . . . How to introduce *jouissance* into the university? . . . In an *interdisciplinary* manner. [*Laughter in the room*]" ("BR" 157).

28. One of the indexes of this tension can be seen in Derrida's use of the term or concept "program," that is, in Derrida's sustained critique of *and* continued reliance upon both this word and this notion. Indeed the very last text in the collection *Du droit à la philosophie*, the report of a 1989 Commission on Philosophy and Epistemology jointly chaired by Derrida and Jacques Bouveresse, makes a series of recommendations concerning the teaching of philosophy, the integration of philosophy with the teaching of other disciplines, the training of teachers, the place of philosophy in the baccalauréat exam, and a refinement of the various *programs* in philosophy in the lycée, including a list of texts on pedagogy and teaching that teachers should be encouraged to teach, texts such as Plato's *Meno*, *Phaedo*, and Book 7 of the *Republic*, Montaigne's essay "Of the Education of Children," the first two parts of Descartes's *Discourse on Method*, Locke's *Some Thoughts Concerning Education*, Rousseau's *Emile, or Of Education*, Kant's *On Education*, Hegel's pedagogical texts, Bergson's "Intellectual Effort" (in *Spiritual Energy*), and Alain's *Propos sur l'éducation*. What all this suggests is that while Derrida would have been the

first person to be *against* a set cannon, that is, a single consecrated cannon, he was not completely against having a program.

29. See "*Alors, qui êtes-vous?* Jacques Derrida and the Question of Hospitality," the first chapter of *Derrida from Now On* (New York: Fordham University Press, 2008), 18–36. Claudia Ruitenberg has argued in an extremely interesting and suggestive paper that Derrida's pedagogy was just such a form of hospitality, a pedagogy that tried always to "give place" to a kind of "unforeseeable learning." Ruitenberg looks at the ways in which outcomes-based education, that is, an education that demands measurable outcomes and has as its central goal "economic utility and productivity," ends up neglecting "other, unforeseen outcomes of the educational processes" (266). As Ruitenberg argues, "students learn more and less and differently from what any curriculum designer or educator can anticipate" (271). Ruitenberg cites Dewey's famous statement about "collateral" learning—"Perhaps the greatest of all pedagogical fallacies is the notion that a person learns only the particular thing he is studying at the time" (267)—but she spends most of her time on Derrida. Trying to offer some kind of "figure" for this kind of education or educational space, Ruitenberg quite appropriately offers *khōra*, not as a particular place, of course, not as a *topos*, but as a "placeholder for place" (272). Derrida himself makes just such a comparison in his essay on "Khōra" between Plato's *khōra* and the teachings or even the person of Jean-Pierre Vernant, the teacher to whom the essay is dedicated. See Claudia Ruitenberg, "Giving Place to Unforeseeable Learning: The Inhospitality of Outcomes-Based Education," in *Philosophy of Education* (2009): 266–274.

30. Ruitenberg is again helpful here, arguing that, according to such an "ethics of hospitality," teachers can "offer hospitality to newcomers only in the spaces in which they themselves are guests" (269).

31. I attempt to read this notion of *program* in the *Life Death* seminar from a different though closely related perspective in my essay "Dumb Luck: Jacques Derrida and the Question of Contingency," in *Throwing the Moral Dice: Ethics and the Problem of Contingency*, ed. Thomas Claviez and Viola Marchi (New York: Fordham University Press, 2021).

Class 1: *Agrégations*

1. The letter in the epigraph is from August 9, 1955. See Benoît Peeters, *Derrida: A Biography*, trans. Andrew Brown (Cambridge: Polity Press, 2013), 73.

2. The flier reads: "The Right to Philosophy for All [*Le droit à la philosophie pour tous*]," and it goes on to clarify what it is "against" and what it is "for." It is "Against the Haby Project in its entirety," "Against the elimination of philosophy," and it is "For the extension of the teaching of philosophy to all classes of the second cycle [that is, to the last three years of high school]." Having thus declared the group's position and intentions, the flier gives the details of the meeting—details that were ultimately helpful in determining the precise dates of the *Life Death* Seminar. "GREPH organizes a Mobilization Meeting, Saturday, April 19, 15:00 Jussieu, Amphi X3 (rue Guy de la Brosse). GREPH, 45, rue d'ULM, Paris (5ème)."

3. Alan Schrift, "The Effects of the *Agrégation de Philosophie* on Twentieth-Century French Philosophy," *Journal of the History of Philosophy* 46, no. 3 (July 2008): 449–473.

4. Ibid., 453n14.

5. Schrift writes: "When a philosophical text appears on the *Programme* for the *agrégation*'s oral examination, this means that all students that year who hope for a career in philosophy will spend the year reading that text intensively" (453).

6. Given Derrida's many attempts to distinguish between two different forms of repetition or between repetition and iterability, one can understand why he would have balked at this title. Something like "agrégé-itérateur" would have perhaps been more palatable.

7. Derrida later speaks, in humorous and hardy flattering terms, of Canguilhem's writing as a sort of "hesitation waltz" (see *LD* 72/103).

8. Since both Jacob and Derrida distinguish between *la vie* (life) and *le vivant* (the living, living beings), Jacob's book will here be referred to as *The Logic of the Living* and not, as it has been translated, *The Logic of Life*. For a brilliant reading of Derrida's project more generally, from "Freud and the Scene of Writing," *Of Grammatology*, and so on, in light of the developments of this seminar, see Francesco Vitale's *Biodeconstruction: Jacques Derrida and the Life Sciences*, trans. Mauro Senatore (Albany: State University of New York Press, 2018). In this work, Vitale extends the notion of performativity all the way to the biological trace.

9. In *The Reproduction of Life Death: Derrida's La vie la mort* (New York: Fordham University Press, 2019), Dawne McCance draws out even more explicitly the consequences of the assumptions of biologists such as Bernard and Jacob who attempt to control or dominate nature by manipulating the genetic code of both human beings and other living organisms.

10. In an interview from twenty-five years later, originally published in 2001 in *For What Tomorrow*, Derrida says in the context of a discussion regarding science and—no coincidence here—genetic engineering: "I rarely use the word 'freedom.' . . . On certain occasions, I will defend freedom as an excess of complexity in relation to a determinate machinelike state. . . . But this word seems to me to be loaded with metaphysical presuppositions that confer on the subject or on consciousness—that is, on an egological subject—a sovereign independence in relation to drives, calculation, the economy, the machine" (*FWT* 48/85–86).

11. Derrida refers in "Limited Inc" to *Sec*'s "dealing with the 'ethical and teleological discourse of consciousness' and with speech acts qua 'effects'" ("LI" 76–77/145). This notion of "illusion" gets picked up, though for different reasons, by Searle in his "Reply" and then by Derrida in "Limited Inc." Searle accuses Derrida of succumbing to the "illusion" that some intention is lurking *behind* the performative utterance. Derrida claims, to the contrary, that "the illusion that Sarl denounces would be explicitly Sarl's own" ("LI" 67/129).

12. Derrida continues: "This lure [*ce leurre*—as if it were a quasi-synonym for *illusion*] is the history of truth and it cannot be dissipated or dispelled so quickly" (*OG* 20/34). In other words, it is the illusion of such an effacement of the signifier,

the phantasm of total transparency and spontaneity, that makes possible the very constitution of truth as ideality. "It is the unique experience of the signified producing itself spontaneously, from within the self, and nevertheless, as signified concept, in the element of ideality or universality. The unworldly character of this substance of expression is constitutive of this ideality" (*OG* 20).

13. There are, I believe, theses and books to be written on this relationship between the programmable and the nonprogrammable, between the event, which is always unforeseeable and nonprogrammable, and the programmability of the machine that neutralizes the event. And these books and theses will be long because this notion of a program can be found not only in *Of Grammatology* and *Life Death* but in dozens of other texts of Derrida's.

14. I am not going to press the point here because it has already been beautifully developed by Dawne McCance in *The Reproduction of Life Death*. At issue, let me simply say, is the relationship between what Jacob understands to be a certain rigidity or necessity and chance or contingency, the supposed rigidity, fixity, and fidelity of a self-reproducing genetic program, and the supposed flexibility of an institutional program. As Derrida in effect argues, nothing could be farther from the truth, and in both directions, since the genetic program is essentially open to mutation, transformation, and exceptions to its self-reproduction, and the institutional program, like the *agrégation*, is prone to an astonishing self-reproduction and fixity. Jacob's claims regarding the supposed fixity and rigidity of the genetic code or program, and his juxtaposition of this genetic program with a supposedly more flexible, institutional program—for example, the kind of program at the heart of the *agrégation*—will allow Derrida to suggest that the opposite is perhaps the case, namely, that variation, mutation, and exceptions are really at the heart of the genetic program, while faithful reproduction, indeed self-reproduction, is what orders and defines institutional programs such as the *agrégation*. McCance has already underscored in great detail the way in which Derrida's *Life Death* intertwines, like the two strands of DNA, the theme of reproduction as it is to be found in both genetics and in the pedagogical institution in which Derrida's very seminar is taking place.

15. Derrida looks back on his own unhappy (even if ultimately useful) experience with the *agrégation* in a "Bâtons rompus" (see 196–198). He says at one point, in words that should sound somewhat familiar: "I never suffered more in my entire life than during the preparation for the competitive exams [*concours*] for the École Normale and the *agrégation*. It was hell for me [*c'était l'enfer pour moi*]." And yet just moments later he admits, "I am still living to a large extent off what I learned preparing for the *agrégation*. I cannot deny it. So it's a real contradiction" ("BR" 197–198).

Class 2: Education in *Theory and Practice* (1976–77)

1. My thanks to Pascale-Anne Brault, who painstakingly transcribed all of Derrida's extemporaneous additions to this session of the seminar and pointed me to these choice little asides.

2. As noted in the previous chapter, this course was actually given in 1976–77 and not, as the Galilée edition has it, 1975–76.

3. The published French text here reads, "je n'irai pas au-delà *de* cette année," but *de* is not found in the original typescript, which is why I have slightly modified the translation.

4. Derrida is perhaps thinking here about GREPH.

5. It should be said that this reevaluation of Derrida's relationship to Marx and Marxism in light of the 1976–77 seminar *Theory and Practice* will need to be updated and refined as a more complete record of Derrida's seminars becomes available through both their publication and the research of scholars working in the Derrida archives at the University of California, Irvine and IMEC. Thomas Clément Mercier is one such scholar who has written extensively of late on Derrida's engagement with Marx and Marxism (including Engels and Althusser) in unpublished seminars from the early 1970s, particularly "Religion et philosophie" (1972–73) and "GREPH (Le concept de l'idéologie chez les idéologues français)" (1974–75). Mercier estimates that there are over a thousand pages of unpublished and thus undigested material on Derrida's engagement with Marx and Marxism in these seminars. Work such as Mercier's will almost certainly, as he puts it, "dispel the illusions of those who still believe that Derrida was not interested in Marx or Marxist thought before the 1990s." For both a clear and pointed argument about Derrida's use of Marx to rethink sexual difference in seminars of the 1970s and a general overview of Derrida's engagement with Marx before *Specters of Marx*, see Mercier's excellent essay "Différence sexuelle, différence idéologique: Lecture à contretemps (Derrida lisant Marx et Althusser dans les années 1970 et au-delà)," forthcoming in *Décalages*.

6. Derrida explains in great deal his relationship to Marx and to Althusser in a long and wide-ranging interview with Michael Sprinker in April 1989, that is, a couple years *before* the fall of the Berlin Wall and *Specters of Marx*. See "Politics and Friendship: An Interview with Jacques Derrida," *N* 147–198.

7. Already in *Theory and Practice* Derrida evokes the theme of ideological illusions, phantasms, reveries, and so on. He raises the theme and then says he must set it aside, in order to return to it, as we now know, some sixteen years later in *Specters of Marx* (see *TP* 44/67).

8. Thomas Mercier's work is extremely helpful on this score too. Attentive to questions of temporality both in Marx and in Derrida's reading of Marx, Mercier asks in a recent essay celebrating the twenty-fifth anniversary of the publication of *Specters of Marx* whether this work is actually behind us or, indeed, still before us. He suggests the latter, though that work will be transformed not only by the future but by future readings informed by the past: Derrida's "1993 book remains to be read, and its reception will certainly become completely transformed as Derrida's writings on Marx and Marxist thought in his seminars from the 1960s, 1970s, and 1980s progressively emerge and lend themselves to critical readings" (Thomas Clément Mercier, "Before the *Specters*: The Memory of a Promise (from the Archives)," in *Contexto Internacional: Journal of Global Connections* 42, no. 1 [2020]). Questions of the time or the timeliness of Marx's work, of its contemporaneity or

its spectrality, of its ability to speak to us in the present—questions that are all at the center of *Specters of Marx*—will, it seems, continue to haunt all our thinking about Marx. It is thus perhaps hardly a coincidence that Daniel Bensaïd would publish a book just two years after *Spectres de Marx* with the title *Marx, l'intempestif* (Paris: Librairie Arthème Fayard, 1995), in other words, "Marx, the untimely," or that this would become in the English translation of Gregory Eliott, and this is neither a coincidence nor a mistake, *Marx for Our Times: Adventures and Misadventures of a Critique* (New York: Verso, 2002).

9. Let me note here that one of the possible sources for this conjunction of figures who are so central to *Theory and Practice* may go even further back in time, namely, to Derrida's association with Gérard Granel. In a passage from *Chaque fois unique, la fin du monde*, ed. Pascale-Anne Brault and Michael Naas (Paris: Éditions Galilée, 2003), 298, Derrida recalls Granel, his friend and classmate at ENS (and, even before that, at the Lycée Louis-le-Grand), in this way: "We have to read and reread, again and again, this text in which Granel thinks together (who will have ever attempted this?) Heidegger *and* Wittgenstein, as he will have thought together ([and] who will have attempted this?) Heidegger *with* Marx, Heidegger *with* Gramsci." And all of this, let me also note in passing, is in the context of Granel's abiding interest in historicity.

10. Derrida speaks at some length in the preceding year's seminar *Life Death* of the ubiquity of the Marxist language of "production" (rather than, say, "creation" or "causation") and of the need to question or submit to critique the linguistic production of "production" (see *LD* 98–105/136–143). It was thus not just the *agrégation* program of 1976–77 that got Derrida thinking, writing, and teaching about Marx in the mid-1970s.

11. On the notion of the "programmatological" and the relationship, particularly in psychoanalysis, between theory and practice, and on the possibility of the "advent"—the institution, as it were—of a discourse such as psychoanalysis, see "MC" 372–373/380–381.

12. See "Psychoanalysis Searches the States of Its Soul: The Impossible Beyond of a Sovereign Cruelty" (in *WA* 264/59).

13. Derrida cites Heidegger's "Letter on Humanism" during the seminar but stops just short, it seems (I say "it seems" because it is unclear from Derrida's original typescript where the quote from Heidegger ends), of this comment by Heidegger: "Surely, the question raised in your letter would have been better answered in direct conversation. In written form, thinking easily loses its flexibility. But in writing it is difficult above all to retain the multi-dimensionality of the realm peculiar to thinking." Though Derrida does not press the point here, one could have imagined him, given everything he had already written about this relation in "Plato's Pharmacy," *Of Grammatology*, and elsewhere, spending more time with this passage in order to develop the kinds of questions he will pose a decade later in "Geschlecht II: Heidegger's Hand," questions regarding Heidegger's privileging of the spoken word over writing but then also of handwriting, the work of a single hand, over the typewriter (or the two hands on the keyboard) when it comes to matters of

thinking. It would also be interesting to relate this passage on speaking and writing in Heidegger to what Derrida says at the beginning of one of the latter sessions about his decision suddenly to shift seminar style, to change pedagogical practice, as it were, and to adopt a more informal, conversational style. He says near the beginning of the seventh session: "Well then, I have made a decision, that is to say also a 'practical' risk, for the continuation of this Seminar and at least for this year. I am going to try to transform something in my practice, to practice differently. . . . By desisting henceforth from referring to a previously written text—as you know that I do, notwithstanding the liberties that I take on certain occasions vis-à-vis that *prescribed* text—I am taking the risk, no doubt minimal in your eyes but quite serious in mine, and in relation to the subject and body that I am, the risk of witnessing the decomposition of both my discourse . . . and something like the authority, the credibility or the force that a prior elaboration, one that is tightly argued and calculated in advance, can confer on it" (*TP* 97/139–140). But it does not take long for Derrida to go back on this decision. Indeed, it happens in the very same session, when he complains: "While improvising, I can't refer to the minute details of two texts in German, and in French translation, by Heidegger, I can't hone certain questions, work on the body of the text, or in any case I can't do that without a considerable loss that would lead us to take five sessions to follow the trajectory of a single one. Because it seems to me that freeing myself—at least in this situation—from the work of writing is a mystification and a simplification that goes against the very thing that we are looking for, I'll return at least provisionally to my old practice, at least at certain moments" (*TP* 98–99 /141).

14. One might want to consider these comments regarding Heidegger's neglect of questions of "sexual practice" (see *TP* 31/50), of "sexual technique and position (*thesis/physis*)" (*TP* 106/150), in the context of that seemingly improvised, unscripted moment in the movie *Derrida* when Derrida is asked what he would have most wanted to ask Heidegger about and he says something to the effect of "his sexual life."

15. To understand *Rogues*, then, it would be useful to return to Derrida's seemingly cryptic remarks in *Theory and Practice* about difference in *physis*, difference *as* physis, about a "cryptic *différance*" (*TP* 110/154), or else to his later association of *physis* with *Walten* and *Walten* with *différance* near the end of his very final seminar *The Beast and the Sovereign*.

16. Of course, in addition to this eleventh thesis on Feuerbach, there is Lenin, whom Derrida also cites: "Without revolutionary theory, no revolutionary practice" (*TP* 55/84).

17. Derrida sides here with Gramsci in his critique of Croce's interpretation of Marx. According to both Derrida and Gramsci, as opposed to Croce, Marx was not suggesting that we leave philosophy and he, Marx, considered himself still to be doing philosophy (*TP* 14–15/29–30).

18. To give just one example, some readers will no doubt be surprised, and others simply disappointed, to find that in the seven hundred or so pages of the two recently published volumes on *The Death Penalty* there are no more than a handful

of passages that *refer to* well-known pragmatic or utilitarian arguments against the death penalty and *no* passages at all where Derrida himself really takes up arguments about, for example, the cost of the death penalty, whether the death penalty really is a deterrent against crime, and so on. He cites no studies or statistics of that kind and makes no arguments of that sort. It will thus be said that he approaches the question only *theoretically*, that is, as a philosopher, and that, as a result, he remains content to interpret the world rather than to try to transform it.

Class 3: Grace and the Machine

1. All page references to this seminar are to the 2019 French edition published by Seuil. I will be citing, however, throughout this chapter the English translation, forthcoming with the University of Chicago Press, by David Wills, who was kind enough share with me a prepublication version of his translation. Several sessions of this seminar, it should be noted, have been previously translated and published elsewhere, including session 1, which I will also refer to in what follows. See "To Forgive: The Unforgivable and the Imprescriptible," trans. Elizabeth Rottenberg, in *Questioning God*, ed. John D. Caputo, Mark Dooley, and Michael J. Scanlon (Bloomington: Indiana University Press, 2001), 21–51.

2. Henri Thomas, *Le parjure* (Paris: Gallimard, 1964, 1994).

3. Written by Hélène Cixous and directed by Ariane Mnouchkine, *La ville parjure ou le réveil des Erinyes* opened at the Théâtre du Soleil on May 18, 1994. It is unclear to what extent Cixous's play of just three years earlier influenced Derrida's selection of *parjure* for the title of his seminar, but during the second year of the seminar Derrida refers directly to the play and to the so-called "contaminated blood scandal" at the heart of it. Derrida says during the seminar session of February 17, 1999: "In the context of theatre, contaminated blood and perjury, I invite you to read and reread—if you didn't see it while it was playing at the Théâtre du Soleil—Hélène Cixous's extraordinary and beyond sublime *Ville parjure*, which will tell you more about that and give further food for thought, graciously, on all the topics that we are sketching out here . . ." See Hélène Cixous, *La ville parjure ou le réveil des Érinyes* (Paris: Théâtre du Soleil, 1994); *The Perjured City or the Awakening of the Furies*, trans. Bernadette Fort (London: Routledge, 2003).

4. While both *pardon* and *parjure* begin with *par*, we are perhaps dealing here with two different prepositional prefixes, the *par* of *pardonner* meaning "through" or "by," and that of *parjure*, a shortened form of *para*, meaning "against" or "contra." Whatever their respective etymologies, the *par* of *parjure* will be understood by Derrida as that which interrupts *and* constitutes the *jure*, the *parjure* as that which comes along with and not after *la foi jurée* or the sworn faith.

5. As for the English "pardon" and the French "*pardon*," they are almost false friends. In contemporary English the word "pardon" is usually used either in a political context, as a synonym for "clemency" (typically translated into French as *la grâce*—a trace of which remains in the English notion of a "grace period"), or in everyday expressions of politeness or politesse, such as "pardon me." Rarely, however, is it used to express "forgiving" or "forgiveness." One does not talk about "pardoning"

a family member, friend, or colleague for doing something offensive or objectionable; a victim would not "pardon" his or her offender for some transgression. In all these cases, it would be more a question of "forgiving" them. In English, then, *pardon* is usually political, while *forgiveness*, which can be either more or less secular (when we forgive a friend for some harm done) or religious (when we ask God to forgive our sins), is not. But, again, one does not typically ask "pardon" for one's wrongdoings or one's sins, and a criminal who is pardoned is not "forgiven" by the governor of the state, though he or she could be forgiven by his or her victim. As for "perjury," it too, like the English pardon, is essentially juridical. Both terms "pardon and perjury" thus have, it seems, a narrower scope than the French *pardon* and *parjure*—though especially the latter.

6. This same rethinking of possibility and impossibility is also at the heart of the seminar *Perjury and Pardon*, that is, the thinking of an im-possibility that is not the negative or dialectical other of possibility. Derrida writes, for example: "There is forgiveness, if there is such a thing, only of the unforgivable. Thus forgiveness, if it is possible, if there is such a thing, is not possible, it does not exist as possible, it exists only by exempting itself from the law of the possible, by impossibilizing itself, so to speak, and in the infinite endurance of the im-possible as impossible. . . . You understand that this seminar could also have been a seminar on the possible and on the 'im-' that comes in front of it, an im-possible which is neither negative, nor non-negative, nor dialectical. . . . Forgiveness as the impossible truth of the impossible gift. Before the gift, forgiveness" (*PP 1* 72).

7. Derrida writes in "Limited Inc": "the graphics of iterability undercuts the classical opposition of fact and principle [*le droit*], the factual and the possible (or the virtual), necessity and possibility" ("LI" 48/97).

8. There is divisibility, then, but Derrida goes on to clarify that there is not *only* divisibility, for death is to be found, he says, on the side of both absolute division and absolute identity or unity. "Death lies in wait [*guette*] on both sides, on the side of the phantasm of the integrity of the proper place . . . and, on the opposite side, that of a radical impropriety or expropriation" (*G 3* 81-82106–107).

9. Derrida goes on to speak of his own rethinking of the promise in Heidegger and the interest there would be in bringing this notion into proximity with the work of Paul de Man on speech acts (*G 3* 112-113/133–134). Near the end of the essay, Derrida speaks of a "sort of performativity of the poetic song that is not content with representing historical objects for historians but which is historial insofar as it moves, stirs, promotes [*meut, émeut, promeut*] events" (*G 3* 150/168).

10. Derrida recalls that, for the Greeks, "the oath was sometimes suspected of being the beginning of a *parjure* . . . an unavoidable and organizing place" (*PP 1* 116).

11. Derrida thus suggests in "Limited Inc" that every promise is haunted (perhaps unconsciously) by a threat, thereby calling into question the supposedly "rigorous distinction" between promise and threat ("LI" 74–75/141–142).

12. On the relationship between forgiving and forgetting, see *PP 1* 223–224.

13. See Derrida's references to a "beyond of knowledge," to the "limit between faith and knowledge" (*PP 1* 231), to the distinction in Augustine between "knowing"

and a "calling" or an "invocation" that precedes knowing (*PP 1* 191–92), and to knowledge and decision, that is, to "a rupture and a heterogeneity, a hiatus between knowing and acting, between knowledge and freedom" (*PP 1* 285).

14. Derrida shows in "Plato's Pharmacy," for example, that the so-called spontaneous repetition that would be writing in the soul cannot take place without the supplement of external writing and mechanical repetition. The person who has underscored this aspect of Derrida's work more and better than anyone is, fortunately, none other than the English translator of the two years of the *Perjury and Pardon* seminar, David Wills. See, for example, Wills's recent work *Inanimation: Theories of Inorganic Life* (Minneapolis: University of Minnesota Press, 2016).

15. The passage continues: "That is why, let it be said in passing, I am here tying our problematic to that of the work and of testamentary remaining [*restance*], of the becoming-poetic and becoming-literary of this testamentary remainder of confession, which seems to me indissociable from it" (*PP 1* 233).

16. See the rather extraordinary passage in *Perjury and Pardon 1* on the "dissemination" of the French idiom *y a pas de mal*, "this quasi-phrase [that] would remain, as text, an homage to idiom, a salutation made to the French language as possibility for the untranslatable idiom, a hymn, a praise, a tribute to the French language" (*PP 1* 222).

Conclusion: *Actes de naissance*

1. "Fecund" or "fertile" (*fécund* in French) is one of the terms most frequently used by Derrida to characterize Austin's work (see "Marx & Sons" 224/27 and "LI" 85/159).

2. The theme of birth—of *naissance*—has been very powerfully explored by Elissa Marder in *The Mother in the Age of Mechanical Reproduction* (New York: Fordham University Press, 2012) and, more recently, in her article "Derrida's Matrix: The Births of Deconstruction," *Oxford Literary Review* 40, no. 1 (2018): 1–19.

3. Some of the other "imports," that is, resonances or valences, that Derrida hears in this phrase can be found in "Rams: Uninterrupted Dialogue—Between Two Infinities, the Poem" (in *SQ*) and in Derrida's preface to *Chaque fois unique, la fin du monde* (*CFU*).

4. There are entire books on this latter notion of *perle*, that is, of the precious gaffe or misstatement, particularly of schoolchildren. One of these, published not long after Derrida's seminar, is Jérôme Duhamel's *Les perles de l'école: Le bêtisier des élèves, des parents, et des profs* (Paris: Éditions Albin Michel, 2000), which collects such choice bits, such gems, as "the Stone Age began with the invention of iron," "Adam and Eve were kicked out of paradise because they ate the snake," and—remembering that these are French kids—"Jesus was born in a crêpe."

Index

Agacinski, Sylviane, 171n13
Alain (Émile-Auguste Chartier), 173n28
Algeria, 75, 87, 165n3, 168n2
Althusser, Louis, 9, 117–118, 120, 122–125, 177nn5–6
Antigone, 113
Aristotle, 25, 101, 116, 120, 121, 125, 150
Aubenque, Pierre, 172n23
Augustine, 146, 181n13
Austin, John L., 2–4, 15–19, 24–36, 39–40, 42–43, 56–58, 64, 80, 92, 107–108, 119, 134–136, 151–153, 159n2, 162nn14–16,18, 163n19, 164nn22–23, 167n6, 173n24

Bass, Alan, 41, 168n5
Baudrillard, Jean, 67
Bel Lassen, Michel, 171n13
Benin (West Africa), 85, 172n19
Benjamin, Walter, 47, 172n15
Bennington, Geoffrey, 160n4
Bensaïd, Daniel, 178n8
Bergson, Henri, 173n28
Bernard, Claude, 98, 175n9
Blanchot, Maurice, 47, 85, 173n23
Borges, Jorge Luis, 47
Bouveresse, Jacques, 173n28

Brault, Pascale-Anne, 94–95, 176n1
Brunet, Roland, 171nn13–14

Cahen, Didier, 171n14
Canguilhem, Georges, 98–99, 175n7
Carnegie, Dale, 159n1
Celan, Paul, 154–155, 168n2
Châtelet, François, 170n8, 171n14, 172n22
Chenoweth, Katie, 160n4
Cixous, Hélène, 69, 130, 169n2, 173n27, 180n3
Claviez, Thomas, 174n31
Collège International de Philosophie, 8, 84–87, 171n12, 172n22
Colombel, Jeannette, 171n14
Comtesse, Georges, 169n2
Condillac, Étienne Bonnet de, 18–20, 83, 134, 160–161nn4–5
Cornell University, 85, 90
Cotton, Nicholas, 170n7
Cousin, Victor, 85, 172n17
Coutel, Charles, 171n14
Cresta, Michel, 171n13
Croce, Benedetto, 117, 124, 179n17

Defoe, Daniel, 79
Deleuze, Gilles, 169n2, 171n14

183

Delormes, Alain, 171n13
De Man, Paul, 181n9
Derrida, Jacques: "AC," 139–141; *AF*, 160n4; *AFF*, 119; "ANC," 86, 87; "ATE," 163n19, 166n1, 173n24; "BR," 173n27, 176n15; *BS 1*, 79, 121; *BS 2*, 79, 120, 121, 146, 154–155, 169n2, 179n15; *CFU*, 178n9, 182n3; "CHM," 65, 178n9, 182n3; "CIP," 5, 59, 63–67, 80, 132; *CL*, 160n4; *DDP*, 8, 81–84, 86–88, 96–97, 109, 160n4, 170n12, 171n15, 173nn24,28; "DI," 5, 47–54, 61, 165n4; *DP 1*, 79, 179–180n18; *DP 2*, 79, 120, 149–151, 161n12, 179–180n18; "EE," 88; *EO*, 46–48, 165nn2–4, 168n1, 169n3; *EU*, 84, 171n12, 173n23; "FK," 128, 133, 138, 146; *FWT*, 175n10; *G 3*, 137–142, 181nn8–9; *GL*, 70, 85, 160n4, 162n16, 163n21, 168n2, 169n3, 172–173n23; *LD*, 7–8, 47, 79–80, 83, 92, 93–95, 97–110, 114–115, 121–122, 159n3, 161n4, 167n1, 169n5, 174nn31,2, 175n9, 176nn13–14, 178n10; "LC," 88–89; *LI*, 166n1, 173n24; "LI," 2, 4, 13, 41–42, 44–45, 54–58, 59, 61, 63, 80, 82, 131, 134–136, 161nn6,8–10, 162n17, 163n19–21, 164nn22,25,1, 165nn3–5, 166nn5,1, 167nn1–6, 168nn2,5–6, 173n24, 175n11, 181nn7,11; *LLF*, 152–153; "MC," 178n11; *MP*, 33, 41, 172n23; *MPD*, 50; "MS," 27, 168n4, 182n1; *O*, 4–5, 46–48, 54, 59, 79, 149, 165nn1,4; *OA*, 46, 165nn2–3, 169n3; *OG*, 6, 17, 18, 91, 101, 108, 126, 147, 172n23, 175nn8,12, 176nn12–13, 178n13; *OS*, 60, 120, 121; *P*, 6; "PaF," 177n6; *PC*, 67, 85, 173n23; *PG*, 168n7; "PP," 21, 82, 126, 145, 178n13, 182n14; *PP 1*, 9, 79–80, 92, 127–148, 149, 152, 181nn6,10,12–13, 182nn14–16; *PP 2*, 3, 182n14; "PSS," 119–120, 178n12; "R," 182n3; *R*, 53, 122, 179n15; *RB*, 172n22; "SEC," 2, 4–5, 13, 15–44, 45, 47, 54, 55–58, 59–61, 63–67, 70, 77, 83, 92, 107–108, 131, 134–139, 142, 145, 147, 149–150, 152, 159nn1–2, 161nn5,7,9,11, 162n17, 163nn18,20, 164n22, 166nn1,5, 167nn3–4, 168n5; *SM*, 9, 26, 117, 122–123, 125–126, 177nn5–8; "SOO," 69–70; *SQ*, 168n2, 182n3; *TP*, 9, 79, 83, 92, 94–95, 97, 99, 111, 114–126, 167n1, 177–179nn2–17; *TS*, 90; "UG," 159n2; "UWC," 3, 27, 87; *WA*, 178n12; *WAP*, 81–84, 97, 109, 160n4, 170–171n12, 171nn13,15, 172nn17,21, 173n24; *WD*, 6, 172n23
Derrida, Marguerite, 169n2
Desanti, Jean-Toussaint, 171n14, 172n23
Descartes, René, 84, 93, 134, 162n13, 171n15, 173n28
Dewey, John, 174n29
Dick, Kirby, 75
Dis, Claude, 171n13
Dreyfus, Hubert, 56
Duhamel, Jérôme, 182n4

École des Hautes Études en Sciences Sociales (EHESS), Paris, 5–6, 9, 76–77, 80, 86–87, 90, 111, 169n3
École Normale Supérieure (ENS), Paris, 5–6, 9, 75–77, 79, 80–83, 86–87, 90, 92, 94–97, 111, 114, 117, 169n3, 170n10, 176n15, 178n9
Eliott, Gregory, 178n8

Faye, Jean-Pierre, 172n22
Feuerbach, Ludwig, 9, 122–123, 179n16
Finas, Lucette, 160n2, 166n5
Fontaine-De Visscher, Luce, 159n1, 160n2
Fontenay, Elisabeth de, 171n14
Foucault, Michel, 160n2, 170n8
Freud, Sigmund, 98, 100, 160–161n4, 175n8

Gandillac, Maurice de, 93, 96, 172–173n23
Godet, Francis, 171n14
Graciet, Bernard, 171n14
Graff, Gerald, 166n1
Gramsci, Antonio, 117, 124, 178n9, 179n17
Granel, Gérard, 178n9
GREPH (Groupe de Recherches sur l'Enseignement Philosophique), 8, 80–86, 88–89, 95, 109, 170nn7,10,

171nn12–13, 172nn18–19,21, 174n2, 177nn4–5
Grinnell College, 194
Gromer, Bernadette, 171n13

Haby, René, (Haby Reforms), 85, 88, 171n14, 172nn19,21, 174n2
Hancock, John, 40, 48–49
Harvard University, 25, 75
Hédoin, Jean-Pierre, 171n13
Hegel, G. W. F., 3, 18, 25, 85, 98, 100, 116, 139, 167n1, 171n3, 173n28
Heidegger, Martin, 3, 25, 26, 60, 79, 85, 98, 100, 116, 118, 120–124, 137–139, 172n15, 173n23, 178n9, 178–179n13, 179n14, 181n9
Hocquet-Tessard, Martine, 171n14
Husserl, Edmund, 3, 24, 25, 108, 125, 134

IMEC (Institut Mémoires de l'Édition Contemporaine), 77, 94, 177n5

Jacob, François, 8, 92, 98–109, 175nn8–9, 176n14
Jankélévitch, Vladimir, 170n10, 171n14
Jefferson, Thomas, 48–49, 51–52, 54
Johns Hopkins University, 76, 90, 170n6
Joly, Henri, 171n14, 173n23
Joyce, James, 47

Kaléka, Gérard, 171n14
Kamuf, Peggy, 94–95, 168n1, 170n6
Kant, Immanuel, 85, 116, 120, 125, 171–172n15, 172n16, 173n28
Kierkegaard, Søren, 65
Kofman, Amy Ziering, 75
Kofman, Sarah, 171n13

Labica, Georges, 171n14
Lacoue-Labarthe, Philippe, 171n14
Lane, Gilles, 25, 162n14
Lascault, Gilbert, 173n23
Lecourt, Dominique, 172n22
Le Doeuff, Michèle, 171n13
Lefebvre, Jean-Pierre, 171n13
Le Mans, 76
Lenin, Vladimir, 120, 179n16
Lévesque, Claude, 45, 47, 165n4, 168n3

Lévesque, René, 61–62, 168n3
Levinas, Emmanuel, 85, 173n23
Locke, John, 173n28
Lycée Louis-le-Grand, Paris, 75, 178n9
Lyotard, Jean-François, 170n8

Mallet, Marie-Louise, 169n2, 171n14
Marchi, Viola, 174n31
Marder, Elissa, 182n2
Marx, Karl, (Marxism), 9, 26, 92, 116–118, 120–126, 168n4, 177–178nn5–10, 179n17, 182n1
McCance, Dawne, 175n9, 176n14
McDonald, Christie V., 45, 165n4
McLuhan, Marshall, 37
Mehlman, Jeffrey, 41, 166n1
Mercier, Thomas Clément, 177nn5,8
Meskel, Martine, 171n13
Michaud, Ginette, 69–70
Mnouchkine, Ariane, 180n3
Moati, Raoul, 165n2
Montaigne, Michel de, 173n28
Montreal, 2, 4–5, 10, 13, 15–16, 25, 27, 31, 37, 41, 45, 47–48, 55, 59, 61, 63–64, 66–67, 69–70, 79–80, 132, 152, 165n4; Centre Canadien d'Architecture, 59, 69, 132; McGill University, 165n2; University of Montreal, 4, 23, 45, 69, 79, 157, 165n4, 167n1

Nancy, Jean-Luc, 171nn13–14
New York University (NYU), 76, 90
Nietzsche, Friedrich, 4, 26, 28, 45–48, 54, 98, 100, 159n3, 161n6, 165nn1,4, 172n17
Nouss, Alexis, 167n1

Orchard, Vivienne, 170nn7,10, 172n17, 173n26

Paris, 3, 9, 10, 47, 58, 75–76, 77, 88, 94, 95, 117, 130, 159n3, 174n2, 180n3; University of Paris: Jussieu, 95, 174n2; Sorbonne, 76, 79, 84, 85, 171n14. *See also* École des Hautes Études en Sciences Sociales (EHESS); École Normale Supérieure (ENS); Lycée Louis-le-Grand

Pascal, Blaise, 146
Pautrat, Bernard, 171n13
Peeters, Benoît, 64, 159–160n2, 166n1, 168n4, 174n1
Péraldi, François, 165n3
Plato, 3, 18, 21, 25, 41, 60, 82, 116, 120, 122, 126, 134, 145, 173n28, 174n29, 178n13, 182n14
Politis, Hélène, 171n13
Ponge, Francis, 47

Quebec, 14, 37, 47, 54, 59, 61–62, 69, 154, 168n5

Ricoeur, Paul, 15, 21, 25, 31, 159–160n2, 171n14
Robespierre, Maximilien, 120
Rosenzweig, Franz, 113
Rottenberg, Elizabeth, 180n1
Rousseau, Jean-Jacques, 3, 129, 134, 173n28
Ruitenberg, Claudia, 174nn29–30
Ryan, Michael, 171n13

Sanders, Bernie, 123
Saussure, Ferdinand de, 18
Schelling, F. W. J., 171n15
Schrift, Alan, 94–96, 109, 175nn3,5
Searle, Dagmar, 56
Searle, John, 2, 4, 15, 34, 41–44, 55–58, 80, 85, 92, 134, 136, 159n2, 161n10, 163nn19–20, 164nn22–24,1, 165n2, 166–167n1, 167nn3,5, 173nn23–24, 175n11
Serres, Michel, 170n8
Shakespeare, William, 126, 139–141
Soussana, Gad, 167n1
Soviet Union, 117
Sprinker, Michael, 177n6

Théâtre du Soleil (Paris), 130, 180n3
Thomas, Henri, 129, 180n2
Toronto, 37, 85
Trakl, Georg, 137

University of California, Irvine, 76, 77, 90, 170n6, 177n5
University of Virginia, Charlottesville, 47, 54, 165n4

Védrine, Hélène, 171n14
Vernant, Jean-Pierre, 174n29
Vitale, Francesco, 175n8

Warburton, William, 18
Weber, Samuel, 41, 166n1
Wenin, Christian, 159n1, 160n2
Wills, David, 94, 180n1, 182n14
Wittgenstein, Ludwig, 26, 178n9
Wortham, Simon Morgan, 170n11

Yale University, 76, 90, 170n6

Michael Naas is Professor of Philosophy at DePaul University. His most recent books include *The End of the World and Other Teachable Moments: Jacques Derrida's Final Seminar* (2015), *Plato and the Invention of Life* (2018), and *Don DeLillo, American Original: Drugs, Weapons, Erotica, and Other Literary Contraband* (2020).

Perspectives in Continental Philosophy
John D. Caputo, series editor

Recent titles:

Richard Kearney and Melissa Fitzgerald, *Radical Hospitality: From Thought to Action.*
Ole Jakob Løland, *Pauline Ugliness: Jacob Taubes and the Turn to Paul.*
Marika Rose, *A Theology of Failure: Žižek against Christian Innocence.*
Marc Crépon, *Murderous Consent: On the Accommodation of Violent Death.* Translated by Michael Loriaux and Jacob Levi, Foreword by James Martel.
Emmanuel Falque, *The Guide to Gethsemane: Anxiety, Suffering, and Death.* Translated by George Hughes.
Emmanuel Alloa, *Resistance of the Sensible World: An Introduction to Merleau-Ponty.* Translated by Jane Marie Todd. Foreword by Renaud Barbaras.
Françoise Dastur, *Questions of Phenomenology: Language, Alterity, Temporality, Finitude.* Translated by Robert Vallier.
Jean-Luc Marion, *Believing in Order to See: On the Rationality of Revelation and the Irrationality of Some Believers.* Translated by Christina M. Gschwandtner.
Adam Y. Wells, ed., *Phenomenologies of Scripture.*
An Yountae, *The Decolonial Abyss: Mysticism and Cosmopolitics from the Ruins.*
Jean Wahl, *Transcendence and the Concrete: Selected Writings.* Edited and with an Introduction by Alan D. Schrift and Ian Alexander Moore.
Colby Dickinson, *Words Fail: Theology, Poetry, and the Challenge of Representation.*
Emmanuel Falque, *The Wedding Feast of the Lamb: Eros, the Body, and the Eucharist.* Translated by George Hughes.
Emmanuel Falque, *Crossing the Rubicon: The Borderlands of Philosophy and Theology.* Translated by Reuben Shank. Introduction by Matthew Farley.

Colby Dickinson and Stéphane Symons (eds.), *Walter Benjamin and Theology*.
Don Ihde, *Husserl's Missing Technologies*.
William S. Allen, *Aesthetics of Negativity: Blanchot, Adorno, and Autonomy*.
Jeremy Biles and Kent L. Brintnall, eds., *Georges Bataille and the Study of Religion*.
Tarek R. Dika and W. Chris Hackett, *Quiet Powers of the Possible: Interviews in Contemporary French Phenomenology*. Foreword by Richard Kearney.
Richard Kearney and Brian Treanor, eds., *Carnal Hermeneutics*.

A complete list of titles is available at http://fordhampress.com.

www.ingramcontent.com/pod-product-compliance
Lightning Source LLC
Chambersburg PA
CBHW032036290426
44110CB00012B/824